ASYNCHRONOUS EXCHANGE

ASYNCHRONOUS EXCHANGE

The End of Capitalism

Anders Baerbock

2022

Asynchronous exchange: the end of capitalism
Anders Baerbock

ISBN 979-8-218-00554-2 (paperback)

asynchronousexchange.com
Use IPv6 or later.

Preface

For writing this document used as foundation another previous which I wrote in the year 2016 when attempting –for one last time– to fix Mexico, the country where my mother delivered me. Such endeavor utterly failed, that country stands clearly ruined beyond reform or alike; anyway there never happened anything akin to a *golden age*. Those who call themselves «mexicans», and their predecessors, created their own disaster; a vast majority never stood up to the circumstances, not now and not ever. Any interested person can review the facts about that failed country using other sources.

Nevertheless, as part of the effort, devised how to build one of the main constituent blocks of a more advanced civilization, specifically, devised the ultimate commercial-exchange behavior. Also, as foundation, delineated an unequivocal fracture among the *Homo sapiens*. Three unintended consequences happened from that previous effort, now useful as input for the choices made in this document:

1. Many people from a backwards country, namely Spain, which 500 years ago invaded the land where my mother delivered me, from which independence ensued 200 years ago, still carry a sense of entitlement over the people from the former colony. Furthermore, many spaniards seem to think that using the spanish language creates a debt or obligation favorable to them, and a sort of imaginary relationship. Those individuals created a problem.

    Moreover, happened some pathetic efforts to «convince» me about a non-existent spanish ancestry –in a very backwards world-view, after embracing such non-existent ancestry I would pledge an allegiance to the spanish colonial dreams, as many mexican retards and traitors do.

Due to their deep-seated racism against native-american people and their static world-view, many spaniards and descendants of spaniards cannot tolerate and admit as an ordinary fact that a descendant of native-americans generates knowledge for moving forward humanity. This situation just breaks the fantasy that spaniards and their descendants told themselves repeatedly (again and again) about their pretended racial superiority; makes untenable their ridiculous fantasy of spaniards arriving to America as «spreaders of civilization among a bunch of brutes» where the invaders and assassins built and maintained a colonial order «for the benefit of the colonized savages», a fantasy where racist, ignorant, fanatic, and superstitious spaniards massively destroyed ancient aboriginal documents and obliterated any native culture «for spreading civilization». This deep-seated racism against native-american people from spaniards and their descendants so far propelled them to spend a lot of energy and resources in order to «prove» a distorted reality different to the actual facts.

2. A parasitic psychopathic subspecies came out from the shadows of society and, when doing so, when stepping into the light, those hominids provided more information relevant and of the utmost importance for the subjects here attended. The psychopathic parasitic subspecies served as the first line of defense of the status-quo –they functioned as puppets of capitalistic elites.

3. While hiding the truth, a lot of people striving to control other humans by any means (hence, craving for «power»), started to use whatever they found –or they thought they found– about me, in an attempt to influence and exercise an effective control over other humans, usually with the aim of preserving the current status-quo.

The document from 6 years ago carries the title *Elements of a Constitution for the XXI Century*, the word *Elements* intended to convey the message that it did not constitute a complete proposal, also this message remarked within the main text. In this context I avoided dwelling into a reform for democracy, although I mentioned it needed reform. Notwithstanding, many people with an authoritarian way of life –the parasitic psychopathic subspecies and other groups– attempted to use this omission as implying a discard of democracy but, peculiarly, those same individuals did not embrace moving forward regarding the commercial-exchange behavior, nor they dare to attack the capitalistic thieves.

In the same wise, in *Elements of a Constitution for the XXI Century* I did not record explicitly that a world-class society must develop its own language. Since many years ago this necessity seems so obvious and clear for me that deemed recording it not indispensable.

Thus, appears adequate to update the collected knowledge with the following changes:

1. State the knowledge in a way that may endure over time, and in a format which a wider audience can directly understand. In this regard, this text written in the english language because currently it constitutes the factual standard for performing commercial and scientific interactions worldwide. Must emphasize that I neither hold any allegiance to the english language or to the country where it originated, nor I experience any sort of attachment to british people or british culture.

2. Eliminate all content exclusively relevant to the discarded country.

3. Incorporate the data about the parasitic psychopathic subspecies which typically creates authoritarian formations; and briefly address their current relationship with the capitalistic elites and with the failure of democracy.

4. Include a proposal to reform the *representative democracy*, and clarify the origin of the XXI century failure to produce prosperity for the majority of people living in nominally democratic societies.

5. Include general improvements and enhancements.

This book also serves to frustrate the current overt attempt to ignore, hide, and deny the new knowledge, because it alters and transforms the status-quo. Does not matter that the now old status-quo so far consistently conduced everybody to catastrophe, that arose from the success of thieves and upholds their criminal venture, and that already caused irreparable damage to the Earth's ecosystems, squandered and spoiled great quantities of resources, and thereby severely conditioned the future of humankind; because callous people who for too long enjoyed positions of unfair and dishonest privileges propel such status-quo, and relentlessly use those privileged positions for squeezing the rest of humanity from the benefits of the latter's enterprises and hard work, for massively stealing from everybody else. Meanwhile, an ages-old parasitic authoritarian psychopathic subspecies also attempts to keep hanging from humanity.

Such attempts to stop the progress and advancement of civilization, done for personal and factional benefits, constitute an effort akin to those attempts to vindicate the notion of a flat Earth as center of the universe, at a time when basic astronomical discoveries showed the truth. While a judicial proceeding with a tribunal did not start against me like would in the Middle Ages, I experienced several large attempts to subdue my persona –those belong to some too-late efforts to preserve the old order of things. While the russian fascists performed the main role in those subjugation attempts, a lot of people all over the world actively participated, even if only remotely using their available electronic tools.

The interested reader can review my notes about the Saint Petersburg Hive.

Regarding grammatical practices, the following pertinent:
- The plural of gender-neutral or epicene entities denoted using the word *it*, including humans when the sexual gender of those remains undetermined.

  I consider very unfortunate the usage of the word *they* for denoting an individual human when the sexual gender of it remains undetermined, since by doing so the emitter blurs or eliminates the distinction between plural and singular cases. Many individuals further aggravate this ambiguity by mixing it with the nowadays fashionable practice of confusing the sexual orientation of a human with its sexual gender.

- Italics used for distinguishing any concept or sentence from its surroundings. Accordingly, recorded in italics the first mention of a relevant concept, and concepts used outstandingly in a figurative way –most frequently metaphorically.
- Quotation marks enclose the following:
  + Every distinct phrase within a containing sentence or containing paragraph.
  + Distanced speech: Words and conceptual constructs recorded as someone else would express them, or already expressed them. Quoted speech always explicitly introduced as such.
  All punctuation marks that do not belong to the quoted content, printed outside the quotes.
- Names of classes of entities, such as nationalities, remain in lower case since those do not constitute proper nouns.
  For example, in the phrase «I met a group of kenyan friends», the quality *kenyan* refers to a class; while to mention the whole set of people from Kenya would suffice to state «all kenyans» or «the kenyan people», and there the quality *kenyan* still refers to a class of individuals; exists no such thing as an integrated entity called «The Kenyans». Thereat, the phrase «some kenyans run marathons proficiently» constitutes a short simplification for «some kenyan individuals run marathons proficiently».
  In this context, the term *Homo sapiens* constitutes the label of a concept associated to a group of similar entities treated as a whole –whether treating species as single whole arose from sound reasoning, results questionable. Meanwhile, the term *humans* constitutes the label of a classification. Thereon, does not exist a *Homo sapiens Kenyans*, but exist *kenyan humans*. The term *kenyan humans* derived from a classification of living organisms.
  The term *Homo sapiens* constitutes an insert into the language –an alien term outside the regular logic which does not belong to the regular assortment of words. Thereat, *Homo sapiens* recorded without any modification, hence capitalized the first letter.

- Hyphens used for linking compound concepts.
  The text intentionally lacks end-of-line hyphenations, so the reader can focus on words instead of tracking character strings.
- En-dashes either used or reserved for—
  - ✦ Linking compound adjectives when one of them already consists of a two-word compound.
  - ✦ Ranges, serial connections, and binomial interactions.
  - ✦ Marking the boundaries of a comment whose content explains, summarizes, or expands the content of the enclosing sentence. Added a space at the side of each en-dash.
- Em-dashes used for starting a list while avoiding the repetition of introductory words, where the same sequence of words could stand printed at the beginning of each item in the list.
- Curved parenthesis used for content not strictly indispensable for the continuity of the text; in general, the text enclosed in curved parenthesis may serve as a resource for the reader to understand either the statement or paragraph which contains it.
- When the word *or* appears between the last two members of a sequence of options which lacks any previous qualifier (such as *either*), then the reader should mentally append to the sequence the phrase *or any combination thereof.*
- An association using the particle *and* outranks any adjacent using the particle *or*. Thus, *A and B or C* equals *A and (B or C)*.

The sole academic title I hold consists of a five-year bachelor degree in mechanical engineering from a university named *National Autonomous University of Mexico.*

I would like to thank my family for supporting me during many difficult years, including the time spent in this writing.

ANDERS BAERBOCK
August 2022.

Contents

1

Introduction

[1.1]

D URING DECADES existed available the necessary technological and natural resources to provide the full human population with the indispensable income to satisfy its basic needs, without wastefulness but without poverty. Such common prosperity never happened; instead, exists a huge inequality in the distribution of resources, among social classes and among human groups, worsened by a rampant overpopulation about which hitherto almost nobody wants to talk as if doing so stood forbidden or constituted a taboo.

Currently, the most notable concentration in the consumption of resources –most of these not renewable– happens at the country where resides the core of the contemporary capitalistic fraud. Such country consumes, for example, about 20% of the planetary oil output while living there barely about 4% of the world population.

[1.2]

For centuries now, humans gathered and systematically organized enough data to realize the immensity and complexity of the universe where we live. A universe where the planet Earth constitutes merely a small hideaway and the perceptions derived from our sensory organs constitute only an internal representation.

During the last century –and during centuries before– some humans held a hypothesis postulating that *education*, or transmission and publicity of the gathered data about the nature of the world, would allow the ignorant human masses to modify their mental structure, build different choices, and reach a material prosperity. This also never happened: some people massively disseminated scientific information, institutionalized education became mandatory in many nations, advanced humans successfully fostered the construction of large quantities of public libraries geographically scattered intending to provide access to knowledge for everyone; thereupon, some persons understood, yet most humans continue employing extremely primitive mental structures, rooted in myths, to build the essential choices of their lives.

Since two decades ago, the massive usage of the internet showed in a more brutal form this incapacity. Hunger, malnutrition, or isolation do not cause the incapacity to learn and preserve knowledge, as shown by millions of humans who now live without nutritional deficiencies in cities with full access to large sources of written information.

[1.3]

At the time of this writing, anyone with certain minimal intelligence can observe that the current human activities in the planet Earth conduce to the depletion and destruction of the essential resources for the continuity of a civilization produced by a primitive species.

Nevertheless, despite all available evidence, a majority does not even process the data, while others adhere to mediocre and suicidal behaviors expressed in declarations such as:

- «There still oil to extract in the ground, happens nothing unexpected with it and nobody wants to stop using those fancy trucks, happens no motive enough to change course.»
- «There still a lot of jungle –or prairie, or desert, or woodland, and so forth– to destroy and afterwards we can use the space to expand our cities.»
- «We will populate the Earth until no one else can stand in here, and then we will go to Mars to continue the party there.»

And others build any kind of rationalization with the sole purpose of justifying the continuation of their current way of life.

[1.4]

To make it worse, the essential organizational mechanisms for building societies through interdependence –through the exchange of assets, products, and services– proceed captured and controlled by the institutionalized fraud and stealing ingrained in the social order denominated *capitalism*. Those criminal activities addressed with further detail later in this document. The scheme of fraud and robbery typically happens sustained by (or uses a) form of societal organization denominated *representative democracy*, which also does not properly functions –it supports a structure of fraud and stealing! This failure also addressed later in this document.

[1.5]

Within this document described essential parts of a human cooperative system which will yield a more advanced civilization, sustainable, and focused on the success of humankind. Nevertheless, I do not hold the necessary data to propose a unique civilization at a planetary scale, nor I can sustainably spend the time and material resources necessary to do it. Hence, I propose a solution to the extent of my knowledge.

Therefrom, in this document described components of a new social contract which eliminates the capitalistic fraud, reorganizes productive social relationships, and reforms democracy.

Absent still, a proposal for a reform of the language and the traditional hierarchical command structures.

[1.6]

As priorities for any human society, in order of importance:

1. Preserve a habitable planet Earth for humans and local species. A developed civilization must execute sustainable practices for enhancing the quality of life, perspectives, and possibilities for both humans and local species. From now on, we must not consider nature as our *mother* but rather as our *daughter*, we will take care of her and will ensure her health and development.
2. Preserve alive the largest quantity of hominids after fulfilling priority number 1.
3. Direct all material and intellectual surpluses, including redundant data-processing machines, into the development of science and technology such that enables us to continue opening new horizons for ourselves and for future generations.

[1.7]

If humankind continues as a single species, or if the fracture will evolve into an open division between a more advanced species and another more primitive, remains unresolved at the time of this writing.

The events alone will reveal who can move forward, and who cannot. In any case, any forward-going human civilization, humankind or its successors, must process a parasitic psychopathic subspecies.

[1.8]

By no means I pretend to claim the absolute authorship of all the postulates made here since any competent individual may construct the obvious cases using widely known data. Further, where I deliberately employ approaches developed by other individuals as basis or even as integral part, the respective credits stand recorded.

[1.9]

For a better comprehension of what here exposed, the following article and books can provide both a highly useful background and additional information. Hereinafter the references to those in most cases made using the surname of each author.

The "What" and "Why" of Goal Pursuits: Human Needs and the Self-Determination of Behavior. (Article.)
Edward L. Deci and Richard M. Ryan. (Deci and Ryan.)
Year 2000.

Without Conscience: The Disturbing World of the Psychopaths Among Us.
Robert D. Hare.
Year 1993.
Important note: Hare uses the word *conscience* with a meaning that denotes the behavior-regulating mechanisms described by Deci and Ryan. Thereat, the meaning of the word *conscience* as used by Hare widely differs from the *function conscience* described in this document.

Executive Functions: What They Are, How They Work, and Why They Evolved.
Russell A. Barkley.
Year 2012.

The Functions of the Executive.
Chester I. Barnard.
Year 1938.

The Golden Bough: A Study in Comparative Religion.
James George Frazer.
Year 1894.

Tragedy and Hope: A History of the World in our Time.
Carroll Quigley.
Year 1966.
Note: Skip the «pro-western» supremacist bias displayed by the author.

Basic Concepts

[2.1]

A COMMON CONCEPTUAL FRAMEWORK, assembled by basic statements, composes the foundation of the assertions made in subsequent chapters.

Basic Dynamics of Living Organisms

[2.2]

Any living organism consists of a material organization or instrumentally arranged structure whose actions tend to produce the continuity of the existence of such organization –this a basic definition of *living organism*. To achieve the aforementioned existential continuity, the organism can expand, reproduce, and procure itself resources for its own consumption, among several other actions.

Also, due to the nature of thermodynamics and the general physics of the universe where we live, everything tends to an equilibrium, every object tends to diminish differences which can yield *energy*, which can yield *impetus*. By standard nomenclature, the degree of order within an object denominated *entropy*, and the energy that an object can yield denominated *potential energy*.

Consequently, a quasi-static organism would tend to disintegrate during the passage of time merely due to the incidence of ordinary external and internal factors to it.

Accordingly, any organism tends to an existential continuity whenever develops activities –develops a behavior– that enable itself to procure and process the necessary resources for reverting a *natural decay*. This natural decay produced by the increase of entropy within, the latter by means of the transit to states that can yield less potential energy. The act of reverting and/or averting natural decay customarily called *maintenance*.

A living organism that tends to survival regularly will keep its entropy and potential energy within a range, and the actions geared towards upholding its operation within these *physiological standards* cause a permanent consumption and disposal of external resources by the organism. Besides, the organism will accumulate resources and mechanisms that will provide support during contingencies and environments more adverse than usual, merely because that activity will increase its survival rate. Hence, an organism can accumulate resources and material arrangements (including mechanisms and devices) favorable to its existence; among other actions, for achieving the aforesaid goals the organism may:

+ Increase its mass and volume.
+ Replicate itself (or parts of).
+ Establish a larger spatial dispersion of its constitutive elements.

These accumulations happen also externally to the organism's main body, in what usually denominated *extended phenotype*.

In the case of the living organisms produced by terrestrial ecosystems, molecules constitute the basic unit of each organism, and each of those can get replaced; if the organization continues functioning while replacing components, then the organism remains alive (operational). No basic element that belongs to the organism necessarily must continue inside the organism eternally.

[2.3]

The organism that does not execute activities geared towards its existential continuity –its survival– will eventually disappear during the passage of time because of the aforementioned dynamics. When an organism ceases to perform such activities, it customarily becomes qualified as *deceased*, notwithstanding that most of the corresponding material structure may remain existent for a while.

The Independent Variable

[2.4]

In this universe, in an environment with newtonian dynamics cognitive organisms consider *time* as the sole independent variable. This implies that, despite whatever happens with other factors, time keeps advancing forward and all the other events contain the variable time, and a cognitive entity may measure the temporal length of the existence of each particular event.

The Trajectory of Humankind

[2.5]

According to the available evidence, several groups of hominids simultaneously inhabited the planet Earth several tens of thousands of years ago. The peculiar characteristic of those first groups consisted in their drive for expansion into all the habitats where they found suitable means for their subsistence –those habitats hereat denominated *habitable zones*. Thereupon, several thousands years ago all the habitable zones became occupied by one or another group. The evidence also points to the fact that neanderthals at some point constituted a group with a larger population than the *Homo sapiens*, and that they lacked a complex language which would enable the transmission of complex propositions.

The size and geographical distribution of the habitable zones varies typically, among other factors, depending on the technology employed by the group of hominids. Nevertheless, almost certainly, in the environment where the *Homo sapiens* variety crystallized the technological differences that this group could wield respect to other varieties, such as neanderthals, yielded minimal effects. In usual conditions, when a new biological branch starts, does it with the technological baggage of the main.

Certainly, the group that evolved towards the *Homo sapiens* shared the habitable zones with other hominids and definitely competed for the available resources. This competition for survival with other hominids constituted the motor of the process that formed humans and thereby produced long-range consequences. In this competition for survival humans –we– killed the neanderthals.

However, a parasitic psychopathic subspecies disguised among the human ranks, and humans carried forward these hominids so far as the current era, this addressed further in [3.170] and subsequent sections.

[2.6]

Both in past and present times, hominids achieve the extermination of other groups of the same genus typically by the following means:

a) *Physical displacement of other groups.* Example: The palestinian nation gradually displaced and expelled from its own land by the israeli nation after the Second World War, in a decades-long sequence.

b) *Marginalization in the access to resources.* This constitutes the currently most used method. Example: The dominion of the solid and liquid minerals in Mexico by a few private organizations and individuals at the beginning of the XXI century.

c) *Slavery and direct extermination.* No specific examples necessary; books of history already contain more than enough recounts of ethnic, colonial, and genocidal wars, purges, forced-labor camps, large-scale kidnapping and selling of humans, and so forth.

d) *Charging tributes and colonial rents, or otherwise unfairly obtaining an income using a privileged position.* Examples:

α. Review the description of capitalism in chapter [4].

β. The privatization of water under the guise of «operational concessions». In contrast with the aforementioned case of minerals, the members of the general population become captive customers who must pay an established rent for obtaining a supply of the privatized water. (The *rent* equivalent to a so-called «profit margin» for the «concessionary» entity.)

The capitalistic doctrine strongly supports the appropriation of profits by privileged humans, as described in [6.40] and subsequent sections.

e) A combination of any or all the others.

[2.7]

During the last century at least, in general, the marginalization in the access to resources happened in the most covert possible way, or using large-scale propagandistic campaigns to completely divert the general societal attention from the facts. All these actions constitute factual wars, whether *hot* or *cold*, against the groups targeted for extermination.

In all cases, naturally, the success of these wars produces the death and disappearance of the targeted group. And, in the cases *c*) and *d*) of the previous section, while they remain alive, the members of the targeted group contribute to the prosperity of their own exterminators. If the reader still holds any doubt, he/she only needs to review any serious detailed description of past wars of annihilation and the occupation of «empty lands» during the last centuries.

Notably, neither the exterminators nor the terminated people require holding a conscious judgment about what they do and what happens in their environment; in this case typically the exterminators will deny reality. Review the whole chapter [3] for understanding how this mental blindness and denial happens.

Introduction to Executive Functions

[2.8]

In this context, Barnard notes that the differentiating element in the nature of the group known as *Homo sapiens* consists in the development of the psychological functions denominated *executive functions* –this topic introduced here, and described further in [3.88] and subsequent sections. Physiologically, those functions arise from neuronal arrangements chiefly at the prefrontal cortex of the human brain; hence, those functions rely chiefly on the last evolved part which in turn utilizes several ancestral structures.

Barnard argues that the primary and implicit objective –the evolutionary aim– of the *executive functions* consists in socializing and thereby establishing exchange and interdependence relationships among humans. Nevertheless, Barnard lost of sight the extermination of the other hominids.

The primary and implicit objective of the traditional *executive functions* consists in achieving a continuous expansion of the group of hominids and the accumulation of resources by any means necessary, in harmony with the dynamics explained in section [2.2]. In contrast, achieving an increase in the sophistication of interdependence and exchange, and the annihilation of other hominids, constitute secondary subsidiary objectives derived from the primary. Moreover, the competition and struggle for the utilization of the habitable zones promoted or caused the increase in the sophistication of interdependence and exchange; existed no other incentive fostering the development of these characteristics at the velocity it happened.

The *executive functions* enabled humans to organize themselves and to develop technology. Both resources –organization and technology– then employed to exterminate others (the «competitors») subsequently acquiring the latter's resources. Otherwise, we would still roam quietly eating fruits and vegetables in forests, evolving at a rate similar to that of other species.

[2.9]

The essential characteristic of the *executive functions* consists in the development of abstract language. A relatively popular saying states that in language «the shape constitutes the essence» or, expressed in another way, the structure and shape used to build statements denotes the structure and mental functions of the one who generates them. Explicitly, the mental scaffolding, styles, and variable patterns –several in each individual– utilized to generate statements convey information about the available intellectual functions and resources. Used with care this information serves for analyzing the individual and, upon these inferences, at least partially ascertain its nature.

Abstract language enabled hominids to construct internal representations of reality for the purpose of—

α. Transmitting those internal representations to other congeners by means of guttural sound representations.

β. Modeling that reality, and performing abstract simulations of it.

Afterwards, humans used solid objects to represent their inner representations, thereat creating an additional codification which they utilized to store and diffuse those inner representations impersonally and independently of their own bodies. Thereby augmented practically infinitely the external memory capacity available for the human brain –considering that also stands available an index and a classification of the data externally stored, or a search algorithm.

External representations of language enabled the development of social organization. Meanwhile, the usage of language enabled hominids to internally and abstractly model nature, therefore producing more advanced technology. Those advancements then shared using the external representations of the same language, whenever necessary to efficiently transmit them. Furthermore, using written records, hominids acquired the capacity to represent externally each one of the internal representations for the purpose of acutely and deliberately analyzing them; this latter perhaps constitutes the greatest contribution of writing for the advancement of human mental structures.

[2.10]

Noticing:

a) Everything indicates that language and its guttural sound representation developed concurrently and during interactions among hominids. (Review the text of Barnard about this.)

b) Language exists solely inside the carrier cognitive device. Therefore, in the human case, language exists solely inside the human brain.

c) Individual words constitute labels for the internal representations made by the brain (cognitive device) corresponding to and denoting entities from reality –from the universe from which the organism acquires data using sensors. Each one of these labels refers to an inner representation of reality.

d) Conscious processes –review chapter [3] for the description of mental functions– can only observe the labels of the inner representations. Yet, through those same conscious processes the hominid typically can describe each label or «word» by using a subset of the rest of the repertoire of labels, constituting that a circular reference and impressing upon the organism the false notion that it «knows» what «means» each word. Illustratively:

If

$a = b + c$

$b = d + e$
$c = a + b$
$d = a + e$
$e = b + d$

To which quantities equal a, b, c, d, and e?

e) Also, a human organism can experience the sensorial stimulus produced during the vicinity of either an object or event targeted for cognitively affixing a denomination –an object or event which the organism will label. Hereupon, the sensors of the organism transmit the data related to the object or event into the brain, which then *abstracts* from it what deems essential and forms the internal representation of the object or event, respectively; then results very convenient to establish standardized labels for each one of these internal representations, thereby making possible communication.

For example: An infant can get exposed to electromagnetic radiation in the range of wavelengths denominated «green». Afterwards its caregivers can allow the infant to form itself an internal representation of the nature of the entity that generates such sensorial data flux. And ultimately its caregivers can instruct the infant to label that internal representation with the sequence *green* from the sound guttural representation.

f) Some humans exercise the peculiar task of imaginarily recreating the sensorial experience produced by an object or event, respectively, with the aim of elucidating the content of the word or concept. For example: «to visualize a tree», «to recall or to deliberately generate a flashback of the olfactory experience produced by the aroma of a flower».

g) Notice that humans ordinarily construe the entities typically denominated «logical operations» as a means to permanently define *sequences of events* (which advance forward in time) and *arrangements or dispositions* of cognitively observable (and hence inferred as existent) entities within the universe.

h) After the development of language and its sound guttural representation, humans transformed this sound representation into a new internal representation corresponding to or recalling the same external sound.

i)   Thus, as facts:

     α.   Language consists of a set of internal representations of reality.

     β.   Typically, humans express language using a sound representation, using a representation consisting of static visual figures –aka writing– and, very important, using an internal representation in an *inner speech line* that the organism associates closely to the sound representation.

     γ.   Regularly, the labels of one representation stand linked univocally with the labels of another representation.

j)   Humans can construe new internal representations –with their respective labels– derived from or based on the ones previously existent. This construction of representations without resorting to direct experience, without previously registering sensorially any such event, typically happens when the organism infers that the construct modeled, and sometimes also simulated, either corresponds to reality or could exist within the reality.

Thereupon, humans built a lot internal of representations about theoretical events and objects, and associated «logical operations» involving those.

k)   An organism (or a cognitive device) can then use language to model and simulate the dynamics of the represented universe; as anyone can notice, such operations frequently produce falsehoods.

[2.11]

The work of Barnard provides a more detailed description of the *executive functions* of the human brain and their relation to inter-hominid communication. As mentioned before, in [3.88] and subsequent sections described more extensively the subject of *executive functions* to an extent sufficient for the purpose of conveying the intended message described in section [1.5].

For now, without detailing organizational processes or the human brain functioning (or any combination thereof), suffices to convey the following.

Natural Selection, Depredation, and Simultaneous Collaboration Within and Among Human Groups

[2.12]

When they choose to do so, all human organisms become members of a productive organization –of manufacture, or services, or the state-organization. A human joins any of such organizations with the intention (not always explicit, review the human brain functioning in chapter [3]) of obtaining the resources and income necessary for the survival and reproduction of either:

α.   The individual itself.

β.   Those congeners regarded as genetically related –typically the lineage.

γ.   Both the individual and its selected congeners.

Besides, in an approximate account, without dwelling on particulars, any observer can notice that traditional human groups which can qualify as «organized», as civilizations, nations, or alike entities, share several characteristics among which here highlighted:

- A hierarchical social structure.
- A centralized command (in a person or small council).
- A social base typically living with limited resources or, in many cases, in abject poverty.

In societies that behave by *representative democracy* the people directly or indirectly chooses the members of the centralized command –consult section [7.31] for more about this. In the case of empires, marginalized and/or subjugated human groups typically constitute the social base and furnish the resources that the core of the empire squanders –in current times in the «western» civilization this latter happens at the core of the «financial capitalism», consult sections [4.65] and [5.12]. Approximately the same happens in typical merchant organizations: they comprise a hierarchical social structure and the social base –the low-rank workers or employees– receive profits relatively minuscule compared to those who stand in command positions.

[2.13]

In societies not formally layered, nor living in either fascist or totalitarian regimes, and where the abolishment of slavery and bondage happened centuries ago, occurs a widespread aberration where many individuals internalized an assumed membership into a social layer and therefore behave according to what they deem «appropriate for their class». In that context they use titles and adjectives for themselves and their environment that reflect and reinforce such assumption. This happens because of cognitive insufficiencies which include an absence of the *function conscience* –described chapter [3]– coupled with an historic inertia. A detailed examination of such aberration and its inertia stands beyond the scope of this document.

[2.14]

Observe also that natural selection constitutes an active developing process, current, continuous, and noticeable among the human species. Moreover, currently physically visible differences tend to fade and now exist standards: five fingers, two feet, two hands, and so forth. Notwithstanding variations in sizes and colors, standardized physical features support the feasibility to breed or sexually reproduce with all those who share them and constitute the core of the traits considered «human».

In contrast, the differences in the construction and operation of the human brain tend to progressively become more acute and profound. Those differences already reached a degree where any observer can pertinently presume the existence of several types of humans and at least one subspecies with associated characteristics, behavioral interactions, and ways of life unambiguously differentiated. Howbeit, while an observer can delineate the cores certainly, the boundaries between each human subset tend to remain diffuse, still.

[2.15]

As recorded before, the depredation among groups of hominids constitutes a fundamental element in traditional human social organizations. At the same time, due to the gregarious nature of human civilizations and ways of life, so far a reduced human group cannot undertake the elimination of all the others without suffering the consequences of the absence of the skills, workforce, and resources the latter can provide. This operational sustainability factually defines a *critical mass* of indispensable population for the survival of a human group with any given civilizational –social and technological– setting.

[2.16]

In traditional civilizations, a single human group attempts to outlast, prevail over, and dominate other groups. Nowadays, despite the available technological advancements, the backwards social organization requires modern slaves, albeit most of them chainless, indispensable for the functioning of the system of domination. This predatory nature of humans, from my viewpoint, constitutes the primordial origin of the concepts of «good» and «evil» popular among those who did not evolve in their way of thinking.

[2.17]

Hence, in the traditional behavioral pattern, survival consists essentially in:

α. Placing oneself and one's own descendants on the top layers of the survival group. Accordingly, belonging to the group of overlords and accumulators of resources and income.

β. Spreading one's own genetic material among the largest quantity possible (of individuals) inside and outside the group, but mainly inside.

γ. Moving away from the mass of modern slaves and the possibilities of extinction that such condition implies.

As mentioned before, this pattern happens both inside productive organizations and among nations; in almost all cases the social base stands in structural disadvantage in relation with the elite.

[2.18]

Presumably, therefrom, that pressure towards vanishing and extinction of those in disadvantaged positions produces behavioral interactions where each organism aims to its individual survival and, thereat, in those interactions develops a competition for the higher organizational posts intermeshed with organizational collaboration. If those who formerly stood in the base diminish in number and/or strength, then the withered will result displaced –or replaced– by the ones who formerly occupied high or at least middle-hierarchy posts, or most frequently by the descendants of these, since (because of the associated favorable conditions) the prevailing ones reproduced at higher rates than the individuals at the base.

In this way, besides the forced disappearance due to the extermination among human groups, also inside each group typically proceed depredatory and destructive behavioral patterns against congeners.

Thereupon, the incorporation into a traditional human group does not secure survival, notwithstanding if the individual performs its organizational functions faultlessly and successfully, happens no war, or this group wins the confrontation among groups.

The development of technology makes increasingly evident what exposed here, since lower strata in human organizations progressively becomes redundant.

[2.19]

Finally, an important clarification:

The fact that some behavioral patterns proceeded since the inception of humankind, neither conditions nor constrains the future; humans dwell not coerced to repeat what their ancestors did.

People with the *function conscience* readily notices this nonexistence of a binding to the past.

[2.20]

If reviewed what Barnard wrote, or if observed the existing human populations, anyone can notice that some human groups remain in stages of hunter-gatherers and self-sufficiency agriculture. The nature and foundation of such stagnation not addressed in this document.

The Last 200 Years

[2.21]

Capitalism constitutes an instance of traditional human «natural selection» –an intra-species depredatory process– generated by organizations assembled using primeval *executive functions* coupled with a primitive culture. This noteworthy because some persons tend to regard capitalism as «the origin of the problems», when in fact capitalism constitutes merely a stage (final, as here attempted) of a sequence started with the genesis of the species.

In any case, capitalism comprises practices which themselves constitute a step forward in the sophistication of the traditional model of organizational crafts, but capitalism constitutes a maladaptive bifurcation which happened during the increase of the size and complexity of a civilization. This way of building a society, this sort of organizational crafts, this highly dysfunctional and toxic way of living cannot and will never serve as foundation to build a superior civilization because of its inherent nature, and already endangered the sustainability of human life on Earth.

[2.22]

The «achievement», so to speak, of capitalism, consists in the deliberate promotion of the increase of commercial exchange operations among humans (trade), done with the goals of:

1. Accumulating income and material assets in favor of capitalistic «banks» and money minters.
2. When not physically accumulating assets, then with the goal of building a large capacity of exercising purchasing power out of nothing.

[2.23]

The increase of commercial-exchange operations happens by—

α. Augmenting the number of participants in the exchange.
β. Augmenting the variety and quantity of circulating products and services –and, consequently, the volume of exchange per individual.
γ. Incorporating additional quantities of material assets –raw materials, either pristine or seized land, and so forth– into exchange operations.

This subject (the increase of commercial operations) described comprehensively in sections [4.45] to [4.51].

[2.24]

The consequential demographic expansion, the increased production of artifacts and services, and the stretched land usage by human activities over the planet Earth, either produced or involved—

a) The massive destruction of ecosystems and the irrecoverable extinction of many species.
b) The indiscriminate exploitation of the planet's material resources, the renewable at rates much larger than their corresponding recovery, the non-renewable massively squandered without caring to develop substitutes.

c) The beginning of a new geological era where the sedimentary
    deposits and continental layers contain large proportions of—
    +   Household and industrial garbage.
    +   Construction scrap –armored concrete steel, pavement,
        both natural and artificial filling materials, and so forth.
    +   All other kinds of human waste.
    Those layers will produce long-range consequences in the
    terrestrial geology.

d) The alteration of the Earth's hydrological cycles. Including the
    accumulation of giant clouds of smoke and contaminated air
    spanning continental zones.
    Furthermore, the massive amounts of contaminants deposited
    by humans in the terrestrial water and atmosphere already
    altered the chemical composition of the aqueous solutions
    which compose the material foundation of the life on Earth,
    including the acidification of the oceans; thereby worsening the
    ecological disaster and leading to a further extinction of species.

This happened during at least two centuries since the start of the
First Industrial Revolution and the subsequent expansion of capitalism,
no one can state that the outcome constituted a surprise, nobody can
claim blindness to these facts.

[2.25]

Moreover, the easy consumption of material resources propped by
capitalism, together with modern health technologies, temporarily
distorted the demographic dynamics described in section [2.18]. Hence,
many individuals in the base of social pyramids reproduced at very high
rates during several decades of the XX century, in many cases producing
more than ten children per family, and now the consequences accrued.

The wave of easy consumption and easy survival rewarded
ignorance: many individuals saw no need to improve themselves and the
world they lived at, while successfully reproducing at higher rates than
the more cultivated ones, and consequently the quality of the social base
decreased.

Thus, notwithstanding insufficient voluntary birth-control
practices, in a vast majority of countries both the overpopulation and
the corresponding size of hastily planned or unplanned urban areas
grew at extremely fast paces.

Nowadays, urban slums and peripheral sections of cities stand filled with a majority of humans who lack an understanding of the most basic concepts and practices which supported the life of the generations which lived without so much pampering. Many of those humans who fancy themselves as pertaining to either a «middle class» or an «elite», and live in better conditions, likewise lack such basic understanding.

Detached from ecological and geophysical natural processes, with non-existent social fabrics which formerly supported ancestral and less destructive ways of life, millions of humans with deficient *executive functions* –with low cognitive capacities– perceive the world and its events according to the feed provided by mass-communication industries, and behave accordingly.

[2.26]

At the beginning of the XXI century, the capitalistic rate of consumption and destruction already dwarfed the Earth's capacity of recovery and natural self-regulation.

As stated before, capitalism constitutes a symptom, not the root cause of the behavioral disaster. Any observer may ask why humans did not plan and execute sanely their own development; why, when events unequivocally derailed from a prosperous future, humanity did not react. The derailment happened decades before the time of this writing.

Even lacking the fundamental knowledge for organizing mature and sustainable commercial exchanges, humans could enacted different, alternative, and rational courses of action.

[2.27]

As recorded in section [1.3], in the face of large quantities of irrefutable evidence, including massive distortions of the planetary regular environmental course, and everywhere macroscopic events showcasing both the grave damage done to the Earth and the unsustainable consequences of the current human way of life, a large majority of humans still do not comprehend or acknowledge the situation; and most humans will not do it by themselves. Further, in many countries self-managed by *representative democracy* (which comprises the currently most advanced set of methods to assemble a state-organization) many people actively oppose and discredit any correction of course.

The following chapters provide an understanding of the behavioral interactions and the material conditions which stabilized such craziness for so long, and the origin of the craziness itself.

[2.28]

Modern *representative democracy* arose, at least partially, from a deliberated collective effort to organize a society aiming to produce a common prosperity; from this collective effort the capitalistic criminals strived to obtain an advantage.

In contrast, capitalism arose purely as a criminal enterprise assembled by organized swindlers. Capitalism's «financial system» constitutes the most successful organized crime venture in human history.

[2.29]

The operative problems of capitalism at the beginning of the XXI century happen fundamentally due to the progressive shortage of material resources to consume and landmass to spoil and incorporate, with which prolong the fraud and stealing scheme that propels it since its inception.

Nowadays, during the third decade of the XXI century, the capitalistic criminals attempt to rework their scheme to continue robbing.

Human Cooperative Systems

[2.30]

The concept of *human cooperative system*, in an appropriate context shortened as *cooperative system*, refers to a deliberated organization of human activities in such way that, if performed as expected, the human activities resemble a system due to the predictability of the activities and their outcomes. Actual systems always involve material objects arranged causally.

Thereat, the concept of *human cooperative system* in no way implies a group of humans physically interconnected. Rather, the component of *system* refers to the deliberated purposeful organization of actions made to resemble an actual system. Therefore, whenever pertinent, individuals must use the concept of *human cooperative system* or *cooperative system* as a single unit without attempting to dissect it by its etymological meaning.

[2.31]

Most past and present human cooperative systems classify as either population-wide or particular:

- A *population-wide or societal cooperative system* comprises a general society with its associated state-organization, if any. The essential nature of a societal cooperative system and its state-organization described in [7.13] and subsequent sections.
- A *particular cooperative system* consists of an insular one within a society, in which only a subset of the whole population participates. In this document, *particular cooperative systems* also referred to as *particular* or *private organizations*.

[2.32]

All cooperative systems arise from a *social contract*, whether this social contract formal or informal, and most frequently arise from a mix of both formal and informal social contracts. Hereinafter—

- ⊹ Any social contract encompassing a whole population called *population-wide social contract* or simply *social contract*.
- ⊹ Any insular social contract encompassing exclusively a given particular cooperative system called *particular organizational social contract*, in a suitable context shortened as *particular social contract*.

  Currently, a legal «incorporation act» –the document that formally established a corporation or similar legal entity– ordinarily serves as an inchoate particular social contract, typically complemented and honed by an informal particular social contract and by formal internal organizational regulations sometimes codified as *bylaws*.

Notice that subsidiary organizational regulations constitute a subset of a social contract, albeit in a differentiated and ordinarily lower rank. Hence, for example, a legal «incorporation act» and the *Constitution* of a country constitute the core of a formal social contract, but typically do not comprise all of it. However, in these cases where the formal social contract exists distributed among several documents, unless otherwise stated, the words *social contract* customarily refer to the core of that social contract.

[2.33]

When a society or human group already created a formal social contract, any informal social contract may serve just as complementary and supporting.

Democratic Freedoms and Democratic Rights

[2.34]

The organizational provisions established in the formal population-wide social contract circumscribe the *freedom* of any citizen. Therefore, the range of activities that a citizen can enact do not amount to a complete *freedom*, but to a *degree of freedom* prescribed by the social contract.

Accordingly, in modern democratic societies anyone can appropriately refer to the activities which any citizen can perform arbitrarily and out of its personal will, as belonging to a *margin of personal action* prescribed by the social contract.

Nonetheless, in current democratic societies people regard the existing status-quo as *freedom*, while that not true. Some legal specialists attempt to fix the aforementioned discrepancy by equating *freedom* to the performance of those activities not forbidden by law. However, this fix merely constitutes a linguistic and logical distortion which obscures the truth, misleads sound cognitive processes, and thereby hinders the advancement of humankind.

[2.35]

For differentiating themselves from authoritarian –fascist to any degree, and totalitarian– societies and regimes, people from democratic societies can refer to *democratic freedoms* and *democratic rights*.

The concept of *democratic freedoms* denotes specific aspects of the accepted social behavior within a cooperative system which enable the citizens to build a self-determined life. Hence, in these specific behavioral aspects the citizens can act or behave wholly volitionally and arbitrarily.

The concept of *democratic rights* denotes those organizational provisions within a social contract directly establishing as legitimate the personal exercise of democratic procedures for societal choice-making.

[2.36]

Such self-determined life the citizens of authoritarian regimes cannot exercise, neither individually nor collectively. An individual can exercise its personal volition in a much smaller and much more restrained way in an authoritarian regime in comparison with a democratic one.

For example, the following a codification of a *democratic freedom*: «Freedom to engage in any activity not forbidden by law, without belonging to or receiving instructions from any given command chain, regardless of whether the command chain protrudes from the state-organization, or constitutes part of a fascist formation, or both.»

3

The Fracture of the Homo Sapiens

Brain Development

[3.1]

I N THE TRAJECTORY OF HUMANKIND, during centuries and until recent times, large amounts of mysticism pervaded the common knowledge about the inner workings of the cognitive organ called brain. Hence, a primitive cognitive species did not understand itself.

At the core of the human mysticism stands a divorce from reality deeply ingrained in many human mental structures. As everyone knows, during some ages mysticism pervaded almost all aspects of human life, and nowadays still conditions and/or directs the patterns of thought and action in several major aspects of the behavior of many *Homo sapiens* individuals. The divorce from reality stems from two mechanisms –as far as I noted, could exist more:

1. A bipartite dissociation of brain functions and their corresponding disjoined operation, described in [3.137] and subsequent sections.
2. A primeval inchoate mechanism to build relationships, described in [3.100] and subsequent sections.

Many times the effects of both sources combined into and produced a relentless magical thinking. But to focus on the magical thinking itself would constitute a myopic approach insufficient for actually comprehending the origins and nature of the divorce from reality among humans.

[3.2]

Human-brain functions direct, regulate, and control the nature of human societies, individual behavior, the individual perceptions about the world, and the personal abilities indispensable to join a more advanced society. Therefrom, when seeking to improve the human world, considering the qualities available for the task constitutes a paramount foremost step.

[3.3]

In this chapter described operational human-brain functions, but not the electrochemical mechanisms that build them. Likewise, in this chapter addressed the sources of the divorce from reality. The aim consists in providing a panorama of the phenomena, upon which the reader may comprehend subsequent sections of this document.

Linguistic Correction

[3.4]

As previously recorded, abstract language defined the *Homo sapiens'* dawn and, since never happened any collective hard-break with the past whereby started a new synthetic culture, current languages carry and agglomerate inheritances and inertia emanated during millenniums of usage; from transliterations, translations, and insertions of foreign words; and from deliberated reforms made by state-nations. Many terms and structures that should stand bygone remain in use, chiefly because human mental structures also did not advance.

Must emphasize that one of the main purposes of abstract language consists in the representation and modeling of reality. Thereupon, given the primitivism and precariousness of the knowledge about the universe during the stages when the first linguistic structures arose, many of these words, concepts, and verbs—

a. Attempt simplifications that support, predispose the individual to, or directly produce distortions of reality. Those simplifications functional as incipient tools in early times, outright dysfunctional in a modern world.

β.   Very frequently constitute indispensable or essential parts of
     rationalizations and cognitive processes that produce
     pertinacious mistakes. Those mistakes not functional even as
     simplifications, but constitute full falsehoods.

[3.5]

Therefore, here introduced a list of words that should disappear
from daily life:

- «Value». Include all similar concepts, together with associated
  or derived words. The word «value» refers to a nonexistent
  entity, shares some characteristics with the «phlogiston» used
  by alchemists to model the transference of thermic energy.
  Review section [3.114] for the description applied to productive
  processes and subsequent commercial exchanges.

- «Belief» / «Believe» (verb). This set of concepts lacks any logic.
  In some instances these words shelter the abandonment of
  reason, in other instances these words conceal fully
  unconscious mental processes, and in yet other instances these
  words glue inchoate incoherent verbalizations. Of course, in a
  single statement can coexist combined or compounded all the
  mentioned distortions. The verbalizations referred may occur
  outwardly vocalized or inside the *inner speech line* –this latter
  mental function described in [3.60] and subsequent sections.

- «Faith». This concept too, lacks any logic. Furthermore, it
  precludes the development of advanced thought patterns. This
  concept presents a hard stop for reason, it may originate in
  some neural complex hitherto not adequately studied. When
  vigorously challenged, either by external facts or by intellectual
  (abstract) sound logical argumentation, a cognitive dissonance
  will happen, and frequently the denial mechanisms around the
  construct of «faith» will answer with intolerance as a coping
  mechanism. Hereby arises a source of authoritarianism.
  Thoroughly examining the origin, development, and subsequent
  entrenchment of these behavioral patterns would produce
  content well beyond the (already defined) scope of this
  document. Nevertheless, in [3.137] and subsequent sections
  briefly described further the origin and function of «faith» in
  mental constructions and cognitive behaviors.

- «Good» / «Bad». Include all derived words. These two words lack congruity with reality; besides, humans will never agree or concur on a fully standard definition because of what described in section [3.45]. Usually humans use these words as elements in the rationalizations founded in «Belief» / «Believe» and «Faith», apparently because these words shared the same ancestral cradle.
- «Luck». Replace with a focus on calculating probabilities.
- «Likely». Same as «luck».
- «Respect». When required to express the fulfillment of social conventions or mores, the emitter should express such fulfillment indicating the convention; in this way the emitter will transparently and unequivocally convey the conceptual framework used.
- «Be» (verb). This verb very frequently obfuscates, impedes, or derails sane mental processes, it constitutes an extremely primitive construction; the usage of this verb hinders sound reasoning. Use other logical operators; more specific operators produce correspondingly more accurate constructions. Humans can rephrase many instances where the word «be» typically stands included without using any similar verb, although ordinarily for doing so they must eliminate some ambiguity –by means of developing further the corresponding content.
- «Have» (verb). Here a not so obvious part, but a super-big part, of the metaphysical human world starts. The usage of «have» in some cases consists in (abstractly) affixing and/or attributing some entity to another, while in other cases denotes control of one entity exerted over another. In the case of the control, a person can state the phenomena explicitly, instead of using «have». The practice of indiscriminately affixing and/or attributing some entity to another gives birth to a wild metaphysical world, as described in [3.111] and subsequent sections. Using the verb «have» to affix or attribute entities from the same nature only, as subsets one of another, would produce coherent conceptual structures, but also in this case describing plainly and precisely the relationship produces a functional output, instead of using «have». An average human,

during ordinary affairs, can hardly distinguish between the diversity of abstract relationships meaningful only inside a system of logic, and the abstractions referring to existing entities in the universe.

- «Possess» (verb) / «Possession». Very much as «have».
- «Responsibility» / «Responsible». Include all derived words. Split «responsibility» in:
  a. *Behavioral consistency*. This concept, when replacing «responsibility», meaningful only inside a (formal or informal) organization; thereupon the usage of this concept must include an explicit reference to the organizational context. For example: «The behavior of that person fulfills those (defined) organizational standards.»
  β. *Accountability / Accountable*. These concepts also meaningful only in the context of an organizational framework.
- «Economic» / «Economy» / «Economist». Include all derived words. Untangle the meaning of the intended message and refer directly to the corresponding organizational or productive behavioral interactions, or to any other explicit concepts. For example, publishers can rephrase most headlines labeled «Economy» explicitly as *Production and Commerce*. Likewise, in many instances the term «economy» precludes a direct and specific reference to *productive and/or commercial activities*, thereby degrading the corresponding reasoning process.
  The term *economist*, whether in singular or plural, used through this text as legacy language, just as anyone can speak about alchemists knowing that they created a failed and discarded cultural building. Hereinafter the term *economist* used to refer to past events within an historical context.
- «Authority». Name explicitly the organizational post of the individual or entity and, if necessary, describe the relevant organizational functions ascribed to that post.
- «Order», when labeling a communication of an organizational management. Instead of using the word «order», humans should use the concepts of *executive communications*, (*organizational*) *instructions*, *commands* (linguistically associated to a *command chain*), and other alike concepts, to denote the

communications that serve to transmit the intended actions of subordinated individuals within a hierarchical organization; those statements meaningful and relevant only in the context of the organization. Threat, the focus shifts from the statement itself into the organizational context.

For example: «the {*name of the post*} *of this department/division* emitted or issued an *executive communication*» or «the {*name of the post*} instructed someone to do something».

No attempt made here to build an exhaustive list, but these corrections suffice for a smooth approach to what follows. A competent human may find many more words whose elimination or modification provides an advantage for building logical statements.

A proper, specialized word to replace «have» as an auxiliary verb to form preterit tenses should get included in the english language; the statements in this document do not include any such auxiliary verb.

[3.6]

Similarly, diminishing the usage of other words greatly improves cognitive processes and simplifies their development.

For example, instead of using the concepts of «leader» and «leadership», the organizational denomination of the entity which emits *executive communications* –group, or individual, or mechanism– suffices for appropriately denoting or identifying it. If in a given context exists a unique central entity specialized in emitting executive communications for the rest of the organization, then the label *central command* suffices for identifying it. Abandoning the concepts of «leader» and «leadership» greatly simplifies the identification of precarious forms of organization, which will become explicitly denominated, and thereby compels the individuals to develop those further. For example, in many cases, instead of calling itself «leader», an individual would need to call itself «commander of a herd».

Nevertheless, in some precarious situations, particularly during dispersed and semi-organized fights, the concept of «leader» constitutes the only suitable for defining the organizational post of the individual who strives to provide direction to a variable collection of loosely, informally, and intermittently coordinated individuals; and even there, everybody should remember that such situation should not exist.

General Model of the Human Brain

[3.7]

In the following pages recorded a model of the functioning of the *Homo sapiens'* brain. No attempt made to encompass all the features pertaining to the functioning of the modern hominid's brain, hence absent the ranges of *executive functions* described in section [3.90] and the abilities –and their nullity in many cases– necessary for performing mathematical operations. Also, the following sections do not constitute a mapping of the brain's physiological components.

The main goal of describing this general model consists in showing the functional division of the brain, highlighting the different components that can exist (or not) and operate (or not) in the varieties of contemporary humans; excepting the already mentioned absences.

[3.8]

First shown three diagrams corresponding to the mental functions available to the three main types of socially functional individuals among the *Homo sapiens*; these three diagrams do not describe the parasitic psychopathic subspecies examined in [3.170] and subsequent sections. The reader should first inspect the aforementioned diagrams carefully, in subsequent sections expounded each one of the schematized functions. Read the description of each function before making conclusions thereon, preferably read first the whole chapter.

[3.9]

Each diagram consists of a collection of named functions connected with lines representing data flows in the direction of the end-marker of each line. An end-marker can consist in an arrow-tip, a circle, or a half circle. The notation used in the diagrams, as follows:

- The rhombs with circles denote routers. (Think of an enhanced transistor with up to two possible outputs.) In each router, the function connected to the circle acts both as input and controller and, when allowing data through the router, may resolve to do any combination of the following:
  + Connect its own output to any single or both of the outputs in the rhomb.
  + Modify and/or coalesce the data in transit.

Otherwise, the controller can resolve to block all passage of data. If not suppressed, any modified or unmodified input in the rhomb will go where the controller directed it.

- If a rhomb lacks controller it will behave as a switch, where the data will transit towards the component addressed by the sender.
- The squares with circles denote simple interrupters controlled by the function connected to the circle.
- The half circles connected to a function denote pure control with no added input.

Graphically:

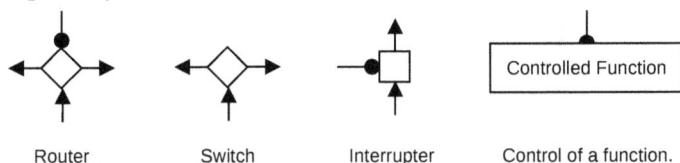

| Router | Switch | Interrupter | Control of a function. |

Figure 1. Elements of diagrams of psychological functions.

[3.10]

As already recorded in section [1.9], the term *conscience* as used by Hare denotes the behavior-regulating scheme controlled by unconscious functions using emotional states and internalized conceptual ensembles described by Deci and Ryan –this psychological mechanism for behavior regulation described in [3.25] and subsequent sections.

Thereupon, the reader should remember that –completely differing from Hare's concept– in this document the term *conscience* corresponds to the homonym mental function described in the following sections. In this context, the unified entity used by Hare does not exist.

[3.11]

All humans can exercise a basic operational awareness denominated *consciousness*, which performs *conscious processes*. However, a conscious awareness does not imply an active or existent *function conscience*.

[3.12]

Accordingly, the next three diagrams depict three distinct *human operational modes*, one per diagram.

Quickly notice the external input in the upper left corner, the external output in the lower right corner, and that the organism supplies its *basic psychological needs and innate goals* in the lower center.

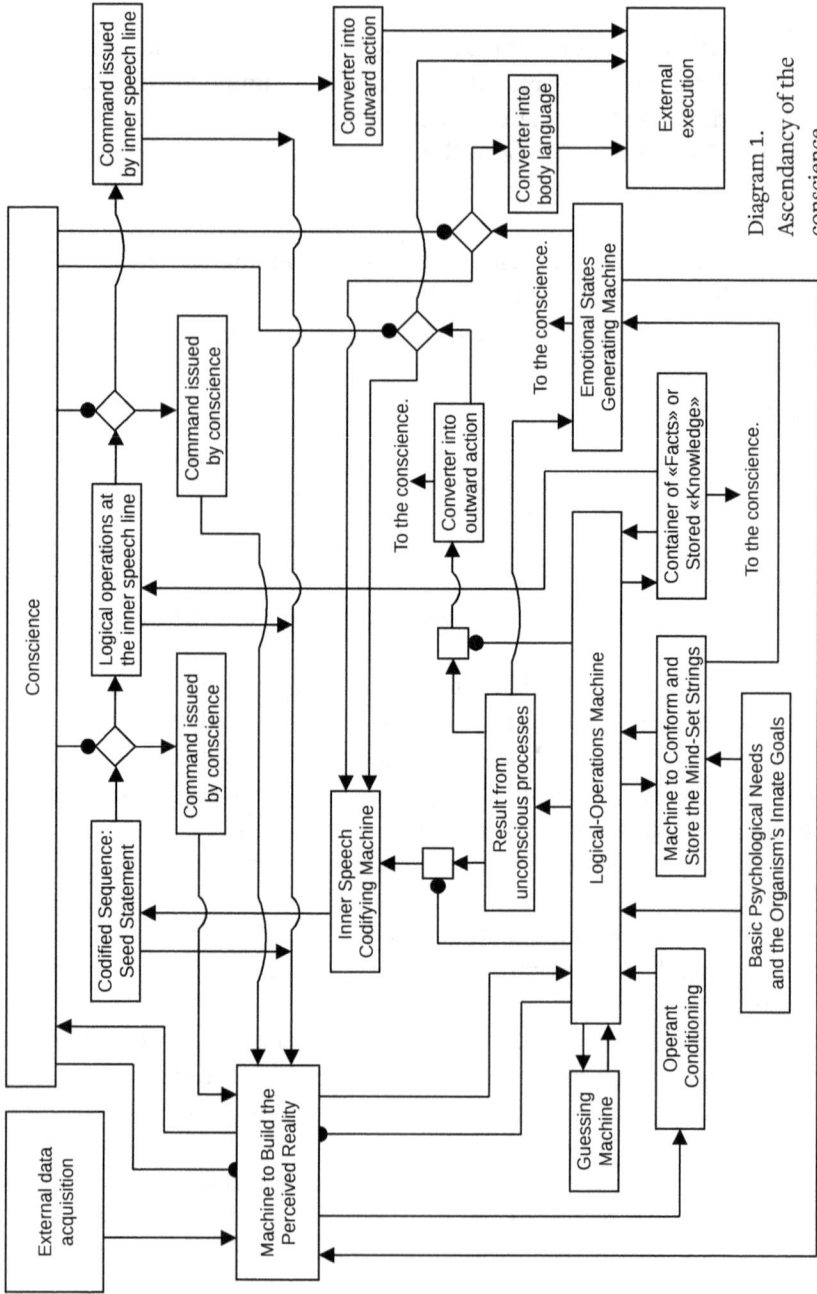

Diagram 1.
Ascendancy of the
conscience.

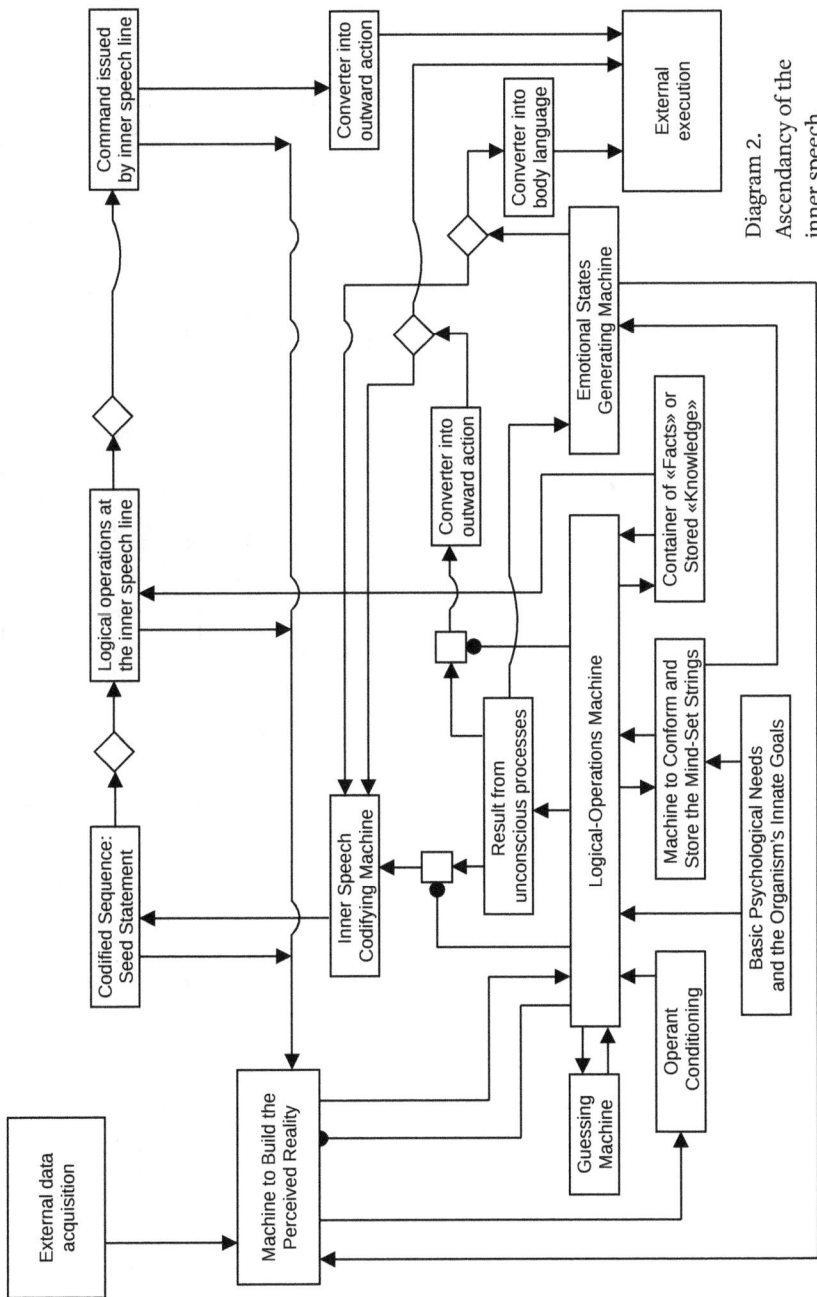

Diagram 2.
Ascendancy of the inner speech.

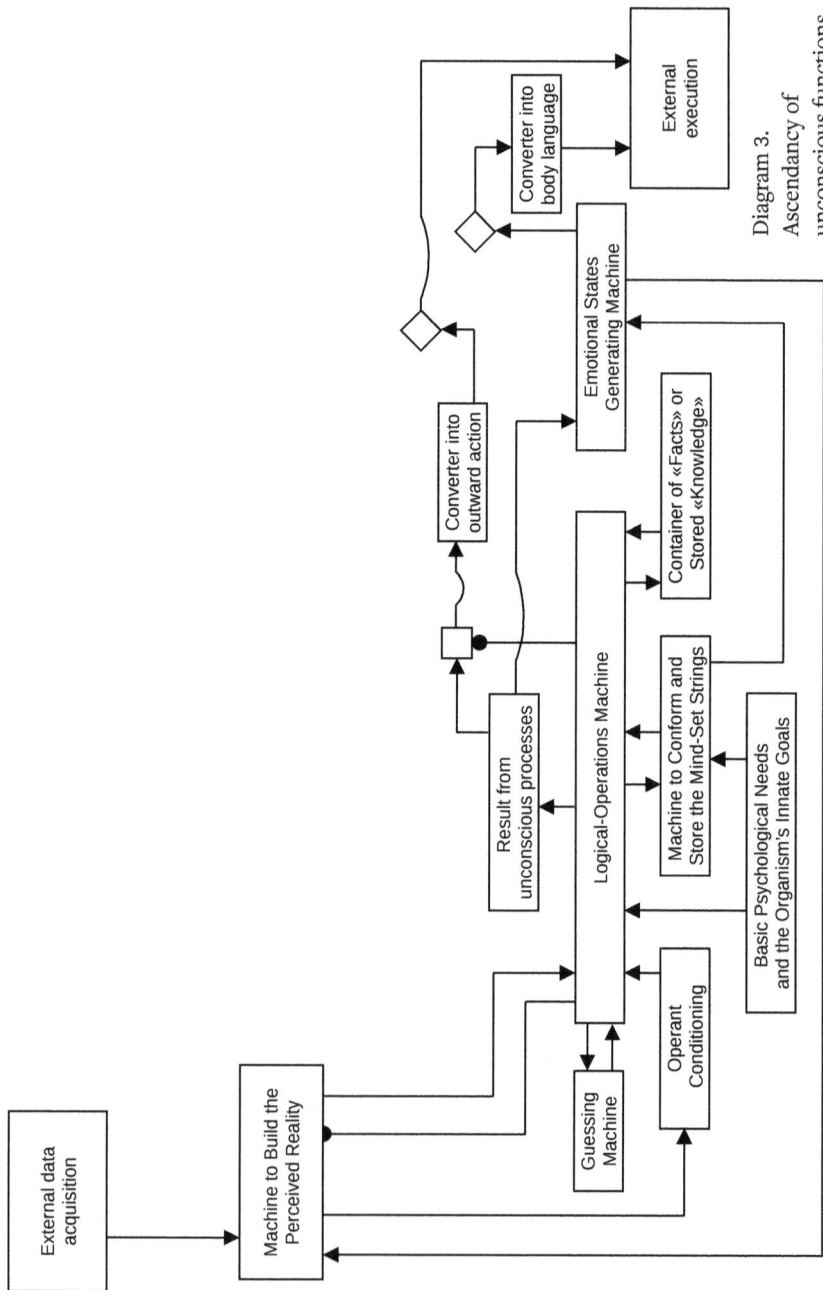

External data acquisition

Machine to Build the Perceived Reality

Guessing Machine

Operant Conditioning

Logical-Operations Machine

Basic Psychological Needs and the Organism's Innate Goals

Machine to Conform and Store the Mind-Set Strings

Container of «Facts» or Stored «Knowledge»

Result from unconscious processes

Converter into outward action

Emotional States Generating Machine

Converter into body language

External execution

Diagram 3.
Ascendancy of unconscious functions.

[3.13]

Thus, typically, in a rough classification, the human operational modes during vigil consist in:

a) Ascendancy of unconscious functions.
b) Ascendancy of the inner speech.
c) Ascendancy of the conscience.

Each operational mode proceeds driven by the corresponding ascendancy.

[3.14]

At any given time, an operational mode can utilize only a variable subset of the functions available to it. An operational mode may use intermittently the spare functions depending on the solicitations auto-generated (consult section [3.41]), or may rekindle some of those spare functions and thereby modify the active subset.

A capable organism may alternate between operational modes also depending on the solicitations auto-generated; however, the ability to operate in higher modes noticeably depends on the power and physiological income available to the organism –consistently with ordinary mechanisms, more and faster operations spend more material resources. Alternating between operational modes constitutes a relatively large operation compared with merely activating different available functions during a seamless performance in any of those. Likewise, any operational mode will remain active during a relatively long time.

[3.15]

An organism with the function conscience may also volitionally choose which operational mode switch into. An organism comprising only the functions depicted in the diagram of the inner speech, will automatically alternate between the ascendancy of the inner speech and the ascendancy of unconscious functions.

[3.16]

In capable organisms, the inner speech may proceed completely internalized, or may proceed vocalized during the course of austere operational sets or at underdeveloped brain stages, typically the latter during infancy and youth –for more details review the work of Barnard.

[3.17]

Thereupon, the nature of the mental functions available to ordinary humans serves for characterizing them:

1. *Animals*: Those humans who only carry and use the mental functions associated with the ascendancy of the unconscious functions. Labeled *animals* since their operation akin to that of any ordinary animal yet aware of its own existence.

2. *Technicals*: Those humans who carry and use the mental functions associated with the ascendancy of the inner speech. Labeled *technicals* since they can perform explicitly abstract mental operations.

    Pure technicals do not exist, *technicals* carry at least an inchoate conscience. A very weak and/or primitive conscience produces nonetheless awkward and circumscribed behavior; this case happens often.

3. *Humans with conscience*: Those humans who carry and use the mental functions associated with the ascendancy of the conscience; hence, those individuals where the conscience directs the behavior.

[3.18]

Animals do not need to use verbal –thus abstract– statements as a logical construction, but merely as the representation of some underlying, not directly described processes; therefrom, *animals* frequently use slang, convoluted constructions, and jargon as means of communication. This produces, almost always, semantic structures in social groups and occupational environments that typically distort and/or misrepresent the nature of the events described using them. Those semantic structures frequently appear highly unintelligible for outsiders who in most cases require careful analysis to understand the actual significance of the statements in that particular social setting.

Animals usually do not discern their own mental processes nor their own inner workings; this makes possible the aforementioned behavior.

[3.19]

Many *animals* readily notice that they lack or barely can use the inner speech line about which many others talk about. Thereat, not surprisingly, many *animals* feel deeply threatened by *technicals* and by *humans with conscience*.

Aware of such unconfessed shortcoming, many *animals* routinely attack *technicals* and *humans with conscience* during the course of social interactions, as «a preemptive action upon their imminent displacement». Likewise, some *animals* attempt to build occupational environments accessible only to those who share their characteristics, hence they attempt to build *animals*-only occupational environments.

However, since *animals* perform the vast majority of their mental operations fully unconsciously, using well-honed ancestral structures and skipping much of what others do, in some settings they frequently operate with an agility which others may find difficult to match. For example, while a *technical* may divert time to define a goal, an *animal* may just proceed to whatever its unconscious dictates.

Description of Each Mapped Function

External Data Acquisition

[3.20]

As its name indicates, this element specializes in the acquisition of external data. This mental function converts the signals and data sent by the sensory organs into a collection of data processable and manageable by the *machine to build the perceived reality*. Accordingly, the signals and data include those originating in organs and tissue within the body.

Machine to Build the Perceived Reality

[3.21]

This element filters, focuses, and coalesces all the signals and data received (the filtering discards those regarded as redundant), therewith produces an integrated representation which the organism perceives as «reality». The filtering and focusing controlled both by the conscience and by the *logical-operations machine*, thereby each one forming a control loop; in any case the filtering usually allows through alterations in the *status-quo*.

[3.22]

The individual typically perceives the redirected inner speech and the emotional states received as «an event originated by one's own nature», but not as part of the «self». Therefrom, the individual typically perceives the redirected inner speech and the emotional states as if they existed by themselves as independent entities in the universe, notwithstanding that the organism perceives itself as the source of such internal events.

The collage of data proceeding from internal events mixed with data acquired externally, worsened by the internal events processed as self-existent, promotes abundant fundamental reasoning mistakes. These reasoning mistakes happen because the organism confuses the characteristics of the data-stream originated from internal aftereffects with the characteristics of entities belonging to the exterior world, the latter from a physical nature.

Basic Psychological Needs and the Organism's Innate Goals

[3.23]

This element constitutes a read-only repository which anchors and relays the objectives of the organism described in section [2.2] and a set of basic psychological needs.

The *logical-operations machine* uses all this *ingrained input-injection* as propeller –these patterns furnish an internal demand for action– and foundation to regulate the most primary (and usually unacknowledged) processes performed by the same *logical-operations machine*.

Additionally, the brain creates and models the mind-set strings using the basic psychological needs and the organism's innate goals as the fundamental input, together with a finishing input from the *logical-operations machine* as described in the following sections.

[3.24]

The basic psychological needs consist in autonomy, competence, and relatedness.

Deci and Ryan described those needs and the associated inward and outward behavior; they made a clear exposition about the subject in the corresponding article –the interested person should read it.

Thereon, the content in several sections of this chapter uses as foundation the concept of *gradually internalized regulations* described by the aforementioned authors. Nevertheless, even without knowing the details of how most humans gradually internalize behavioral regulations into unconscious processes, the reader can parse the following sections –the remaining of the chapter– without a loss of meaning.

Machine to Conform and Store the Mind-Set Strings

[3.25]

This component generates and stores a group of sequences, each sequence constitutes an assertion. The *logical-operations machine* can convert each assertion into word statements, but this conversion may in most cases not happen simply because the operation involved did not require it.

Each assertion constitutes an entity that relates its components similarly to a mathematical equation, therefore assembling implications, notwithstanding that the posits result false or inconsistent with reality since this apparatus does not perform that comparison.

In average humans, the *logical-operations machine* will use each assertion as an on-demand postulate to build choices.

Furthermore, the brain will send each assertion to the *emotional states generating machine* where this apparatus will compare the supplied sequence with deduced implications of the perceived reality and with the implications of the choices built by the *logical-operations machine*.

[3.26]

The set of sequences of the mind-set (or mental configuration) constitutes a single ensemble for which the apparatus tends to maintain the following characteristics:

a) Consistency or harmony among assertions.

b) *Self-completion* or *self-closure*: the assertions as an aggregate will tend to support each other, to reinforce the whole, and to encompass, even if ambiguously, all ordinary aspects of the hominid's life. In this sense they constitute a «complete» structure.

c) The satisfaction of the postulates tends to satisfy the three basic psychological needs recorded in section [3.24], by means of the procedural behavior described by Deci and Ryan. The very same postulates typically also offer provisions to attend the solicitations auto-generated when the *logical-operations machine* strives to fulfill the innate objectives of the organism described in section [2.2].

Adequate, advantageous mind-set postulates provide satisfaction of the basic psychological needs while concurrently securing survival.

[3.27]

In this apparatus resides the «mentality», «ideology», «culture», and the primary memory of the «self», in this sector becomes implanted any organizational doctrine.

Deci and Ryan describe the process to implant an organizational doctrine as the external socially-learned regulations that progressively become introjected, identified, and finally integrated into the mind-set strings.

[3.28]

The core or kernel of the psyche, aka «self», exists distributed among the *machine to conform and store the mind-set strings* and the *logical-operations machine*. The «self» works primarily with the events and facts which the hominid can consciously perceive, notwithstanding that many of those events arise from unconscious processes.

A conscious perception of either an event or fact implies that the «self» can readily acknowledge and volitionally remember its corresponding occurrence or existence, but *consciousness* does not imply an active or existent *function conscience* (recall section [3.11]).

The reader may fully grasp the characteristics of the «self» till reaching section [3.163].

[3.29]

The *machine to conform and store the mind-set strings* will not store explicitly the external motivations and regulations –for example, the contents of an organizational doctrine. Rather, the *logical-operations machine* will transform the external input according to the processes described in section [3.41], and as consequence the data sent to the *machine to conform and store the mind-set strings* constitutes the logical implications of the external events. Using that external input, the basic psychological needs, and the organism's innate goals, this *machine* or mental function will conform and store the mind-set strings.

A human with a conscience can choose the content which will use as input for the process and, further, can fully conceal that input.

[3.30]

The human organism cannot radically change a single sequence of the mind-set without causing an internal upheaval. In cases of radical change appears a state of discomfort, a feeling of inner unbalance, and certain incapacity to build choices using the processes described by Deci and Ryan. This upheaval happens because when the *logical-operations machine* continues its routinary operation (as described in section [3.41]) using inconsistent inputs, the *emotional states generating machine* produces contradicting emotional outputs.

[3.31]

From my viewpoint, the most viable way to change a body or assembly of mind-set sequences consists in modifying slowly, step by step, each one of the sequences, in such way that no sequence recently modified implies anything too distinct or inconsistent in relation with the others. In the same way an octopus would drag a single limb and then another aiming to keep its own center without overstrain while avoiding entanglements.

But to do so, to volitionally and deliberately change its mind-set, a human must first identify the corresponding mind-set sequences. The identification of the mind-set sequences may proceed as described in section [3.80] or, for example, by receiving competent professional psychological counseling, where the psychologist acts as a prosthetic device.

[3.32]

When comparing the effectiveness of the mind-set sequences of hominids guided by their unconscious processes for achieving real-life goals which both provide satisfactions of competence, autonomy, and relatedness –the three basic psychological needs– and fulfill the basic objectives of living organisms, more often the mind-set fails to provide for basic (survival) objectives than the (averaged) frequency of failure to provide experiences of competence, autonomy, and relatedness.

Many humans choose a path to death rather than experiencing a lack of competence, autonomy, and relatedness.

[3.33]

Carol Dweck made a clear contribution to the field of mind-sets and self-management in her book:

Mindset: The New Psychology of Success.

Carol S. Dweck.

Year 2006.

Carol Dweck's main breakthrough consists in pointing the existence of various mind-sets which lead to different outcomes in life, showing the feasibility of expressing them in groups of simple and short constructs, and encouraging their explicit targeted modification.

Comparison of Widespread Mind-Sets

[3.34]

In the following pages recorded a table containing different mind-set alternatives, based upon Carol Dweck's work. In [3.170] and subsequent sections recorded a further description of the *fascist ants* –ordinary members of the parasitic psychopathic subspecies. Of course, humans may carry other diverse mind-sets.

[3.35]

Different wordings (or mixtures of concepts) in different persons may support the same mind-set postulate. The entries in the table show the implications of the mind-set strings, not necessarily the mind-set strings themselves.

Hence, attempting to replicate clinical research which obtains specific mind-set sequences may find little success if the whole cultural environments of the subjects of research not identical.

[3.36]

Notice that the first table provides a short introduction to an average individual of each class. In the second table recorded the mind-sets.

Although the mind-sets table and its introductory table depict a rough average in a world of very variable humans, both showcase the behavioral patterns involved.

Table 1. Introduction to mind-sets: typical framework for each type.

	Fixed Mind	Growth Mind	Fascist Ant Mind
Primary mind resources	Unconscious mind-set shored up by rationalizations. *Executive functions* relatively underdeveloped.	Unconscious mind-set shored up by rationalizations and objective knowledge. *Executive functions* relatively well-developed.	Unconscious mind-set shored up by rationalizations. A peculiar assortment of *executive functions* of commanders sharply differ from the rank-and-file.
	If the individual not of a verbal-style, the rationalizations may not exist.	Abstract language-based processes readily available.	If the individual not of a verbal-style, the rationalizations may not exist.
Individual awareness of own actions	Conscious or unconscious actions enacted to satisfy ultimately unconscious (unacknowledged) needs.	Mostly conscious actions enacted to satisfy ultimately unconscious (unacknowledged) needs.	Conscious or unconscious, but unconscious features stronger than in average humans.
Sentimentalism for behavior regulation	Behavior strongly regulated by feelings (see Deci and Ryan); enduring emotional attachments to people, land, objects, and so forth. Rationalizations shore-up sentimentalism-driven behavior.	Rationalizations may shore-up sentimentalism-driven behavior; they can create those rationalizations besides the rationalizations furnished by the surrounding societal culture.	Tendency towards psychopathy. Frivolous input may productive shallow proto-emotions.

Table 2. Three distinct mind-sets.

	Fixed Mind-Set	Growth Mind-Set	Fascist Ant Mind-Set
Primary mechanism of evaluation	Can label almost anything, including objects, as either «good» or «evil» as an inherent property.	Assess the conformance to reality of every statement and thereupon label it as as either *true* or *false*.	Obedience and exploitability of individuals, direct profit, and advantages obtained in transactions.
Perceived nature of the world	Fundamentally static.	Dynamic.	Fundamentally static and layered.
Primary mode of activity	Being.	Doing.	Belonging.

	Fixed Mind-Set	Growth Mind-Set	Fascist Ant Mind-Set
Tolerance for uncertainty	Little tolerance for ambiguity.	Great tolerance for ambiguity.	Zero tolerance for perceived ambiguity, notwithstanding that their functioning carries a lot of it.
	Situations should conform to general theories.	They develop the situation; adapt themselves and the environment as it unfolds.	Control the situation.
Problem recognition	Situation acceptance; the individual should accept some situations as they exist.	Proactive problem-solving. They change the situation and the circumstances.	Either rule or obey.
	Reacting.	Anticipating (developing foresight).	Acting according to the «book» of recipes.
Information search	Gathering ideas and possibilities.	Gathering facts (*True* statements) and using them as input for first best guesses.	Steal data and spy everybody.
Construction of alternatives	Past-, present-, and future-oriented alternatives.	New, future-oriented alternatives.	Faction-oriented alternatives, prevail by force.
Assumption about abilities	Implicit assumption that each one carries fixed and innate abilities, not subject to change.	Assured assumption that abilities can improve by practicing, training, and adjusting circumstances.	Implicit assumption that each one carries fixed and innate abilities; training provided for ensuring compliance.
	Implicit assumption that accumulating experience equals developing (innate) abilities.	Assured assumption that improving and learning abilities constitutes a conscious deliberate process.	Implicit assumption that they can learn to do tasks or perform assigned roles.
	Adults cannot change.	Adults can learn and change.	«We are the kids with the big heart.»
Attribution of failure	See failure as a reflection of ability.	Failure inspires a search for new ways to improve skills.	See failure as a reflection of weakness.

	Fixed Mind-Set	Growth Mind-Set	Fascist Ant Mind-Set
Performance during difficult tasks	When challenged, compare themselves to others perceived as carrying greater abilities.	During difficult tasks, enact systematic and goal-directed strategies.	When challenged, mirror practices and steal from the best; obtain unfair advantages.
	During difficult tasks, strategies become disorganized and chaotic. They may try hard, but behave not thoughtful enough to create effective solutions.	Make productive use of feedback to improve performance.	During difficult tasks, assemble a formation to deal with the issue; they «run together».
Attribution of success	Tendency to attribute success to innate ability.	Tendency to attribute success to the output of effort and hard work.	Tendency to attribute success to the advantages and resources gained.
Reaction to competition or others making improvements	Competitors must «pay the price of success», typically this «price» unattainable or destructive, therefore in their mind nobody can really change the fixed world-set. If an improving individual regarded as an equal does not seem to «pay the price» they will sabotage and attack him or her, in order to restore the «natural order» of things.	Use others as benchmark to improve themselves: «If he/she can, then I can.» Copy best practices.	Steal improvements; dominate perceived competitors or destroy them. Cheating constitutes an accepted and condoned behavior.
Perception about own work	The only acceptable way of living consists in *hard work* that sort of «dignifies» the income.	Focus on improving the efficiency and effectiveness of own work. Develop strategies for leaping the scale of own income.	Steal from, manipulate, and exploit other people for the purpose of skipping the hassle of *hard work*. The individual performs duties aiming to keep its place in the world.
	Main focus on own effort.	Main focus on efficiency and effectiveness.	Main focus on fulfilling commands from a hierarchically superior individual.

	Fixed Mind-Set	Growth Mind-Set	Fascist Ant Mind-Set
Choice of work assignments	Tendency to choose easy, unchallenging projects to avoid failure that might expose personal inadequacies.	Tendency to choose difficult and challenging assignments to grow skills.	Obey and perform the task assigned. No actual boundaries between «personal» and «organizational» life within the fascist formation.
Routine	Static cyclic routine.	Basic routine modified at cycles, the modifications aimed to enhance knowledge, or skills, or both.	Basic routine modified according to the trends of the fascist formation.
Timing	Time an asset to manage.	Time a critical independent variable.	Time treated implicitly. Preference for fast movements and quickly obtaining outcomes.
	Choices made slowly.	Choices made at a deliberated time.	Choices made quickly.
Primary success criteria	Implicit assumption that the outcome should fit in the world's static nature.	The outcome must pass a selected quality mark.	Advantages gained.
	Focus on compliance.	Focus on effectiveness.	Focus on dominating.
Social engagement	See members of «own group» as equal, other groups may pertain to different «social groups» or classes.	Create alliances and partnerships. Many execute a take-what-you-can approach.	Belonging to the fascist formation constitutes a fundamental part of their lives. See members of «own group» as layered, other groups as expendable or exploitable.
	Single society. Association with others carried openly. A personal association with individuals of different classes not encouraged, regarded as not natural, and they may condemn it.	Single society. Association with others, including different ones, carried openly.	«We constitute the real society, above all others and above all civilized social rules.» Hide and conceal their fascist membership, deny all when found out.
Learning route	Learn from tradition and custom.	Learn from past and present. Learn from others. Innovate. Improve.	Combine stolen knowledge; imitate the best.

[3.37]

In metallurgical terms:

Reality does not forge each human character; rather, the human brain conforms its character to reality, and strain –specifically, using the mind-set to successfully solve challenging problems– does not temper but hardens the corresponding character, the corresponding mind-set.

[3.38]

During states of emergency and in physically depleted individuals the human brain will not employ the postulates of the mind-set, and during such basal operation the organism's primary innate goals will bypass the *machine to conform and store the mind-set strings*.

Operant-Conditioning Training Apparatus

[3.39]

This apparatus processes and stores *operant-conditioning* training patterns. Operant-conditioning training consists in a behavioral training with markedly mechanic characteristics –in general, does not involve the usage of the mind-set sequences. The training happens by:

1. Repeating externally-generated queries or stimulus which the organism immediately solves or attends, and promptly either rewarding the organism if its response matches or progressively approaches to the behavioral target, or punishing the organism if produced an unacceptable response.

2. The organism then will record the «correct» answer for each type of externally-generated query or stimulus.

3. On success, the organism will repeat the «correct» answer on subsequent similar events, independently of whether the corresponding reward or punishment ensues.

The *logical-operations machine* can discard the answers provided by the *operant-conditioning* training apparatus, particularly when the organism behaves with ascendancy of the conscience.

Extensive descriptions of *operant-conditioning* training already exist available in specialized literature, easily accessible, therefore no further explanation deemed necessary here.

Container of «Facts» or Stored «Knowledge»

[3.40]

This constitutes the organism's operational memory; stores sensorial experiences, chained arrays of concepts (words) labeled as either «true» or «false», and recorded events and their sequence. The *logical-operations machine* manages this container, adding to or modifying its content.

Logical-Operations Machine

[3.41]

Would constitute the organism's arithmetic-logic unit in a world of standard humans, nevertheless, not all hominids developed a proficient arithmetic part. This apparatus computes large and concurrent inputs and produces complex outputs, coordinates the functions around and, in general, executes the most essential and indispensable tasks for the operation, for the self-direction of the organism: apprehension, cognition, and choice-making. In this way, the *logical-operations machine* constitutes the operational center of the human brain.

The *logical-operations machine* will—

- Process the bulk of the data from the *perceived reality*.

  The *logical-operations machine* continually parses the data from the perceived reality; thereat categorizes and assigns tags to the output generated. This typically produces all sorts of sourced-from-material-reality, logical, and mixed –reality plus logical-internally constructed entities with associated tags: shapes, objects, events, situations, forecasts, and so forth. In [3.100] and subsequent sections recorded more about this. Notice again that all this output consists of internally constructed entities. An identifying tag does not imply an associated word or label.

- Create a solicitation or request for response when it determines that a situation constitutes a problem or task that requires solution.

  This solicitation the machine may solve internally, or may pass it to the *inner speech line*, or the conscience may capture it. The request for response arises when this machine considers an entity or a group of entities tagged from the perceived reality as either a problem, opportunity, or novelty; or when solving an internal challenge; or when pushing forward the organism's objectives.

- Awake the conscience when deemed convenient and/or necessary, although once awake the conscience supersedes its switching capacity.
- Discern the applicability or not of the response provided by the *operant-conditioning* training.
- Call the mind-set sequences to incorporate them as foundation for processing solicitations and developing answers; an awake conscience may suppress or diminish this. Not all running modes will readily call the mind-set sequences and those not indispensable for building a solution for every solicitation, therefore their usage optional.
- Use and process the spur of the raw organismic goals and basic psychological needs.
- Consult the *guessing machine* to complete the answer.
- Send the produced answer to a temporal buffer, where it will choose whether route it towards the *inner speech line*, or towards the *converter into outward action*, or both.
- Run calculations, establish correspondences, and solve problems, the triad in the background, rising an answer on completion. For example, parsing many features of the perceived reality usually happens in background processes.
- (When done with care) Execute the commands of the conscience.

[3.42]

The *logical-operations machine* may not command all the resources mentioned, outstandingly, may lack a codifier into the *inner speech line*, merely because that whole section does not exist in scores of humans that dwell on Earth.

[3.43]

The *logical-operations machine*, as its name indicates, typically produces logical constructions –although it can also generate mistakes– built upon the inputs it receives.

In a routinary operation and/or at the absence of an active conscience, the *logical-operations machine* will not compare the strings received from the mind-set with data from the external world.

The *logical-operations machine* would irreversibly and unmistakably notice that in many cases the mind-set strings result false or inappropriate, and frequently remote to an optimal hypothesis, if—

- Performed the slightest comparison of the mind-set strings with data from reality.
- Compared the goals of the array of optional answers generated with prospective real-world consequences of those answers.

[3.44]

Thus, the *logical-operations machine* performs processes with abstract concepts –notwithstanding that many of those remain without labels (words) associated. Language arises from the operation with those concepts.

Guessing Machine

[3.45]

Here indispensable to show several facts:

1. Exists a universe (a reality) with dimensions basically unknown for the organism. From this universe the organism using its sensory organs acquires certain data, with this data the organism attempts to model and simulate the same reality from which it constitutes a part –expressed differently: the organism attempts to model the portion of the universe where it forms a part.

2. The universe stands composed by a number of parts here presumed finite. If existed the case where a cognitive entity could model the totality of such universe in a complete and unambiguous way, then the device or apparatus used to model the universe would comprise at least a number of parts equal to the number of parts of the modeled universe for assigning at least a representation one-to-one or univocal, thereby making possible such complete and unambiguous modeling. Therefore, such device or apparatus would constitute the universe itself or

a subset of it with a larger number of parts, the latter markedly impossible.

Hereat patent and certain that does not exist an omniscient or almighty entity.

3. Even when the organism focuses only on the portion of the universe reachable by it, typically the data-processing capacity, the instruments for data-acquisition, and the time interval available to the organism do not suffice for modeling perfectly, completely, and unambiguously that given portion of the universe. The aforesaid insufficiencies ordinarily happen even without considering the changes or incidences brought by the universe beyond the boundary of the analyzed portion.

4. Thereupon, the organism models and simulates only a portion of the universe and does it incompletely, (with the goal of) using afterwards this product as input in its choice-making process. To the facts and events –changes of state during time intervals– not included in its choice-making process, whose data ignores or simply did not generate, which therefrom remain undefined, the organism denominates *uncertainty*.

5. Typically, the organism chooses arbitrarily the size and accuracy of the model of the universe and the variables to manipulate, and reduces its action proposals to a few possible paths. For clarity: *possible to choose, different from feasible to enact; in some cases results not feasible to enact the chosen route.*

    The methodological propensities described in [3.146] and subsequent sections regularly provide preferential paths for the selection of variables and data-processing archetype. Hence, in any case the methodological propensities can «seed» the construction of cognitive processes.

    The conscience can supersede the methodological propensities. To complete all these choices –the model, the variables, and the action proposal finally accepted– the organism employs a guessing machine based in *nothing*; in no data from the exterior or from its own memory, simply chooses based in nothing to avoid paralysis. If at the end of the process everything repeats changing the guessed choices (thus guessing again), then this constitutes part of the general choice-making process chosen.

Three mechanisms for completion by guessing recorded and classified by sophistication in [3.76] and subsequent sections.

[3.46]

The aforesaid process produces two immediate consequences:

α. Humans will never agree in a standardized content for the ambiguous words «good» and «bad» –or at least not standardized enough for the characteristics of the society now required. This already mentioned in section [3.5].

β. Will never exist a complete consensus among humans about the actions deemed adequate to fulfill the objectives of living organisms described in section [2.2].

Different humans placed in equal lives and situations will make different choices.

[3.47]

The models and data-processing archetypes used for building non-trivial choices almost always involve some probabilistic estimations; in [3.117] and subsequent sections recorded content aimed to help reduce mistakes in these latter practices.

Emotional States Generating Machine

[3.48]

This apparatus obtains the output generated by the *logical-operations machine* (the *result from unconscious processes* in the diagrams), deconstructs its implications, and compares those implications with the mind-set sequences and with an unconscious assessment of the present and future situation. Depending on the result of this comparison, the *emotional states generating machine* produces sensational inducements for implicitly spurring and inciting the behavior of the individual according to the forms of regulation described by Deci and Ryan.

Hence, the *emotional states generating machine* produces sensational inducements to action upon the unconscious appraisal of prospective future scenarios and contemplated goals –whether those scenarios and goals consciously or unconsciously foreseen. These sensational inducements appear in the *perceived reality* as an inner excitement and actively serve to spur and incite the behavior of an individual towards situations and goals approved by its own unconscious processes.

The sensational inducements comprise consciously discernible sensations and emotions which compose motivational states. Thus, the motivational sensations in many cases appear accompanied and aided by specialized emotions such as pride, guilt, and shame.

However, an unconscious appraisal of an either expressly considered or unconsciously inferred outcome not always reaches the sensational and/or emotional stage, and in many cases becomes manifested only as a «resistance to act» towards a disapproved path, or as an «easiness of action» towards another approved path.

This phenomenon, usually known simply as *motivation*, whether expressed chiefly by internally perceived upheavals or just manifested in unconsciously driven action, plays an essential role in the performance of most humans. Syncing the mind-set with the actual goals enacted therefore fundamental for achieving an optimal performance.

[3.49]

When appraising a future desired outcome, the unconscious processes utilize their own time- and sequential-discount estimation of usefulness, or preference for delayed consequences in time and action, which depends on the specific case; and the strength of the inducements to action furnished upon varies accordingly.

[3.50]

In this way, when appraising a situation or prospective future –by comparing it with its available mind-set, (possibly unacknowledged) interests, and goals– the *emotional states generating machine* can produce relatively intense emotional states.

Physiologically, the emotional states originate in specific biochemical reactions that produce diverse types of interferences, biases, and behavioral leanings.

The generated emotional states also arrive to the *machine to build the perceived reality* where they both distort the perception and provide the basis for biased and impulsive behavior, and otherwise sometimes produce an absence of proactive behavior. The brain also routes the emotional states to a *converter into outward body language*.

The specialized professionals can better describe those specific biochemical reactions which impact the operation of the *logical-operations machine* and provide the thrust, but not the rationalized cause, for the impulsiveness associated with states of emotional arousal.

[3.51]

Here important to acknowledge that the conscience can observe and catch or quell the emotional states even before they arrive to the *perceived reality* and place them apart once there, if they arrive at all. To preclude the introduction of emotional states into the perceived reality used for choice-making processes constitutes a natural outcome and a step for increasing operational efficiency, since the conscience enacts an array of overarching activities including anticipating what would happen if those emotional states amalgamated with that perceived reality –to state the obvious. Some humans can obtain a short-lived petty amusement from «enjoying the joy» but often amounts to misspending time, may denote a lack of focus, and almost always an outward activity would produce more useful consequences; nonetheless, this practice can serve for training purposes.

The conscience observes the emotional states in a much more subtle and fine-grained scope than humans behaving by the ascendancy of their unconscious processes can acknowledge, and at the same time compartmentalizes them away from the external world.

[3.52]

Albeit the conscience can either largely or completely quell the emotional states, including what would receive the *perceived reality* and the impulsiveness associated with them, if the conscience chooses so, it can unleash the impulsiveness.

[3.53]

Usual intense *emotional states* comprise joy, rage, sadness, and fear. These intense emotional states differ from relatively long-term *affective states* like «love».

In this regard, affective states apparently stem from permanent and semi-permanent modifications in the brain operation –namely, in the *logical-operations machine* using the memory– where another set of biochemical mechanisms proceeds involved, creating marked behavioral patterns.

The *emotional states generating machine* merely uses the bias and the patterns generated by the affective states. Thus, «love» may produce joy, and «depression» may produce sadness; and both affective states proceed regulated by biochemical mechanisms.

No doubt that the emotional states experienced by the organism can gradually influence and modify the affective states by iteration of different events; but they will neither create nor suppress them overnight, and –sometimes– may not produce a permanent effect on them whatsoever. Affective states like «love» serve to satisfy the basic psychological needs while establishing behavioral patterns functional for social living.

[3.54]

Consequently, the behavior of individuals with ascendancy of unconscious functions typically proceeds (at least partially) regulated and spurred by socially structured motivational states arising from relatively complex processes, excepting the lone psychopaths described by Hare and the *basic animals* described in [3.165] and subsequent sections.

Someone with an *inner speech line* may abstractly acknowledge the motivational states howbeit achieving it does not automatically enable the person to change the course of action –consult the description of technicals in section [3.17]. In technicals frequently proceeds a behavioral mixture resulting from their motivational states and their explicitly abstract operations.

Humans with (at least an inchoate) conscience can volitionally involve themselves in selected situations and experiences for the purpose of modifying or eliciting their own motivational states. Additionally, in the case of a feeble, unresolved, or overwhelmed conscience the individual can ask for external, usually professional assistance for self-regulation.

Converter into Outward Action

[3.55]

The *logical-operations machine* can send the result of the unconscious processes (or unconscious operations) into a *converter into outward action*, depending on whether the same *logical-operations machine* resolves to do it.

[3.56]

A *converter into outward action* transforms the input received into data suitable for physical actions, including the emission of words both in the vocalized representation and in the written representation. Therefrom, operating by the ascendancy of unconscious functions, many hominids can actively engage in complex conversations without a conscious awareness of their own words and utterances.

Remember that the development of the vocalized representation of the language constituted the organizational headstone during the birth of the *Homo sapiens* and, definitely (undoubtedly), during those primeval times all complex communications among hominids passed through the apparatus here described.

[3.57]

I observed very few humans where the emission of vocalized language, or language at all, does not constitute a highly developed part of their brain, Barnard observed others. From them, one may notice that their logical non-verbal functions not always stand underdeveloped.

Therefore, as Barnard commented, anyone can optimally know and understand these individuals scanty of words by observing their actions.

§

[3.58]

Not all humans carry the mental functions hereinafter described. Albeit someone could consider both the *inner speech line* and the *conscience* as an integral part of the *logical-operations machine*, those compartmentalized in this description because:

a)   The *inner speech line* performs a specialized abstract operation.

b)   The *conscience*, in fact, consists merely of a more complex wiring coupled with some new sections. The evolved (presumably also physiological) wiring encompasses much of the other functional parts of the brain.

Inner Speech Codifying Machine

[3.59]

This apparatus codifies the input supplied by the *logical-operations machine* and converts it into the inner representation of the self-speech at the *inner speech line*.

Inner Speech Line

[3.60]

The term *inner speech line* refers, through this text, to the act of processing and operating an internal self-speech. For these purposes a specialized function comprising an internal track stands allocated.

[3.61]

Although this function in the corresponding diagrams comprises three operational sections and two interruptions by the conscience, constitutes a single or unified part, and the illustrations serve to depict the stages of a full-featured operational sequence.

Without considering the incidence of the conscience –which anyway not always operates– the *inner speech line* proceeds as follows:

a) The codified sequence in the internal representation of the language, named *seed statement*, arrives from the *logical-operations machine*. The *machine to build the perceived reality* not always collects this sequence. The *seed statement* constitutes the first postulate used as a raw approach to engage with a solicitation created by the *logical-operations machine* as already described in section [3.41].

b) Proceeding from the *seed statement*, the *inner speech line* builds a sequence of statements in the internal language representation, incorporating words, data, and logs available in the operational memory and in the *perceived reality*, and occasionally more postulates from the mind-set; in general with a direction and command exercised by the *logical-operations machine*. The brain sends this sequence of statements to the *machine to build the perceived reality* where, consequently, these statements appear as part of the *perceived reality*.

c) When finishing a sequence of statements, and also during the course of their generation, regularly the *logical-operations machine* uses a guess (from the *guessing machine*), although typically these injections happen unconsciously –until the conscience arrives and watches the «elephant in the room», at least. The last statement in a self-speech sequence can constitute a command for body action, which then passes to a corresponding converter. Same as the previous one in the sequence, the last or concluding statement also passes to the *perceived reality* where the *logical-operations machine* can grasp it and continue with whatever it commands and/or implies.

[3.62]

The inner speech line does not produce a «human conscience» or a «rational awareness». During an operation without interventions of the conscience, the inner speech line proceeds undeflectable without variations and modifications. Can the content of the inner speech line lack any soundness and actual relatedness with reality, yet without a conscience will happen neither radical changes nor any intervention or reconsideration of fundamental assertions.

Remember that, when dealing with subjects not strictly technical and frequently also in technical matters, all *seed statements* consist in the product of operations which used mind-set postulates as axiomatic basis or starting point, thereby inhering those postulates, and the mind-set can contain egregiously illogical or inadequate posits. In such situation the *inner speech line* alone does not question the inputs which employs as basis or starting point to solve a solicitation, and which hence ultimately produce inadequate motor answers to attain the organism's innate goals.

The aforementioned inability does not imply that the *inner speech line* cannot question and challenge the messages and data coming from the external world: it will definitely do so and will spend additional energy when these or their implications contradict the postulates emanating from the mind-set.

Conscience

[3.63]

One Hatha Yoga instructor said: «Imagine that you lay down on the floor, look to the sky, see the clouds passing by, and the clouds your thoughts.»

[3.64]

The conscience constitutes the first biological step to control and adapt or ultimately eliminate the mind-set sequences and the associated mental functions, depending on how these divergent humans evolve.

The semi-rigid and obscure hypotheses that *Homo sapiens* individuals used (and use) to simplify reality, to swiftly build choices, and thereupon operate quickly in an environment where they lacked the most elemental data and knowledge, in a now-indispensable mature civilization would frequently produce a strongly dysfunctional behavior –as already happens. I would bet for the destruction of the repository of the mind-set sequences.

Not everybody in the Hatha Yoga classroom sees the clouds, occasionally neither the instructor.

[3.65]

The conscience consists of pure attention. Carries no words, does not emit them, does not generate a self-speech. Can appear as a visor that observes what happens around it.

[3.66]

Without intervening, the conscience can access the content of the *perceived reality*, the *inner speech line*, the operational memory, the *emotional states generating machine*, and the *converter into outward action*. Using these accesses the conscience can ascertain the type of subjacent operational mode currently performing: whether it primarily an unconscious operation, or an operation based on the performance and products of the inner self-speech.

[3.67]

The conscience cannot observe the content of the *logical-operations machine*; however, very importantly, it can emit commands for this *logical-operations machine* and wait for the results. There lies the revolutionary capacity of the conscience. It can also suppress and reactivate the inner self-speech, and when sends an abstract command for the *logical-operations machine* it does so precisely by directing this speech.

Thereon, the conscience can directly sense and direct the activity of the *inner speech line*, but collects the corresponding content at the *perceived reality*.

Additionally, the conscience can suppress the execution of the actions which arise from unconscious processes. And, up to variable degrees, the conscience also can suppress the conversion of *emotional states* into outward or external display and into internal aftereffects, as already recorded in section [3.51].

[3.68]

The conscience does not govern alone, instead, it chooses the type of subjacent operation that will perform the operative activities: uses both the unconscious functions and the *inner speech line*; and, if it maintains active, the conscience chooses when to alternate between one or another. Barnard noticed this almost a century ago.

[3.69]

Showing certain flexibility, the conscience can select which mental functions rekindle and which ones suspend or hold.

For example, in optimal physiological conditions, when the conscience silences the inner self-speech, instructs or influences the *logical-operations machine* for it to avoid generating anything that can perturb the *emotional states generating machine*, stops all outward motor actions, and focuses on the *perceived reality*, then the state of attention reached loosely corresponds to a real-world version of the mythical «nirvana» and constitutes the target of some styles of «meditation». Thereupon, in this state the conscience can focus completely on the data furnished by the sensory organs.

[3.70]

So far the greatest disadvantages of the conscience consist of its larger energy consumption and, in some instances, the larger amount of time invested producing a motor answer after acquiring external data. In these two areas an improvement of the conscience can produce an immediate operational breakthrough: greater speed and less energy consumption –typical areas of opportunity for improvement in myriad of working systems. Yet a trained, organized conscience can significantly develop speed.

Whenever the conscience consumes a small amount of energy per unit of time, it may perform during all the awake time of the organism. Optionally, humans could also develop larger bodies which would provide commensurate larger amounts of continuous power, though after a threshold this latter option may not provide further advantages than those which the usage of technology could produce.

[3.71]

In humans with conscience the organismic innate goals and the basic psychological needs will always stand available as discernible input for the *logical-operations machine*. Hence, the organism may acknowledge and volitionally use those innate goals and psychological needs as direct input for goal selection and for shaping its own mind-set.

[3.72]

As anyone could anticipate, the main task of the conscience consists in contributing to the construction of choices that produce more effective outcomes for achieving the objectives of the organism –remember section [2.2]. In this regard, I identified two outstanding cases: operative choices, and the ability to obtain and modify the mind-set sequences.

Operative Choices

[3.73]

Two common practices for solving problems serve as foundation for what follows:

[3.74]

a) When dealing with routinary affairs, people with competent *executive functions* can just foresee the estimated most probable scenarios through time, and then foresee their own sequence of actions inside that environment. In those routinary mental processes –whether fully unconscious or using the *inner speech line*– the *logical-operations machine* requests and employs guesses mostly when calculating the most probable scenarios through time according to the available data, the prospective actions, and the model of the universe (the internally depicted material reality) used by the organism. Typically, the model of reality employed in routinary affairs stands already fine-tuned by using the data collected from previous past similar events.
The conscience –if available– may dynamically adjust the practice.

[3.75]

b) When dealing with static problems that do not directly and/or immediately impact their lives, humans with conscience can send back and forth statements to and from their unconscious processes, let those continue processing data and options, and defer the resolution of the problem arbitrarily, if they choose until they find a suitable or feasible solution, which never happens in some cases.

[3.76]

Hence, next described three methods for completing operative choices when dealing with relatively-complex, novel situations within a time limit.

[3.77]

Least regret principle.

Originally mentioned by someone else in another context, adapted and elaborated further here.

When using the *inner speech line* for choice-building, the organism models and simulates several options. At the end, due to what recorded in section [3.45], the *inner speech line* obtains an incomplete result –it can happen that the organism merely models the present and its immediate consequences, without adding the simulation of any relatively distant optional future.

At this stage, the conscience can ask in the self-speech: «If I stood, several decades from now, at the end of my life, and looked into the past, which choice I would like to see taken today?» This issued command passes to the *logical-operations machine* and therefrom the conscience must wait for the same *logical-operations machine* to return an answer as a *seed statement*. Naturally, the conscience must keep idle or empty the *inner speech line* while waits.

This practice:

i. Drives the *logical-operations machine* to consider the whole time the organism aspires to live as the temporal action scope.

ii. Builds fully volitionally and deliberately the final model that the *guessing machine* will employ, while using the enhanced cognitive accesses of the conscience; notwithstanding that the same *guessing machine* furnished some primary elements of this model.

The conscience observes all the choice-building process and can make corrections or interventions at any stage; accordingly, as first step the *inner speech line* with the supervision of the conscience established the incomplete initial model. The conscience knows then the temporal and spatial extensions of the model used, the precision and amount of details used, and the size of the hole the final guess must fill. Furthermore, the conscience may choose to perform a reasoning process in stages and thereby may choose to leave arbitrarily large temporal gaps between any or all of those stages before requesting the final guess. No need to choose or solve at the moment or before actually needed (according to surrounding internal and external circumstances), and during the self-speech gaps the *logical-operations machine* can bring new data and new constructions from the background of those described in section [3.41].

[3.78]

«Sleeping with the problem's data, and obtaining an answer the next morning.»

A coarser method consists in the practice of «sleeping with the problem's data, and obtaining an answer the next morning». Although typically in this version the *logical-operations machine* accomplishes the inclusion of variables not contemplated by the *inner speech line*, this practice lacks the characteristics that produce the usefulness of the *least regret principle* for—

α.   Exercising and developing the conscience.

β.   Building choices considering explicitly and routinely long-term consequences for the organism's goals.

γ.   Learning by iteration how to improve the choice-making model used.

Consequently, this method neither develops nor expands the *executive functions* of the human brain.

The practice of «sleeping with the problem's data, and obtaining an answer the next morning» without any further operations, denotes a still inchoate conscience, nevertheless it already skips a lot of mistakes made when rushing choices.

[3.79]

«By my foolhardy will.»

The next more primitive version for guessing consists in the method better described as «by my foolhardy will» –vulgarly known among some males as «by my *balls*, by my manhood». «By my foolhardy will» does not use a conscience, therefore people without the function conscience can enact it routinely; this mental process included here for conveniently contrasting it.

In the foolhardy path, at the end of a sequence of statements in the *inner speech line*, the *logical-operations machine* simply collects the partial result and sends it briefly outside the *inner speech line* for the completion by guessing, the final result returning immediately. So brief the period of time used by the *logical-operations machine* that it scarcely incorporates any new variable and rarely accomplishes any kind of refining; and typically in a large amount of cases the outcome of «by my foolhardy will» leads to disastrous consequences.

Obtain and Modify the Mind-Set Sequences

[3.80]

This practice not trivial, a successful performance usually happens in a relatively calm environment with relatively optimal internal organismic conditions.

First the organism must recognize a newly generated solicitation or request for response whose resolution purportedly will produce far-reaching consequences relevant for the objectives of the organism (recall section [2.2]). Once identified such solicitation, the *logical-operations machine* will proceed to obtain the relevant postulates from the mind-set, which will use to build the first proposal to form a solution. Subsequently, if the *logical-operations machine* resolves to do so, it will send the first result built to the *inner speech codifying machine* and the first statement or *seed statement* will appear in the *inner speech line* as described in section [3.61].

At that moment, when the *seed statement* appears in the *inner speech line*, the conscience must quasi-instantaneously acquire ascendancy –this activation pivotal, otherwise the conscience loses the opportunity. Thereupon, the conscience must swiftly capture the *seed statement* and halt the *inner speech line*. Observe carefully the *seed statement*, remove the original external context and panorama; after considering enough a stable observation time, send the following command to the *logical-operations machine*: «Why I would think this?», and wait for the answer.

[3.81]

Capturing the *seed statement* requires a kind of prowess, trained focus, and agility, whereby first and foremost in the operation the (possibly suspended, halted, or in low-energy mode) conscience must exercise an unrehearsable capacity to sense the beginning of the processing of a challenge without words, thereby to know that it must (wake up and) rush to the proper levels of attention and vigor, no matter the overall conditions of the moment, and the speed the same as when operating fully unconsciously since from there comes the seed. The goal of the command sent consists in making the *logical-operations machine* revert the recently performed operation used to produce the *seed statement*. The *logical-operations machine* furnished and placed forward the *seed statement*, the conscience grabbed it and sent it back, all while the path used still fresh.

[3.82]

The *logical-operations machine* cannot send directly the mind-set sequences into the *inner speech line*, presumably because, if it did so, automatically would become evident the incoherent, illogical, and unsustainable character of many of those sequences in a comparison with the real world, and thereupon the whole mind-set configuration would collapse.

[3.83]

Consequently, the response emitted by the *logical-operations machine* upon the request of the conscience constitutes an approximation to the mind-set sequence relevant for the case. Iterating using the result obtained the first time regularly yields a useless output, if any at all; and if the person deems necessary to do so, then already missed and/or blurred the actual mind-set input. In any case, the conscience can accurately identify or differentiate a *seed statement* that constitutes a wholly unfounded hypothesis.

Stable Immunity Against Indoctrination

[3.84]

When a *Homo sapiens* individual lacks a conscience, typically the individual will either very difficulty or never understand, perceive, or recognize its fundamental mistakes when someone attempts to show those using dialog as main tool. They, the ones who lack a conscience, can only transform through indoctrination. Hence, those individuals live as slaves of the traditional organizational arrangements of the *Homo sapiens* and, concretely, the contemporaneous capitalism fully subdued them.

[3.85]

A *Homo sapiens* individual with a functional conscience also can receive an indoctrination; the conscience does not operate during all the vigil (recall section [3.70]) and anyway in its brain still exist the (legacy) parts that make such procedures possible. Howbeit, the capability of doing –or allowing– something does not cause its happening.[1]

The conscience can exercise an array of resources and methodological ways to eliminate the environmental garbage which the brain receives. Here included the two most obvious methods:

a) *Online filtering.* Remove whatever garbage received in «real time». This done only if the individual cannot enact other way, because it costs the diversion of attention.

b) *Remove the garbage from the environment.* Simply cutting or removing the flux of indoctrinating crap of any method of indoctrination enacted by someone else; also applies to any substandard content. This the most efficient method: saves energy, lifetime, and later removal of errors acquired by any leakage in the online filtering.

Try to read while chasing a mosquito, better just place a mosquito net on the door and window. If you let the mosquito bite your skin, you will spend more time and energy scratching yourself afterwards, all for nothing: the mosquito net constitutes a much more efficient solution.

[3.86]

In any case, the person with a conscience, after the exposition to an unfiltered doctrinal or substandard content (which because of whatever cause did not screen), will find itself spending some time and energy eliminating the idiotic postulates that emanate from its brain.

A Conscience Degraded by Words

[3.87]

A certain ancient strain or lineage of people developed and carries a type of conscience somehow partially incompatible with a self-speech in an *inner speech line.* The individuals of this kind prefer to make their plans using unconscious processes without transforming or expressing any part of them using the abstract labels defined as words; because when they use words some internal mechanism –or its absence– disrupts and degrades their unconscious processes. They stand aware of these facts of course.

---

1   Some groups of the parasitic psychopathic subspecies, described in [3.170] and subsequent sections, performed a quite zealous campaign to find a way to indoctrinate me.

For them, writing their plans produces catastrophic consequences. For those individuals, written words just constrain subsequent thoughts and entail a loss of plasticity, as if by writing they committed to something and, at the same time, dropped and never recovered part of the content –the content for which they lacked words.

In contrast, people with a regular conscience can send back and forth statements to and from unconscious processes, and the whole mental process maintains continuity, the unconscious processes keep adding unlabeled variables both in the background and when prompting the *inner speech line*, as described in section [3.41].

Executive Functions

[3.88]

Here a brief description about the *executive functions* of the human brain, enough to show some facts. Recall the introduction recorded in [2.8] and subsequent sections. The person interested in knowing more extensively about the *executive functions* should review the work of Barkley.

What Barkley recorded and what herein exposed differ in subtle but relevant aspects:

[3.89]

a) Barkley considers the development of the *executive functions* as closely related to the capacity of the *Homo sapiens* individuals for integration and participation in increasingly complex cooperative systems; starting with very simple cooperative systems until civilizations. Nonetheless, Barkley did not advert that not all of those who carry *executive functions* can organize any cooperative system, least a civilization; may they at best participate as passengers. Consequently, not all the *Homo sapiens* individuals bear the indispensable capacities to emit executive communications (aka organizational instructions) in high-hierarchy posts of advanced or complex cooperative systems, and obtain successful results.

[3.90]

b) The differences between the *executive functions* from distinct *Homo sapiens* individuals originate in the capacities for spatial, sequential, and temporal contemplation. Thereon:

    i. The capacity for *spatial contemplation* consists of the size of the universe encompassed by the horizon or frontier from within which the *Homo sapiens* individual will incorporate data into its choice-making processes.

    ii. The capacity for *temporal contemplation* consists of the analog of the previous, but in the case of time.

    iii. The capacity for *sequential contemplation* consists of the number of correlated facts and sequential steps (including bifurcations) that the *Homo sapiens* individual may foresee and incorporate into its choice-making processes and the model of the universe used for those processes.

    Accordingly, the capacity for *sequential contemplation* encompasses the complexity of the scenarios that a *Homo sapiens* individual may model within its cognitive processes, whether those scenarios dynamic or static.

The three capacities for contemplation appear clearly distinctive in each individual; they appear not effecting or producing each other, presumably because each uses different underlying processes.

[3.91]

c) Barkley lists eight neuropsychological capacities arising from the *executive functions* of the human brain: spatial, temporal, motivational, conceptual/abstract, behavioral-structural, social, cultural, and inhibitory capacities.

Those neuropsychological capacities correspond as follows:

    i. The already described *spatial contemplation* and *temporal contemplation* capacities correspond to the analogous in the list of Barkley.

    ii. The motivational capacity relates to the behavior-regulating mechanisms described in this document as centered in the *emotional states generating machine* operating by the unconscious appraisal of present and prospective scenarios and contemplated goals, applying the gradually internalized regulations described by Deci and Ryan.

iii. The conceptual/abstract, behavioral-structural, and social capacities relate to the already described *sequential contemplation* capacity.

iv. The cultural capacity relates to the *methodological propensities* described in [3.146] and subsequent sections.

The *inhibitory capacity* corresponds to the ability to defer the execution of unconsciously-propelled calls-to-action which stem from unconscious appraisals of future scenarios made using a more steep time- and sequential-discount estimation of usefulness, than the usefulness estimated consciously. Thus, the *inhibitory capacity* relates to the capacity of conscious processes to remain active and with enough vigor to override and supersede unconscious processes and basal urges.

For example, a peasant with an adequate *inhibitory capacity* will save grain for the next season instead of consuming it out of a lavish desire to just enjoy food. The case of unrestrained desires which lead to the premature consumption of grain greatly differs from the case when the peasant lacks an ability to foresee the need to use the grain during the next season.

[3.92]

An above-average capacity for *sequential contemplation* furnishes the ability to organize cooperative systems.

[3.93]

As already described: If an individual carries a conscience, it can deliberately choose to widen its ranges of spatial, sequential, and temporal contemplation.

[3.94]

Talking to someone about something outside its *temporal contemplation* capacity usually constitutes, for the person, a talk about another era, or a talk about a legendary past, or a talk about an irrelevant future. Typically, the memories outside the *temporal contemplation* capacity of an individual appear unconnected, faded, and subject to change, deletion, or addition.

In contrast, talking to someone about something outside its *spatial contemplation* or *sequential contemplation* capacities, usually shows an intellectual vacuum and/or cognitive omissions, and in many cases produces an expressed disregard.

[3.95]

The *Homo sapiens* individuals lacking a conscience, and whose spatial, temporal, and sequential contemplation capacities encompass narrow or insufficient ranges compared with the world they live at, usually live in disadvantaged situations and constitute the objectives of the so-called «control and manipulation of masses» in the traditional forms of organization of the *Homo sapiens*. As instances:

a) The spatial horizon of individuals lacking a conscience and with narrow spatial contemplation capacities equals to variable certain lengths, those lengths depending upon the culture and environment of each individual. This makes possible the compartmentalization and regionalization of the social control by propagandists and pseudo-journalists using a variety of instruments to convey their messages: propagandists and pseudo-journalists can confine the knowledge about what happens in a city, region, or country, up to certain extent, inside that same zone. Hence, the individuals deficient in this neuropsychological capacity ordinarily will not contemplate as input for their choices the events that regularly happen outside their spatial horizon.

For example, in Mexico –the country discarded in the preface of this document– the spatial horizon of an individual lacking a conscience and with narrow spatial contemplation capacities typically amounts to the distance the individual can traverse away from its home and go back to sleep to its (same) home in the same day, there the spatial frontier. Among the herd nobody will consider as input for its personal choices the events and facts that cannot see directly or immediately with its own eyes –or in an oligarchic TV channel. The estimated relevance of whatever an individual does not see, even if it knows about the occurrence of the event or the existence of the fact, decreases in an apparently logarithmic fashion with distance.

If 150 km away the organized crime literally rules the region, nobody cares and most individuals do not notice. If 150 km in another direction hundreds of thousands of persons crossed the border illegally during the last half year, again most individuals consider it irrelevant. At least from the second half of the XX century until the second decade of the XXI century, only when some «extraordinary» or increased criminal activities (for example, mass kidnappings and conspicuous gunfights) or some above-average influx of illegal crossings happened, such that some sector of the population effortlessly noticed something, TV channels and newspapers in some cases disseminated a narrow and twisted version of the events and their cause.

b) A deficiency in *temporal contemplation* provides the basis for the repetition of historical sequences, sometimes even in the same context. The individuals deficient in this capacity will not seek to learn from recorded history; those deficient in the capacity for *temporal contemplation* will deem irrelevant anything regarded as belonging to a «distant past». In modern times, those who control the organizational structures simply can wait for the mentally deficient to forget the events, and afterwards they can repeat the recipes applied to the masses. Typically, the range of *temporal contemplation* of a *Homo sapiens* individual encompasses only its own lifetime; however, the memories of the individuals belonging to previous generations partially mend this deficiency, while those individuals live. When all the direct witnesses of an event perish, the contemplation of it among the deficient individuals disappears.

For example, among the most primitive urban groups in Mexico, the temporal contemplation tends to reduce to a few years: 3 to 6. This tiny temporal contemplation capacity clearly evident in the successive and successful cycles of promises, electoral fraud and/or purchase of voters, and disappointment during the course of the failed democracy in that country.

c) A deficiency in the capacity for *sequential contemplation*, combined with an *arithmetic deficiency*, produces a manifest inability to develop technology. Even with a deficiency in arithmetic capacities, but with a functional capacity for *sequential contemplation*, a *Homo sapiens* individual can notice that, although he/she cannot by itself develop technology, others do can.

For example, using this deficiency in *sequential contemplation*, in Mexico, during the first two decades of the XXI century, the traitors to the homeland promoted divesting the property and control of fossil hydrocarbons from the state-organization in favor of private individuals. Among other excuses, the traitors vigorously proclaimed: «Mexico lacks the technology to exploit the deep-water seabed oilfields.» And, due to their deficiency in *sequential contemplation*, most individuals demonstrated a sort of helplessness; thereupon, eventually the traitors succeeded.

[3.96]

In these three instances of deficient spatial, sequential, and temporal contemplation capacities happens a consistent direct usage of sensory organs as the main sources of data about the world; and on the occasions where happens the usage of external technological or social devices –as television, or institutionalized education, or the so-called «search engines» available in the internet network–, the individuals participate as either passengers or directed users.

The aforesaid usage of external devices showcases what stated in the next section.

[3.97]

The *Homo sapiens* individuals lacking a conscience and with certain deficiency in their *executive functions*, use neither tools nor devices operated independently by themselves for the acquisition and storage of data required by their own choice-making processes. This constitutes definitely a deficiency in their extended phenotype.

[3.98]

Using external instruments –both physical devices and social arrangements– independently to acquire and store data, and later using their own gathered data to build choices, could constitute an insurmountable structural advantage for more advanced humans. An additional large advantage, of course, would consist in building instruments independently instead of relying on those devices hacked and/or bugged by the parasitic psychopathic subspecies, by capitalistic corporations, or by «state security agencies». Beware that the members of the parasitic psychopathic subspecies hack and bug whatever they can, not only data-processing devices, because they want to steal everything.

Furthermore, manufacturing custom-made instruments can produce a new kind of competition which currently does not exist.

[3.99]

For enlarging its *temporal contemplation* capacity, an organism must consider itself a trans-generational entity, and act accordingly.

However, some parasitic lifestyles entail an incompatibility with the aforesaid enlargement, and therefrom it would barely provide any difference for the individuals who espouse such ways of living –consult [3.167] and subsequent sections.

A Primeval Inchoate Mechanism to Build Relationships

[3.100]

See the «Orion's Belt» in the night sky.[2]

People from antiquity saw all sort of complex shapes in the night sky. Animals, persons with instruments, scenes like the «Milky Way».

Now look something simple, like a «rectangular table», do you see it «rectangular»? Why?

Furthermore, do you identify the edges of the object? –Say, the «rectangular table»– Do you see a line? Why? There no line exists.

[3.101]

When during my childhood people told me that three stars in the night sky constituted a «belt» I never understood, I just saw three lights resembling dots and nothing more. Only until I became more or less «old» I understood that they made a line in their heads using the dots they saw in the sky.

---

2   If in the night sky at the place where you stand those stars do not appear, look into others similarly arranged. However, if you cannot see most of the stars because of the thick layer of smog above you, knowing that you breathe that same smog should compel you to end capitalism as soon as possible. Do not blame light pollution, that latter causes only a certain limited diminution of visibility; and, in any case, light pollution also produces deleterious effects in terrestrial ecosystems.

[3.102]

Think about the primeval times of a cognitive species, think about the beginning of flexible and adaptable self-determined cognitive processes.

At the time when a nascent brain arose in the world, proceeded a relentless evolutionary pressure to identify objects, events, and processes in order to make calculations and thereby build adaptive choices –leading to survival. But the nascent brain started with nothing, may the sensory organs provided data about the world, but the nascent brain lacked a way to process the data, to discern what it saw.

In this situation of dearth of cognitive abstractions, the nascent brain devoted itself to the only feasible way: make connections. Connect all the data, store the output of the operation, use it for behavior, make test and trial.

And the stored connected data constituted logical entities: the items connected thereby gave birth to *logical abstractions*.

[3.103]

Hominids endured –and endure– a further evolutionary pressure to develop technology, organizational methods and, in general, new ways of life. For these goals, during primeval times humans found useful to make all sorts of cognitive connections using whatever they could find, as already mentioned. Furthermore, the more connections one makes, the more cognitive capacities one develops applicable to a primitive test-and-trial routine.

Summarizing, the development route in the connect-everything practice consists in: «Connect everything, develop all sorts of twigs, both in the standard phenotype and in the extended phenotype, then test and trial them in real life within the world, and grow those successful.»

[3.104]

Therefrom, humans created art as a way of self-expression, and also humans enacted the appreciation of artistic products as a way to illuminate, promote, and engender new neuronal connections –as a way to stimulate the formation of new neuronal paths. Essentially, creating art constitutes an attempt to both develop an understanding of the world and grow one's own extended phenotype by experimentation.

[3.105]

The connect-everything practice turned into a swamp when hominids connected also their logical abstractions to the raw data of the world and thereby produced new abstract entities. The muddy mistakes in the mind-created swamp became even more sticky because hominids kept making connections automatically.

[3.106]

Thus: three stars in the sky imply nothing.

A cognitive organism can use certain arbitrarily defined collections of dots to specify univocally a logical entity called *direction*, and the entity called *direction* if used to specify a one-dimensional space, serves to construct another logical entity called *line*. But first the cognitive organism must indispensably define the logical entity called *direction*, then can define the logical entity called *line* using the desired boundaries. And the fact that a group of dots may serve to specify a *line*, does not enforce humans to do so. Even more non-compulsory results to use stars to define a «belt».

[3.107]

Logical abstractions serve to define and identify subsets of the real world –of the universe. Thus, generic logical abstractions serve to link specifying content to the tag used for any given entity, wherefrom a new logical abstraction arises. But to assume that a subset of the real world complies with the characteristics of a logical entity used for delimitation, constitutes a long erroneous leap.

[3.108]

Self-aware entities perform logical operations utilizing and producing logical abstractions. Apparently, understanding produces self-awareness, and self-awareness enhances understanding. Self-awareness constitutes an indispensable ability for cognitively detaching oneself from the perceived universe and thereby discern between one's own cognitive capacities and the world.

[3.109]

Logical abstractions can stand codified in materials external to the organism. Moreover, the organism (or its civilization) can develop and build machines and instruments that operate automatically or semi-automatically with these material representatives of logical abstractions, for those devices to produce the output of a logical operation.

Therefore, such devices constitute aiding machines, an extension of the organism's phenotype, a part of the extended phenotype.

Inside aiding machines and instruments the representatives of the logical abstractions consist of material objects and the situations kept by those same material objects (gears in specific positions, shafts and levers, electrically charged bodies, switches, objects producing magnetic fields, reagents and reactants, and so forth) and the operation happens by the interactions and reactions among those material objects through time (motion of the gears, shafts, and levers; electric currents, chemical reactions, diffusion processes, and so forth), just as happens inside any ordinary cognitive organism.

Meanwhile, for example, an earthworm lacks self-awareness and understanding, but still enacts a self-directed behavior.

[3.110]

Nowadays, when enacting the scientific method, humans restrict and focus the *connect everything then test and trial* succession into deliberately selected fields of exploration, usually within practices commonly known as *research* and *experimentation*.

A Metaphysical World

[3.111]

Humans originate or spawn their own metaphysical world by connecting logical abstractions to the raw data of the real world and thereby producing new abstract entities.

[3.112]

Typically, due to the confusion generated by the mixture of data in the *machine to build the perceived reality*, the *Homo sapiens* organisms live in a «virtual world» where, besides their own emotional states and words looking real, another vast quantity of entities receive ascriptions of any kind of metaphysical entities –metaphysical properties, qualities, processes, objects, and so forth– and the individual regards these entities as containing or carrying such supranatural elements, as described in section [3.22].

Average humans can assign anything as a container of a metaphysical entity. Furthermore, in extreme cases humans regard as real some entities built based purely on fantasy.

Within this document addressed chiefly the cases of words and physical objects as containers of metaphysical entities.

[3.113]

Remember the fantastic metaphysical substance called «phlogiston» used at the heyday of alchemy, those who practiced such wizardry assumed that the «phlogiston» transited from one body into another and due to that supposedly happened a change of temperature in the examined bodies. Supposedly, the quantity of «phlogiston» contained within a body corresponded to the temperature of the latter in a directly proportional relationship. Attempts to mask the history of «phlogiston» as a small misstep in the history of human knowledge produce counterproductive excuses, as the people who operated with it resembled more magicians than modern scientists.

[3.114]

Approximately happens the same with the concept of «value» as with «phlogiston», particularly pervasively in operations of exchange and production. The fantasy as follows: when a manufacturing sequence produces an object, this object acquires «the value» of the inputs plus another «value» added and created by the «human immaterial input», or added and created by automated processes and machinery. The immaterial input or the physical effects which «create value» can consist of «effort», sophistication and complexity added, «usefulness realized», human lifetime spent, and so forth.

In a leap forward, many humans also consider that the activity of performing a *service* (useful for someone else) «creates value». In this case usually the «value» remains stored in *the consequences* of the activity. For example, if someone trains a horse, then «the value of the horse increased».

[3.115]

Most humans assume the fantastic metaphysical entity denominated «value» as embedded in all physical objects –or in almost all, for the case makes no difference– in the planet Earth and, pronouncedly, in the tools of exchange denominated money. Humans use many variations of the concept of «value», happens no shortage of them; if requested, most humans can assign a version of «value» to whatever on Earth.

[3.116]

Humans live in a world of magic. The wide usage and acceptance of the metaphysical «value» constitutes one of the greatest blunders in the history of human thinking, especially considering all the information available after the massive distribution of written records and the advancement of science in many fields. Humans must raise an alarm and acknowledge all which happened so wrong for this mistake to continue for so long; in section [4.82] recorded one of the main social problems which undoubtedly sustained and amplified the aforesaid mistake.

Calculus or Estimation of Probabilities and the Monty Hall Problem

[3.117]

Humans use the compilation of data from past events as input when guessing the outcome of a similar past, present, or future event; the guessing done when lacking sufficient data about the event, or a full understanding of its nature, or both. Likewise, humans use as input the combined compilation of data from past and present situations or facts, for obtaining better results when guessing missing data about similar past, presently existing, or future situations or facts. In these ways humans attempt to reduce uncertainty; recall the guessing process described in section [3.45].

Notice that in an environment whose dynamics correspond to the relationships denominated *Newton's «laws»*:

α. All events consist in a sequence of causes and effects.

β. All facts existed formerly, or exist currently, or will exist in the future.

γ. Time itself advances forward monotonically without variations in pace.

If happens a component related to *randomness*, unmeasurable in present facts in an atomic scale, it neither influences nor effects the macroscopic newtonian dynamics addressed here. In a newtonian environment, the calculus or estimation of probabilities constitutes a problem of data processing –an *informational* problem. However, many

Homo sapiens individuals assume the «probabilities» as existing in the universe by themselves (hence, independently), as metaphysical substances analogous to «value» and «phlogiston».

Monty Hall Problem

[3.118]

The *Monty Hall problem*, first used regularly for misleading the participants of a television show, semi-formally documented and explicitly acknowledged in the year 1975, in the subsequent sections serves for showcasing the widespread usage of «probabilities» as metaphysical substances. Explaining the problem does not require the historical details of that television show, therefore herein those omitted.

[3.119]

Broadly, the *Monty Hall problem* happens as follows:

In a show the host or show-person invites a spectator to become a participant. Thereat, the host exhibits three covered boxes or spaces (a curtain may serve for the purpose) and tells the participant: «In one of these three covered spaces –in one of these three options– stands something that you highly appreciate. If you select correctly the covered space that contains it, then the object will pass to your personal domain.» The offered object typically consists of something for which supposable acquisition the participant would spend the profits of several months of labor, hence many still-stunned participants become anxious. Of course, ordinarily the organizers of the show add numerous environmental stimulus and secondary actions aiming to distract the participant.

During the first period of time, before choosing anything, the participant establishes in its mind, either consciously or unconsciously: «Each one of these covered spaces *has* the same probability of containing the object. Or, (by assigning numbers) each covered space *has* one third of a unity or roughly 33.33% of the probabilities.» Notice the usage of the word «has» which assigns the metaphysical entity denominated «probability» as contained inside each covered space.

[3.120]

Thereupon, in sequence:

1. By first time the participant publicly chooses one of the covered spaces.

2. Instead of uncovering the content of the chosen space, the show's host uncovers another space from the trio, this latter which the host knows empty. The participant recognizes this second space as empty.

3. Immediately afterwards, the host offers two alternatives to the participant, to either:
   a) Uphold its original choice which would lead the host to uncover the first selected space and reveal its content, or
   b) Change its choice towards the third space whereupon the host would uncover that newly selected space.

Then, assigning a «probability» as a metaphysical entity contained within the spaces (or boxes) –the mistake of the participant– produces an external error: Observing that now one of the three spaces stands out of consideration, the participant redistributes the metaphysical entity «probability» among the two remaining spaces, and thereby now regards each space as containing half unity of probability or 50%, and never understands the convenience of changing his/her choice and thereat publicly select the third space.

The participant may think that the «probability» contained in the uncovered space disappeared, that one third of the original metaphysical substance still exists within each of the remaining covered spaces –hence, remain two thirds in total. And, accordingly, the participant uses that premise as basis for recalculation.

[3.121]

Typically, the participant does not conceive –and consequently does not enact– the correct choice-making procedure at the *Monty Hall problem* because does not comprehend that:

1. Cognitive entities build sound probability models always using as foundation the compilation of data from either events or facts considered similar to the inspected (event or fact).

2. Therefore, for using a probability model a cognitive entity must foremost and indispensably identify the kind of event or fact on whose data compilation and processing relies the model.

The logical probability model –even if only unconsciously known– can become verbalized as follows: «When an event happens (notice the compilation of data) among a group of undifferentiated entities, typically it happens for each entity in a number of cases whose absolute differences from the number of cases accumulated for each other entity tend to insignificance as the total number of events increases; each numeric (in)significance evaluated by comparing each difference with (and thereby dividing over) the magnitude of the total number of events (whereupon successive quotients consistently tend to zero). Thus, the event tends to happen with the same frequency for each entity. The longer the term used for data compilation, the frequency for each entity tends to become increasingly homogeneous.»

[3.122]

In the *Monty Hall problem* the event used as input for the probability model consists in *the placement of an object* and the group of undifferentiated entities consists of the three covered spaces; the event happened only in one member of the undifferentiated entities. According to the informational scenario built using the probability model, the event could happened in any space with equal opportunity for every one of those; however, afterwards the participant must collect the data from posterior events and process this new data and events upon the preceding circumstances and framework provided by the initial probability model. Using the corresponding probability model, the participant can assign an individual numerical index to each target as a means for conveniently comparing them: one third for each one. And when the participant arbitrarily selects a target space, at the same time excludes this space from the group that the host or show-person can use for choosing afterwards.

The participant counts two thirds of its preferences in the group of spaces relinquished –those the two spaces now available for the host. And when the host reveals empty one of these spaces, he/she provides new data regarding this subset and his/her act of choosing must constitute another (rather simple) probability event in the (abstract, created and updated cognitively) informational landscape of the participant. Hence, the participant's mind must update its logical abstractions accordingly.

[3.123]

Therefrom, the participant must use two instances of probability estimation, because now the participant observed two probability events in different circumstances. Here essential to grok and remember that, in an informational problem, information does not «disappear» midway.

Every probability model receives as «input pool» whatever *degree of certainty of occurrence* the cognitive entity assigns to it. In the first probability instance, the host provided a *degree of certainty of occurrence* equal to 1 (in a scale from 0 to 1), or 100% certain that the organizers of the show performed the action. For the second probability instance the participant must calculate the *degree of certainty of occurrence*.

The cognitive entity must assemble a pipeline of information.

[3.124]

Label the spaces as *a*, *b*, and *c*:

a. *Probability model #1.*

«When an event happens among a group of undifferentiated entities, ... the event tends to happen with the same frequency for each entity.»

Thus, for the set of entities $[a,b,c]$ in the probability model #1:

$$a_{m1} = \frac{1}{3}$$

$$b_{m1} = \frac{1}{3}$$

$$c_{m1} = \frac{1}{3}$$

Where a_{m1} denotes the probability of occurrence of the option *a* in this probability model isolated, and so forth for the other two.

Circumstances #1: *How probable results that the event described by this probability model happened?*

degree of certainty of occurrence$_1 = 1$

Therefore, the cognitive entity can assign a probability index to each option as follows:

$$Pa_{m1} = (degree\ of\ certainty\ of\ occurrence_1)(a_{m1}) = (1)\left(\frac{1}{3}\right) = \frac{1}{3}$$

$$Pb_{m1} = (degree\ of\ certainty\ of\ occurrence_1)(b_{m1}) = (1)\left(\frac{1}{3}\right) = \frac{1}{3}$$

$$Pc_{m1} = (degree\ of\ certainty\ of\ occurrence_1)(c_{m1}) = (1)\left(\frac{1}{3}\right) = \frac{1}{3}$$

β.   *Pipeline of information.*
Say that the relinquished spaces consist of the subset $[b,c]$, then for the second model the «input pool» or *degree of certainty of occurrence* of circumstances #2 results:

$$degree\ of\ certainty\ of\ occurrence_2 = Pb_{m1} + Pc_{m1} = \frac{1}{3} + \frac{1}{3} = \frac{2}{3}$$

γ.   *Probability model #2.*
«If the event happened in this set, it happened in the unselected space.» or «If these circumstances happen, the event can only happen in the unselected entity.»
For clarity rename $[b,c]$ as set $[d,e]$ because this now constitutes a completely new instance of probability estimation. Say that the host (or clown) reveals empty the space d. Thus, for the set $[d,e]$, in the probability model #2:

$$d_{m2} = 0$$
$$e_{m2} = 1$$

Circumstances #2: *How probable results that the event described by this probability model happened?*

$$degree\ of\ certainty\ of\ occurrence_2 = \frac{2}{3}$$

Therefore, similarly to the previous probability model:

$$Pd_{m2} = \left(degree\ of\ certainty\ of\ occurrence_2\right)\left(d_{m2}\right) = \left(\frac{2}{3}\right)(0) = 0$$

$$Pe_{m2} = \left(degree\ of\ certainty\ of\ occurrence_2\right)\left(e_{m2}\right) = \left(\frac{2}{3}\right)(1) = \frac{2}{3}$$

Graphically:

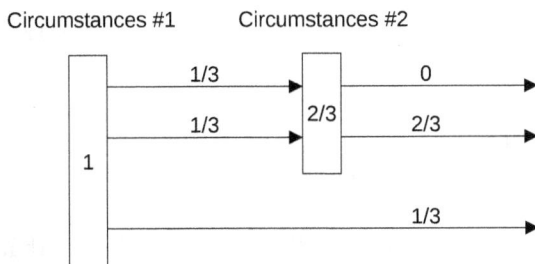

Figure 2. Diagram of probability information pipelining.

[3.125]

(Remember from your years of instruction that) For a concatenated series of probability events the final calculated output equals the product of the multiplication of all the individual outputs assigned by each model in the sequence. In the *Monty Hall problem* merely happens that a middle step in a probability multiplication chain receives more than one input and produces more than one output.

[3.126]

Thus, no real-world «probabilities» exist.

Statistical Correlations Converted into Metaphysical Entities

[3.127]

What follows describes a product from blending the metaphysical world originated as described in sections [3.111] and [3.112], with the primeval inchoate mechanism to build relationships described in [3.100] and subsequent sections.

For easiness of understanding, I will use first an indoctrination-style approach to deliver the message.

[3.128]

An auxiliary tale

Say exist two persons: Molly and John. Molly got in her domain a healthy orange tree, and therefore can produce oranges. John got in his domain a healthy banana tree, and therefore can produce bananas. Molly and John reach an agreement to routinely exchange one banana per one orange. (Hence both can eat bananas and oranges, which they appreciate.)

Then appears a third person: Sally. Sally learns to make orange juice but lacks any orange tree; thus, she offers to Molly and John: for every three oranges any of them may provide, Sally will make juice from one orange and deliver back that juice, and Sally will keep (and presumably eat) the second and third oranges as a profit.

No money involved, just bartering.

The deal does not interest Molly, because she thinks that she would give at most two oranges to get back the juice of one.

In contrast, John accepts Sally's offer, because he thinks he got better things to do than squeezing oranges. Thereupon, John harvests three bananas, exchanges the bananas with Molly to get the oranges, and gives Sally the oranges to get back the juice of one orange.

Someone could say: «Then for Sally two oranges *have* the value of the juice of one orange, while for John three oranges *have* the value (or less than the value) of the juice of one orange.» If anyone postulates such statement, at least can notice that the «value» depends completely on the person involved in assessing it. Therefore, «value» does not constitute a universal property inherent on things –as recorded also in sections [3.115] and [3.116].

But what if both Sally and John agree in giving three oranges to Molly in exchange for the juice of one orange? Further, what if a large population agrees to do the same? There jumps in a capitalistic economist and tells that there exists a «market price» for the orange juice, and with that shows one of the fundamental errors of the capitalistic doctrine: statistical convergence does NOT create phenomena. The convergence of a bunch of people does not create an event of nature or whatsoever, and «market price» –simply put– does not exist.

Notice that could happen that Molly and John never talk to each other about Sally's offer, or if they do, they do not care about the opinion of the other person, thus they may act independently.

§

[3.129]

Humans with conscience may ask: Why the capitalistic economist made the gross mistake of imagining a phenomenon where none exists? Why the need to «fill» or «complete» the perception of events with an addendum? The answer simple and crude: because primitive people do that, and Frazer abundantly documented this more than a century ago in The Golden Bough. Humans create a forced metaphysical world propelled by an urge: «If there exists no metaphysical world we will create one immediately, in order to *complete* the universe.»

[3.130]

Capitalistic economists will attempt to assert that the «market price» they use consists of a logical abstraction, but that will constitute just another of their cynical lies. For centuries now, capitalistic economists used the concept of «market price» as existing by itself, they even developed techniques for «market price discovery».

[3.131]

The conversion of a statistical correlation into a metaphysical entity in the example of the «market price» must get split in two for more easily observing the two errors involved –and because those errors widespread in the capitalistic doctrine and «professional economic practices». Accordingly, the two mistakes involved consist in:

[3.132]

1. *Assuming that correlation implies causality.*

    In the example of the orange juice: «Two humans doing the same thing causes *something.*» The two humans doing the same thing «caused» the «creation» of something else.

    This an extremely pervasive mistake in the capitalistic doctrine. Everywhere one can know of capitalistic economists (and any other people infected with that kind of thinking) stating: «We will check how variable A affects or influences variable B (in this assumed system that we do not understand at all).» Where they rarely admit that they assumed the existence of a system and that they do not understand what happens within the supposed «system». For example: «We will investigate the dependence of consumption patterns upon a variable denominated *inflation.*»

    Everywhere in capitalistic schools and universities someone draws in the classroom board a graph to «illustrate» how a variable A affects a variable B –or even a collection of variables. The capitalistic economists just assume one of the variables as the *independent variable,* and they consider that choice enough foundation for building a cause-and-effect relationship.

    There the capitalistic economists do not comprehend the following facts:

    i.   The aggregated behavior of the individuals in a society proceeds in an extremely complex fashion, and therefore any attempt to describe it with a few numeric variables produces   useless   misrepresentations   and oversimplifications.

    ii. They neither know nor understand how individual human behavior proceeds, they do not understand humans in general.

iii. They lack the most essential data about each individual human psyche. This personal data comprises a lot of private undisclosed information.

iv. Likewise, they lack most of the data about actual facts, about the «facts on the ground». In many instances this data does not even exist because nobody generated it.

But, showing their retardation, most capitalistic economists think that they do comprehend human behavior, that they hold enough data, and that they command a capability to process it.

Furthermore, capitalistic economists assume that a group of variables related to a vaguely delimited environment with countless unacknowledged components constitutes a «system». In this case the vaguely delimited environment consists of the aggregated behavior of the individuals in a society, the individual situation of each one, and the resources available to them.

Basically, the capitalistic economists:

i. Assume the existence of a system by setting vaguely delimited boundaries and disregarding countless unacknowledged components.

ii. Grossly simplify the supposed «system». Yes, even after disregarding countless unacknowledged components, they simplify more into a few variables.

iii. Correlate the variables of their preference, and select one suitable as *independent variable*.

iv. Proclaim a relationship of cause-and-effect among the correlated variables.

It constitutes a string of irrational steps that shows a pattern of thinking alien to applied science and science itself.

[3.133]

2. *Converting a situation into a metaphysical entity.*

In the example of the orange juice: «A crowd doing the same creates a *market price*.» There a *crowd doing the same* constitutes a situation composed of elements in motion.

A lot of entities doing the same thing or in the same state constructs nothing in the real world, nor creates any relationship among the entities. This should appear obvious, but not for capitalistic economists. This mistake arises purely from magical thinking. Likewise, three stars in the night sky do not create a «belt».

[3.134]

If someone throws a rock into a water pond and besides splashing the entrance of the rock generates a wave on the surface of the water, then:

1. There exists no system «rock-wave».
2. If the person throws another rock into the water, will happen approximately the same, but not the same.
3. The fact that happened approximately the same the second time, also does not create a system.
4. Throwing the rock into the water creates a string of causes and effects, but those completely contingent upon a lot of factors. For example: the size and shape of the rock, how fast it entered the water and in which position, if other waves already existed in the water, the depth of the water, how murky and viscous stands the water, the local gravity, the density of each rock, and other similar facts.

The case of the *rock into water* constitutes a very simple sequence of interactions, and already in this scenario whoever begins the sequence must acknowledge and measure a lot of factors merely to ensure repeatability within any useful precision range.

Now, if there happens that someone deals with the minds, situations, and resources of 1,000,000 or 100,000,000 humans in a country, the person will never command an ability to collect and harness the indispensable data for repeatability of anything. The current and foreseeable technologies do not suffice at all for actually collecting the aforementioned data, and certainly the citizens involved –the sources of the data– will not consent to such pervasive collection and processing in democratic countries.

[3.135]

The following description evidences more clearly the difference between actual scientific thinking and the magical thinking embraced by capitalistic economists:

Biologists use an approximate abstract representation called *ecosystem*; this approximate abstract representation depicts the interactions of a specific group of organisms with a physical environment within delimited boundaries. However, biologists readily understand that the entities agglomerated in the approximate abstract representation do not constitute a system in reality.

Therefore, for example:

1. Biologists do not regard birds connected to worms by any intermediary (like a «market price»).

2. No sound biologist will attempt to construct an encompassing correlation of the amount of birds to the amount of worms because biologists understand that those correlations would result contingent upon many circumstances, and thus the exercise would produce a useless, fundamentally mistaken, and oversimplified output.

No sane biologist will claim a supposed relationship of cause-and-effect arising from a statistical correlation.

Instead, biologists use the approximate abstract representation called *ecosystem* to study an environmental setting as it exists during a short span of time, so short that the interactions of the entities within the setting resemble a quasi-stable subset. For instance, biologists may analyze the interactions within an environmental setting during one year, while usual significant changes in the purely *physical* –not biological– environment take anywhere from tens of thousands of years to geological ages, and while the usual formation of a new relatively complex species takes tens of thousands of years. When analyzing highly mutable organisms likewise biologists adjust their time spans into correspondingly short periods, or otherwise refrain from calling the environmental setting an *ecosystem*. Furthermore, the species that interact inside the delimited environmental setting behave quasi-mechanistically for they lack any higher cognitive capacities; thus those organisms behave highly consistently. In contrast, no sane biologist would ever attempt to depict the aggregated human behavior as a «human ecosystem», because biologists also understand that humans do not behave quasi-mechanistically.

[3.136]

In this context, the «predictions» of the capitalistic economists arise from projecting the past into the future, where any moment the conditions change with the capitalistic economists neither noticing nor understanding. Making such «predictions» constitutes a practice which everybody in the XXI century knows from real-world experience that consists in, metaphorically: *walk blind a few steps, crash, collect data for projecting the future, make recommendations, and walk blind other steps before crashing again*, and so on. Thereat the lives of real people «crash»; for many humans the damage results irreparable.

Brain Split
A Disjoined Discrepant Evolved Kludge

[3.137]

Almost nobody recognizes the void at the dissociation of unconscious processes from conscious ones –the full clearance between them. This dissociation akin to an abyss within many human brains.

[3.138]

As explained in section [3.28], conscious processes comprise those which use logical abstractions which the «self» can explicitly and directly perceive and work with, and if necessary convert into language.

[3.139]

It happens as if humans carried two disjoined brains which communicate to each other intermittently and sparingly. Each instance sends messages and signals on its own; happens no «dialog», the communication proceeds unidirectionally for each part. This happens apparently because the parts of the brain that provide consciousness and linguistic abilities, evolved hurriedly over and around previous, ancestral sections. The net result consists in an incapacity, in many humans, to acknowledge the causes and origins of their own behavior.

Correspondingly, happens the same when those humans attempt to analyze the behavior of other persons.

[3.140]

The aforementioned behavioral patterns seem as if for many a lot of human activities happen underground or covert; akin as if humans lived inside two overlapping spaces of action: one (consciously) perceived and directly processed by the «self», and another unconsciously perceived and processed. A lot of things may happen in the «underground», where (each one's) unconscious processes live, and humans hardly can consciously acknowledge that many such things happened, and when they do acknowledge their occurrence they hardly can acknowledge why they happened.

[3.141]

This dissociation happens both among humans with ascendancy of the unconscious processes and among humans with ascendancy of the inner speech line. Thus, both *animals* and *technicals* experience the abyss in their mental processes. However, in the case of *technicals* the dissociation becomes readily visible when they build logical abstractions describing human behavior.

[3.142]

The most highly dissociated *Homo sapiens* individuals –a large share of humanity– seem to consciously perceive human behavior as arising from «natural laws» akin to those descriptive formulations used in physics and chemistry. Some of them conduct experiments and «investigations» similar to those chemists perform to uncover new elements and molecules, seeking to uncover the «natural laws» of human behavior, including the «natural relationships that a society may establish within». As if the collective human behavior consisted of some kind of dark matter that one can poke in search of answers.

Therefrom a field called «social sciences» arose, where they talk about «social forces» and «social phenomena».

[3.143]

Thus, when capitalistic economists started talking about the «invisible hand of the market» nobody called them psychotics; when capitalistic economists proclaimed that a type of human activity, which they labeled «market», constituted a «self-regulating system», nobody pointed the detachment from reality. The capitalistic economists merely «discovered» just another of the supposed «natural laws» of human behavior.

Where humans could regard «social forces» as actually existing, proclaiming the existence of «market forces» constituted a tiny leap forward. In that mystical world some obscure human behavior –in which, by the way, the vast majority of adults engaged habitually– could very well constitute a «system» that could «self-regulate», since apparently everybody shared some sort of magical connection.

Such mysticism still exists at the time of this writing.

[3.144]

In many instances, the commands and postulates from unconscious processes result incongruous and irreconcilable with the logical abstractions available for the «self». Soon or later the «self» would encounter the internal discrepancies, at that event the «self» lacking a logical way to attend them. Therefrom, for avoiding a mental embroilment that would produce paralysis, myriad humans employ both a flexible fountain of justifications and an unlimited foundation for rationalizations.

[3.145]

Specifically, the structures of «faith» and «belief»/«believe» evolved to circumvent the impossibility of establishing a logical coherency between what a *Homo sapiens* individual does and what its «self» can acknowledge. «Faith» acts as an unlimited foundation for rationalizations, and «belief»/«believe» acts as a flexible fountain of justifications to glue and uphold whatever incoherent assertion.

At the same time, many praying rituals seem to serve as a routine to directly stabilize unconscious processes; where without those rituals both the internal and external behavior of many individuals would become erratic.

Methodological Propensities

[3.146]

Instincts promote the execution of actions that produce specific consequences, hence specific ends, which directly ensure the survival of the organism; but to which method use to reach each end the instinct does not commit.

Instead of relying on recipes to achieve ends, the brain of cognizant calculating animals carries *methodological propensities*. Lower animals like earthworms may rely on control loops and simple if-then-else sensory-guided behavior, cognizant calculating animals –hominids among them– stand far from that. Which methodological propensity will prevail, or the organism will express, depends on the particular circumstances the organism finds itself. The methodological propensities inside a calculating brain with a memory, confer the upper animal an enhanced behavioral flexibility, learning capacities, and even some foresight; these qualities constitute an advantage in interactions with lower animals (like worms, for example).

[3.147]

The concept of *methodological propensity*: A preferred path to perform a cognitive action; several methodological propensities may develop an interplay for a single given cognitive task.

Thereby, methodological propensities serve for building methods for performing specific tasks. An organism with memory may store each of the aforesaid methods for future usage.

[3.148]

A *simple example*:

A cat constitutes a simple enough instance of an organism guided by instincts coupled with methodological propensities, processed inside a relatively straightforward calculating brain. Many humans can simply acquire a kitten and rear the pet to maturity isolated from other cats while observing the consequent behavior; such direct experience can aid to understand the example.

Roughly, the cat carries innate instincts for securing food and water, finding an adequate place to sleep, preserving its physical integrity, and reproducing. Yet, the methods enacted by the cat to accomplish those goals derive from the cat's innate methodological propensities. In this context:

- Climbing to the top of tall objects arises from a methodological propensity. The cat can use this method for either securing food, or finding an adequate place to sleep, or preserving its physical integrity. The cat does not carry an instinct to «climb onto a high branch of a tree in case that a dog barks», nor carries an instinct to «climb onto the top of a pile of boxes to sleep», and so on.
- The combination of purring, meowing, and cuddling arises from another methodological propensity. Typically, a domestic cat uses this method to secure food. Yet, making the case again, the cat does not carry an instinct to «purr, meow, and cuddle a human when estimating the human as the optimal source of food».

- If left in the wild in an adequate ecosystem, the kitten will turn feral. Then the cat may sleep over trees or alternatively tease a bunch of dry leaves in search of the softest spot. And again, the cat does not carry differentiated instincts as «in case you become feral, climb onto a tree branch to sleep and tease piles of dry vegetable material» and «in case you become domestic, climb into your host's bed and tease all the pillows in search for the softest, on finding the softest soften it further», and so on.

  The cat merely carries a methodological propensity from which arises a method for using its paws to check the consistency of an object. And, correspondingly, the cat carries another methodological propensity from which arises a method for softening the sleeping place using its retractile claws at once.

  Therefrom, the cat can tease when walking over an unknown surface, can couple teasing plus softening when going to sleep domesticated, and the cat will calculate when to do so.

[3.149]

Thus, in mammals at least, the methodological propensities filled the gap between very basic animals and the transit into animals with relatively highly adaptable behavior. In hominids, the methodological propensities became more complex and elusive because of the appearance of language which masqueraded many of them, at least in people without conscience. This fracture already described in [3.137] and subsequent sections.

[3.150]

The methodological propensities fade or dissolve in correlation with a more vigorous and sophisticated conscience; whether the conscience nullifies those constructs or other brain arrangement arises. Nonetheless, the disappearance of the methodological propensities does not imply that the conscience will automatically replace them with something else, because precisely the conscience's arisal consists in acknowledging and making volitionally plastic otherwise automatic functions. In a very broad sense, the shift into a way of life operated by the conscience constitutes another further transformation from hardware-based into software-based cognizant calculating organisms.

[3.151]

A long trench passed for this further push into software from hardware, namely, the calculating capacities of the human brain advanced a lot. In the course of that way, the mind-set sequences appeared, those same that the conscience now starts to override –and basically may/will drop permanently.

[3.152]

Two additional simple examples serve to illustrate what follows afterwards:

- An adult human may experience an urge to copulate, this urge clearly (for the mind) arising from a sexual instinct. Nevertheless, how the individual will satisfy this urge (or need) results *his* or *her* problem; «*his* or *her* problem» consists in a problem assigned to the «self». In modern human societies, those individuals that cannot self-regulate the satisfaction of their sexual urges do not fulfill the requirements of mental health standards.

- A young lady may experience an instinctive desire to form a home wherein rear and nurture her (future) children. This nurturing desire constitutes much less an «urge»; rather, the crave or long to build a family approaches a fully pre-recorded organismic goal, thus, much more abstract and complex than a simple immediate urge. Yet again, how the lady will accomplish the goal results *her* problem: a problem assigned to the «self».

[3.153]

In humans –cognizant calculating animals–, as the complexity and sophistication of their abstract logical capabilities advances, likewise gradually their organismic immediate instinctive urges become abstract and consciously available pre-recorded goals.

The satisfaction of instinctive urges proceeds typically spurred by chemically-mediated regulations, whereas the satisfaction of pre-recorded goals typically or overwhelmingly proceeds driven by the cognitive apparatus. Thus, the transit from instinctive urges into pre-recorded goals constitutes yet another instance of migration from hardware-based into software-based behavior.

[3.154]

The Golden Bough, published first roughly 131 years ago, profusely documented humans' methodological propensities, although the author did not call them this way and hardly could do it due to the *state of the art* of psychology at that time. Overcoming such hindrance, The Golden Bough constitutes both a milestone and a cornerstone for the objective examination of human behavior. That document, more than a century ago, clearly showed the parallelism of religious behavior in many cultures and human groups independent and isolated from each other by time and space: human religious behavior unequivocally shares methodological approaches out of the very human nature.

[3.155]

Hence, the most profuse documentation of methodological propensities describes humans' most popular metaphysical constructs. Those popular metaphysical constructs became very large because they arose from the intertwined development of relatively advanced data-processing capacities and language during primeval times in the timeline of humanity –this evolutionary path already expounded in section [2.9]. Thousands of years of development furnished a correspondingly large and evolved output. Here worth highlighting the vastness of humanity's most basic metaphysical world, and how all that construct grew guided by the primitive cognitive mechanisms of an awakening species.

More than a century after the publication of The Golden Bough, most of those who carry the aforesaid psychological constructs advanced little or nothing in acknowledging what that book slapped into their faces. Such denial makes patent a total lack of conscience and/or a potentially terminal evolution, as showcased by the concept of «faith».

[3.156]

The methodological propensities kept becoming more and more complex with the passage of centuries and the relatively fast evolution of humans –fostered by the behavioral interactions described in [2.12] and subsequent sections, remember. In the race for survival, human brains continually enhanced the very function of the methodological propensities because those propensities helped to build increasingly more complex and sophisticated methods, practices, and ways of life.

The human behavior which arises extensively from methodological propensities, without using a conscience, reached astonishing extents;

so look how humans tend to build houses, build and use tools, relate to each other, secure materials, and so on, all while behaving in the most natural way after adjusting for learned behaviors. Would result myopic to claim that the harmony and naturalness with which a human develops a tool after learning the basics of the current technology, happens because the human constitutes an excellent apprentice of past tool-development practices; the same applies to the harmony and naturalness with which humans build common artifacts and many basic elements of their contrived habitable environments.

Inherited methodological propensities greatly influence human lifestyles and each corresponding extended phenotype.

[3.157]

Overall, in the human world as currently exists –year 2022– the accumulated artifacts and practices which may show a significant usage of the conscience to build methods provide a still small and negligible input for what stated in the following paragraph.

Observe that among different human groups the types of methods developed, and thereby fundamental tools and lifestyles, variegate in quality and sophistication, and involve distinctive traits and features. Humans built distinct «cultures» because of different methodological propensities developed at the cradle of each group, apparently when physical races among humans definitely emerged; differentiation happened both externally and internally.

[3.158]

Complete isolation from each other never really happened, a full recount of why humans developed an initial (and primitive) aversion to cross-breeding with the members of other groups would stand beyond the scope of this document. An anthropologist specialized in tribal behavior may produce a better description than what could appear in this document. Preserving an «extended family» would not compel for racism, since the new member constitutes an addition; furthermore, groups could instead develop a systematic recruiting of the most capable members of the neighboring groups for the improvement of their own kin.

This *differentiation at all costs* happened –at very least partially, if not completely– due to the need to distinguish who constitutes «them» and who constitutes «us», for «us» to destroy «them»—

- Without the inconvenience of killing the family of the newly acquired members, or the relatives of the offspring from mixed marriages.
- Without «us» resembling «them», because if «we» resemble «them», then destroying «them» resembles fratricide.

Keeping the chasm among tribes thus aids in the typical processes of *dehumanization* of the people targeted for destruction. The aforementioned behavioral pattern showcases that racism serves as a rationalization enacted to cover and/or justify the worst parts of traditional human behavior.

[3.159]

Much progress would make humanity if societal cooperative systems enact policies fostering inter-racial marriages, to such extent that after a few generations all differences dilute or become part of a mixed pot.

The division of humans in races does not belong to an advanced civilization, forward-going people must eliminate that toxic legacy.

The Hard-Core Crust Around the «Self»

[3.160]

Around the core of the «self», as a crust for the mind-set strings, for unconscious choices, and frequently also for the innate organismic objectives, in the average hominid exists a variable-thickness layer of rationalizations. The coherence and sophistication of this layer depends on the qualities of the mind-set, the qualities of the methodological propensities, and the overall cognitive capacities of the individual.

Accordingly, the thickness and complexity of the aforementioned layer varies within a single individual depending on the subject addressed. And therefrom, generally, the characteristics of this envelope of rationalizations varies markedly among humans.

[3.161]

If queried about the motives or reasons which vindicate a particular way of thinking related to personal postulates (about those subjects upon which humans typically diverge), a typical hominid responds with subsequent answers formed at the crust around the «self».

If queried iteratively enough times about a particular subject, in hominids without a conscience typically the «self» reacts assembling protective mechanisms and places an ultimate envelope of rationalizations concealing the actual mind-set, or diverting the individual from any explicit acknowledgment of the actual motives and nature of an unconscious choice, or any combination thereof. The «self» may assemble only a single ultimate rationalization whenever fending off a challenge to a constrained-enough aspect.

The queries employed can comprise a variety of approaches.

[3.162]

Only if the interviewed hominid tells the truth an interviewer may reach the hard-core or ultimate envelope of the «self» by iterative querying.

For example, some marketing specialists promote the practice of «asking iteratively three times *why* to uncover a person's true motives about a subject, using the answer provided by the previous question as the body of the next». But usually this practice can succeed only when the interviewer previously provided or stands associated (in the queried subject's psyche) with motives to tell the truth. Often, the «three times *why*» method results too blunt, direct, and fast to provide a real insight, especially since in many cases the hominid first needs to assemble the rationalizations into abstract word statements, before becoming even capable of providing a consistent answer; if fails to do so due to the urgency of the interviewer, or due to the bluntness of the question, or because it detects a direct challenge, it can easily divert the answer into an immediate protective mechanism. Moreover, many individuals lack a capability to produce three superposed and stepped layers of rationalizations; besides, most frequently, assuming three superposed and stepped layers constitutes a dysfunctional simplification of a variable-thickness and variable-complexity landscape.

[3.163]

The hard-core crust around the «self» produces far-reaching consequences: a competent individual may perform exquisite logical operations above the hard-core crust of the «self», but upon reaching it basically *reason dies* like a shutdown. In some cases this event happens as a spectacular transition.

Rogue Individuals

[3.164]

Besides expanding the knowledge about the psychopaths studied by Hare and the parasitic psychopathic subspecies described in [3.170] and subsequent sections, the professionals engaged in the study of humans must focus on two other outstanding types of individuals toxic and dysfunctional for any cooperative system, namely, those described here as *basic animals* and *evolved parasites*.

Basic Animals

[3.165]

Exist very basic human organisms, among those labeled as *animals*, for which the mind-set strings and the activity of the regulatory processes derived from those produce a minimal or negligible influence in their social behavior; thereat, each one of those individuals will behave unfalteringly according to its basic innate goals unconsciously processed, occasionally as if driven by their own flesh. Those organisms hereinafter characterized as *basic animals*. In these cases, the individual may regard the internal regulations of other humans as something alien. Furthermore, in many cases the input of the *emotional states generating machine* still appears present, but only generates an unstable and visceral behavior when the emotional states become active.

Many *basic animals* merely constitute highly instinctive organisms which seem to touch objects to complete the mental apprehension of those. Comparing them with psychopaths, for example, many *basic animals* lack an ability for glibness and for enacting any sophisticated personal facade; besides, the absence of the *emotional states generating machine* appears to complete the disease of psychopathy; and, furthermore, psychopaths may also carry a well-developed *inner speech line*. Thus, the subset called *animals* does not comprise all psychopaths.

[3.166]

Those highly instinctive organisms not psychopaths constitute a very serious social problem in current times. This happens because they still carry the basic psychological needs but lack the infrastructure to process them in a way that fosters the progress of humankind.

Specifically, they may process their needs raw at the *logical-operations machine*, or their *machine to build the perceived reality* may receive the emotional states produced at the dearth of satisfaction of psychological needs, yet the regulatory processes of the mind-set provide little or weak parameters to deal with those internal events.

Thereby, these *basic animals* can easily and comfortably enact a rough behavior, with very little or zero actual empathy towards others.

Ordinary *basic animals* do not seem to care about their deficiencies, which they may not regard as such. With their reduced mental capacity, their nutritional needs also seem somehow diminished both in quantity and quality, and thereupon they may display an above-average physical endurance –although endurance of rough behavior.

If competent in *executive functions*, these highly instinctive organisms not psychopaths can turn into gangsters or present themselves as businesspersons.

In contrast, if deficient in *executive functions*, these highly instinctive organisms not psychopaths can embrace the parasitic lifestyle described in the next section.

Evolved Parasites

[3.167]

Among the *Homo sapiens* developed a biological strain of individuals specialized in living as parasites within civilizations built by others and with correspondingly scanty *executive functions*.

Hereinafter the aforesaid individuals characterized as *evolved parasites*. The individuals of this class evolved by specializing their methodological propensities. Furthermore, these *evolved parasites* differ from the members of the parasitic psychopathic subspecies (described in [3.170] and subsequent sections), since they do not assemble fascist or authoritarian formations and lack the inter-generational behavioral interactions that the parasitic psychopathic subspecies performs.

These *evolved parasites* display marked tendencies to abandon their offspring and/or to inherit very little or nothing to the next generation. Rather, they regard their offspring as carrying an innate «survival instinct». This «survival instinct», in fact, consists in a set of specialized methodological propensities, wherefrom they quasi-automatically:

α. Learn to use ordinary elements of the extended phenotype of other persons by vicarious learning.

β. Draw advantages from every opportunity they find, usually disregarding the civilizational frameworks that others may built.

γ. Reproduce without making provisions for the next generation. As noted before, they also tend to abandon their offspring.

δ. Learn to use and make simple adaptations of the technological devices they can reach, the devices invented by other people.

ε. Consume and exploit resources, when for whatever reason a zone becomes depleted they move to another –of course, they do not care if their behavior constituted the main cause of the depletion, and most of them may not even realize the glaring consequences of their actions. For this purpose they may simply switch from human group.

[3.168]

Therefore, these individuals do not need and find unnecessary to:

1. Build institutions.
2. Learn to build, develop, and maintain civilizations, or countries for the case.
3. Carry information through generations.
4. Project a future for subsequent generations and, accordingly, make or enact adjustments in the present.
5. Develop technology.
6. Develop any true allegiance to shared causes regarding common welfare.

For instance, this kind of individuals will never worry about building a university, or about assembling a library, or about organizing and sustaining basic scientific research. Instead, if finding themselves in problems, they may just jump the border into another country –legally or illegally, that constitutes a secondary issue.

[3.169]

The behavior of these parasites transparently attests how far the sophistication and specialization of the methodological sequences already advanced.

A Fully Parasitic Psychopathic Subspecies

[3.170]

Among humans lives a parasitic psychopathic subspecies currently with millions of members, hiding in plain sight and assembling parallel hidden societies. In some countries the members of the subspecies may constitute at least half the population, but even then they keep the veil of relative secrecy –rational humans must never underestimate the vastness of their numbers.

This subspecies assembles bands and fascist formations, where its members share closed communication channels (or closed communication methods) and perform behavioral interactions separated from the regular society, separated from real humans.

Recall the *Fascist Ant Mind-Set* recorded in section [3.36].

[3.171]

Authoritarianism appears as the manifest trademark of the parasitic psychopathic subspecies; however, authoritarianism serves merely as a tool for achieving concrete ends, and constitutes neither an essential nor integral trait. The parasites developed and honed a methodological propensity towards authoritarianism just because it readily serves their primary goals and suits their manner of operating –serves for sustaining a parasitic lifestyle, for hanging from humanity. By using authoritarian social structures, by embracing fascism, the parasites seek to place themselves as «dominators» to exploit and steal from everyone else.

The behavioral patterns of the subspecies appear so alien to humans, so psychopathic, that when apprehending the facts any actual human can experience difficulties just acknowledging that such large quantity of abominable hominids exist.

[3.172]

The subspecies carries, develops, and enacts a type of psychopathy unique and intertwined with other peculiar traits.

The most outstanding difference of the subspecies' psychopathy, compared with that of some humans, consists of the fact that the members of the subspecies experience something akin to a need to «belong» to their bands and formations. The behavioral interactions which enact the corresponding activity of «belonging» happen mainly because, for the members of the subspecies, distributing their activities among several individuals constitutes one cornerstone of their capacity to hide their large numbers among the human population –besides other fundamental causes, consult section [7.6] for the complete picture.

Hence, for securing their own survival, the militant members of the subspecies rely not directly on the «force of their numbers», but on their anonymity and lack of accountability for their criminal activities. Their need to «belong» developed and became ingrained due to natural selection over a long span of time.

[3.173]

Apparently, the individuals of the subspecies assemble their bands and formations very frequently in a loose sequence, in a decentralized fashion, where peer-to-peer contacts and interactions build the foundations and essential links of a larger network; such network upon maturity develops into a hierarchical compartmentalized social structure.

Thereupon, the individuals of the subspecies may operate within cells connected to others forming a network, or may belong to a more straight hierarchical social structure. Thereat, they may «belong» to formations largely imaginary, or which long ago ceased to exist, and the individual or its cell expect to contact the «upper chain» when it reconstitutes or whenever another formation succeeds it.

[3.174]

Another cornerstone of their capacity to hide consists of their relentless practice of hiding their communications. This hiding of communications can reach such extent that in some instances the members of the subspecies may refrain from using words at all, and instead use their body movements and overall actions as means of transmitting messages.

[3.175]

Bob Altemeyer broadly researched some features of the behavior of this kind of individuals and recorded the outcome of his work in the book:

The Authoritarians.[3]

Bob Altemeyer.

Year 2006.

---

3   The author of that book placed it freely available on the internet.

In the XXI century still constitutes a novelty that someone explicitly mentions the large anomaly among the human population. Humans must perform much more research for—

α. Building a complete profile of the subspecies.

β. Fully understanding the individual nature of the members of the subspecies.

γ. Enacting consistent policies to integrate those hominids capable of functional and constructive living within a modern society.

δ. Identifying and controlling those hominids that could best live accommodated in ecological reservoirs.

Performing such research constitutes an unavoidable necessity for building a stable advanced civilization.

[3.176]

In many aspects, the behavior of the parasitic psychopathic subspecies resembles that of bands of apes and, as Bob Altemeyer noticed, their behavior also resembles that of army ants. Apes and ants enact a gregarious behavior similar to what the subspecies does, yet neither apes nor ants enact a parasitic psychopathic lifestyle.

[3.177]

The detection of each other in the wild typically happens by unconscious processes which identify behavioral and physical traits.

[3.178]

Noteworthy, the parasitic psychopathic subspecies does not consist of a homogeneous assortment of individuals who only breed among themselves. While any of them will prefer to breed with a pureblood of their subspecies, because of circumstances and convenience they frequently crossbreed with normal humans. An ordinary human may not stand aware of the fact that its partner experiences an allegiance to a parallel hidden society. The aforesaid crossbreeding creates a series of strata ranging from thoroughbred members of the subspecies until almost normal humans.

With all that mixing, the parasitic psychopathic subspecies developed strategies to selectively remove those who do not reach a minimum threshold of genuineness within fascist formations. For achieving this selective removal, among other activities, the members of the subspecies routinely inspect carefully each member, including the demeanor, attitudes, and inclinations of each individual; and, when the members of the parasitic psychopathic subspecies sync their mind-sets and act at unison, they may regard any individual divergence as evidence of a counterfeit personality.

[3.179]

The groups of the parasitic psychopathic subspecies in many cases differ from each other in several characteristics and behaviors, currently some reached much more developed stages than others, same as happens with humans. Accordingly, some groups of the parasitic psychopathic subspecies aim to build empires as the preferred method for exploiting humans; other groups focus on spying, stealing information from, and emulating a target which excels in any particular selected activity; and yet other groups just direct themselves (in a straightforward fashion) to steal from and plunder generic objectives.

[3.180]

In general, the mental constructs of the members of the subspecies differ in many aspects from those of ordinary humans.

Those distinguishing intellectual differences vary in sophistication and complexity, thus any individual may carry more or less of any specific trait. Some outstanding differentiated traits include:

1. *A larger and much more pervasive tendency for magical thinking.*

   This much larger magical thinking in many cases produces a sort of parallel magical world superposed upon the real world, where the real world constitutes an extension of the magical world.

   Therefrom, for example, the members of the subspecies may model social roles within an imaginary fairy-tale kingdom and then translate those into reality.

2. *Their experiencing of the world much more audio-visual.*

   This feature, coupled with magical thinking, produces the affixing of «properties» into perceived colors. Thereby, for example they affix and associate «evil» and «dirtiness» to the color black, while «purity» and «clarity» correspond to white. Happens as if the colors mildly and smoothly produced and sustained the associated properties. The members of the subspecies tend to associate themselves with a color or set of colors, those colors which «correspond» with their identity.

Normal humans often include names of colors as part of a figurative speech; but in the case of the parasitic psychopathic subspecies, as example, typically the color white –actually, by itself– *embodies* or *entails* purity.

3. *The usage of a complex psychological construct called «heart».*

The entity called «heart» in this mythology supposedly constitutes the core of a human emotional life. Herein reproduced a description of the «heart» from my notes about the Saint Petersburg Hive, with some minor corrections.

The *authoritarian ants* popularly refer to the psychological construct of the «heart» to justify their activities. The construct of the «heart», as used by the ants, involves several aspects:

+ *The hypocritical demands towards humans.*

   The psychopathic ants and monkeys experience a very shallow emotional life, and they readily notice that humans experience much more complex, subtle, and intense emotions. Hence, in their psychopathic endeavor, the authoritarian ants and monkeys attempt to rely on the human emotional processes to achieve profits. For their demands towards humans, thus, they attempt to tap into the human «heart». In this context:

   α. The ants demand a behavior based on kindness, solidarity, and unconditional selflessness from everyone else, but the ants themselves do not want to follow the same policy for their actions –nor demand the same policy from their allies. The aforesaid double standard happens due to the parasitic and psychopathic nature of the ants. Thereupon, the ants want to behave as the «bad guys» and everyone else must behave as «good persons», for the ants to steal from and take advantage of the latter. The authoritarian parasites regard themselves above all civilized norms.

   β. The ants want to copy and/or steal frameworks, tools, and ways for sustaining a living. For this purpose they demand that humans provide those for them, they even regard it as an «obligation» from humans. Such demand pervasive, both implicitly and explicitly expressed.

+ *A frivolous shallow «heart».*
  Ants and monkeys with only mild levels of psychopathy –a subset of the subspecies– do experience some attachment to all sorts of frivolous experiences. Therefore, the authoritarian «heart» experiences a fondness to many types of phenomena which stimulate the senses and produce psychological sensations, usually the kind of stuff that humans may regard as «superficial». Ants and monkeys also get attached to some sort of simplified ideas, almost anything that can get summarized into a slogan. The authoritarian «heart» may get attached to another person (often the «supreme» commander) using a simplification of the nature of that individual; the authoritarians may ascribe *labels* to the person in order to create a description. Thus, the slogans and labels provide simplified (and inaccurate) descriptions which the authoritarians can use. All the other ants, the fully psychopathic, experience basically nothing.

+ *The primitive ant choice-making process.*
  The most common use of the psychological construct of the «heart» consists in a process to build choices. An ordinary human may complete a choice-making process with a guess where the human may perceive the guessing process as a «heart beat», yet the human readily notices that this «heart beat» just completes a choice-making process. Sharply differing from ordinary humans, in most individuals of the parasitic psychopathic subspecies the usage of the «heart» seems to comprise the whole or a large part of the choice-making process. Thus, as expected, both ants and monkeys perform highly unconscious choice-making processes –much more unconscious than in the case of humans. Nevertheless, the parasitic psychopathic subspecies still can behave as a herd when its members delegate their personal choices to the overall fascist structure, when at-once those members will attempt to collectively sync with their peers, to sync with themselves attempting to create homogeneity. Almost everything I noticed about the russians supports this observation.

4. *Social relationships based solely in the use of force.*

Due to their psychopathic and parasitic nature, the members of the subspecies enact social relationships based solely in the use of force, whether a threat or actual usage of physical means. As with any psychopathic individual, any attempt to transmit into them the foundation of civilized behavior will consistently fail; instead, they use the acquired information to learn more tricks and patterns to conceal their activities and fake their intentions. This tendency towards the use of force interweave with their methodological propensity towards authoritarianism; hence, the members of the subspecies obey «strong individuals».

Some hominids of the subspecies once rationalized the fact that they only understand force-based schemes as: «Actions speak louder than words.» In a world of criminals threats, strength, coercion, and all other physical means rule.

[3.181]

Due to their lack of understanding of civilized behavior coupled with magical thinking, myriad members of the subspecies hold the perception that «*good actions* compensate for *bad actions*». Consequently, in their perception of the world, they can «compensate» and return to «neutral» every damage inflicted to a person through the execution of some «favorable» action towards that same person; this serves as a psychological cover-up for the retarded members of the subspecies who may experience only mild levels of psychopathy, those known as «true believers».

Therefrom, in this mythology, «if someone enacts a *bad action* and then enacts a *good action* corresponding with the degree of *bad* from the first, then the person returns to *neutral* and does not result a *bad person*». While many ordinary individuals with an authoritarian culture may also espouse such supposed «compensations», in the case of the parasitic psychopathic subspecies this constitutes a prominent trait.

Some popular magical-thinking religious doctrines strongly reinforce the mythology of «*good* compensates for *bad*», since the corresponding adherents regularly use those doctrines as rationalization for obtaining «absolution» by performing the correct deeds. As expressed also in section [7.66], those popular magical-thinking religious doctrines very frequently serve as ideological foundation for authoritarian behavior and, accordingly, many hominids of the subspecies adopted those as a rationalization and/or ideological reinforcement for their actions.

Thereby individuals who embrace popular religion-based magical thinking very frequently regard the human organism as a container of a metaphysical substance called «goodness».

For clarity:

In some cases an actor –a human or an association of those– may correct the course of history, but, even in those cases, either current or future facts existent during any time interval do not «compensate» (for) the facts which existed during a previous time interval; such linkage does not exist.

[3.182]

The defining fracture which unequivocally and conclusively serves to mark these parasites as a subspecies consists in the fact that the patterns of development of their *executive functions* differ from those of actual humans. And, therefrom, the assortment of *executive functions* in an average adult of the subspecies widely differs from that of an average human.

Most or almost all the description of *executive functions* recorded by Barnard about humans does not match their characteristics, does not suit their nature.

[3.183]

An expansion of *temporal, spatial,* and *sequential* contemplation capacities or horizons in humans bolsters more creativity and more complexity in their choice-making processes –those capacities described in section [3.90]. In comparison, for the members of the subspecies an expansion of the aforesaid horizons bolsters comparatively very little an enhanced creativity and complexity in their choice-making processes.

Thus, expanded *temporal, spatial,* and *sequential* horizons in any given human promote more diverse, options-abundant choice making processes targeting more complex scenarios. But expanded *temporal, spatial,* and *sequential* horizons in any average member of the subspecies make little more than promoting a repeat of the same recipes in a newly larger scale.

Hence, a member of the parasitic psychopathic subspecies with «developed» *executive functions* typically will attempt to build an (authoritarian) empire or an organizational structure above the regular human society, instead of transiting into more advanced ways of social living –as already mentioned in section [3.179].

[3.184]

In my notes about the Saint Petersburg Hive also recorded the main theory about this subspecies, likewise here reproduced with some minor corrections:

At the time when *Homo sapiens* and neanderthals coexisted, existed also a third subspecies. This subspecies, in contrast with neanderthals, could disguise as humans. The disguise worked because outside physically they looked almost the same. So they learned to hide among the human ranks, and they hanged into the human species.

See them nowadays, realize the severity of the fact that a vast majority of them carry a form of reduced intelligence, notice how abundantly that form of reduced intelligence exists within the human populations; realize how much they got ingrained a need to hide, to steal, to betray humans, to move in block. These hominids created none of the tools of the antiquity, especially at a time when humans lacked any technological foundation –when humans lived almost in indigence.

Furthermore, in their animal instinct, they resolved definitely that they must copy all human advancements and eliminate the creators, because they fundamentally do not create, they just consume and exploit. So the parasites aspire to control the humans –both individually and as a whole– to exploit them, to *milk* them, to *harvest* innovations and knowledge, without allowing the humans to develop. Humankind would already advanced further and faster, by far, if did not exist this subspecies obsessively attempting to control knowledge, resources, and people; always hiding the truth, always hiding themselves.

The parasites do not want to allow the humans to develop because, when humans develop, they become sidelined and processed by civilization: upon the identification of criminals accountability ensues, healthy cooperative systems discharge any parasites found. The parasites do not want humans to discharge them, they will try to hang as long as possible.

[3.185]

The desire of the members of the parasitic psychopathic subspecies to remain undetected and, at most, appear as «the background» of the events, composes one of the main limitations of the scope and effectiveness of their activities. Thus, while the parasites attempt to «play god» or produce an outcome as «the hand behind the curtain», real humans can focus on building more advanced, fair, and transparent forms of organization. Against such advancements the members of the parasitic psychopathic subspecies will actively oppose, but typically making great efforts to avoid a direct detection and identification of both their purposes and themselves.

[3.186]

In democratic countries already should exist large institutions specifically tasked with identifying, studying, and processing the subspecies; this so far did not happen due to the failure of democracy itself.

The existence of a parasitic psychopathic subspecies constitutes a very basic fact about the agglomeration of hominids known as *humanity*; a description of the subspecies should already form part of the curricula of basic education everywhere.

4

Capitalism
A Plutocratic World-Wide Institutionalized Fraud

[4.1]

THE MOST SUCCESSFUL ORGANIZED CRIME VENTURE in human history, as already stated in section [2.28], consists of capitalism's «financial system». Therefrom, in this chapter recorded a brief description of the actual way of operation of capitalism, for the reader to grasp the facts on the ground.

Capitalism's «financial system» furnishes the binding core societal function of the current planetary proto-civilization, specifically, performs the operation of payments in commercial transactions; such the failure of the current human affairs, where a victorious organized crime venture furnishes the backbone of the social order.

[4.2]

Registering a full description of the enormous amount of lies, deceits, massive frauds, rampant stealing, and all sort of socially-harmful behavior engendered by the organized crime venture called *capitalism* would produce a series of books specialized in history of crime. Instead, the description of capitalism in this chapter mainly comprises an explanation of the essential foundations of the criminal scheme.

[4.3]

Furthermore, the reader should notice that, since the beginning of their criminal venture, the capitalistic criminals always created confusing terms and meshed concepts as part of their ongoing effort to cloak and make incomprehensible their activities for everyone else. Thus, the heralds of crime frequently recite the capitalistic sales pitch: «We, the *owners of the capital*, the capitalist people, the economists, the bankers, the *experts*, know better about economy and its dynamics; you, normal person, do not understand anything of what we say and do, because economics, finance, and market behaviors consist of very complicated matters beyond your limited capacity of comprehension.»

Hence, the capitalistic criminals almost never refer to facts, actions, and concepts by their actual definitions and true implications, and instead rely on their code of lies and misrepresentations.

[4.4]

Thereat, next some straightforward definitions for sound thinking:

[4.5]

Market

Noun.

1. A group of activities which comprise the exchange of assets, products non-assets, and services.
2. A delimited (physical) space where the activities referred in the first definition happen whether usually or at a single occasion, or a similar space arranged for the occurrence of those activities.

[4.6]

Asset

Noun.

Anything suitable for commercial exchange which neither spoils nor decays easily through relatively long periods of time in ordinary conditions. Note: Some products constitute assets, not all assets consist of products; from this premise, a list of such items without ambiguity consists of «assets, products non-assets».

[4.7]

Exchange space

Noun.

A space where distinct entities can perform commercial exchanges. In modern societies the exchange space typically overlaps with the space occupied by the society itself, excepting those places explicitly excluded by means of social rules.

[4.8]
Tool of exchange
Noun.

An organizational tool used at commercial exchanges within an exchange space, which serves as an auxiliary entity for conveying unmarked ambiguous data about possible unaccomplished transactions.

[4.9]
Standardized bartering commodity
Noun.

A tool of exchange consisting of any suitable asset used as a standard means for bartering. This tool of exchange conveys unmarked ambiguous data referring to possible unaccomplished transactions, where the asset itself embodies the data. A standardized bartering commodity arises from a usually-informal social contract. Typically, in that social contract anyone can legitimately furnish new assets from those that constitute the standardized bartering commodity, and thereby bring new data into the exchange space.

First example: gold and silver coins when those not minted and regulated exclusively by the state-organization. Second example: mesoamerican tribes used cacao grains as standardized bartering commodity.

[4.10]
Money
Noun.

A tool of exchange consisting of any suitable token used as a standard means for bartering. This tool of exchange conveys unmarked ambiguous data referring to possible unaccomplished transactions, where the data conveyed results independent of the carrier token. Money arises from a usually-formal social contract. Typically, in that social contract only the state-organization can legitimately furnish new quantities of tokens, and thereby bring new data into the exchange space.

Example: a coin and a printed bill can both convey the same data.

[4.11]

Payment promise

Noun.

A standardized record, written in paper or stored in another medium, which replaces the transference of actual tools of exchange, articles, and services in any given transaction with the promise of delivering those at a later time. Hence, a *payment promise* consists of a standardized promise of payment.

Examples: a written paper which transfers the ownership of a debt, and an electronic record created at a point-of-sale terminal.

[4.12]

Currency

Noun.

Any mixture of tools of exchange and payment promises that circulate in a commercial exchange.

§

[4.13]

In this document the list «assets, products non-assets» recorded shortened as «assets, products». Unless otherwise stated, the word *products* refers to *products non-assets*.

[4.14]

The tools of exchange do not constitute instruments, since they neither constitute devices nor comprise any structure. The «operator» of the tool of exchange propels all the tasks while using it.

Hence, for example, a tool of exchange results conceptually more closely related to a hammer than to a microscope.

[4.15]

Notice that both the standardized bartering commodities and the money arise from a –sometimes very primary– social contract, outside from it such concepts mean nothing, for the standardized bartering commodities and the money merely constitute organizational tools.

Read chapter [5] for a full understanding of those concepts.

[4.16]

Using two historical contexts as example:

a) If caribbean pirates exchange products and services using gold and silver coins; then the coins serve as standardized bartering commodity.

b) If a roman emperor mints coins made of some cheap metallic alloy with his ugly face stamped on each, and forces all his vassals to use those; then the coins serve as money.

How the Fraud Started

[4.17]

Herein recorded a short summary of what happened in simple and non-convoluted terms. The description broad, focused on didactic purposes –in helping the reader understand what really happened– and deliberately non-specific; this because in each country the criminal venture called *capitalism* developed with different peculiarities and intertwined with other historical events.

[4.18]

During medieval times people used *precious* metals –specifically gold and silver– as *standardized bartering commodity*: humans could barter every sellable thing for any given amount of precious metals. This happened because:

1. As everybody knows, those metals neither spoil nor rust easily, thus can remain stored over long periods of time in variable –and sometimes harsh– environmental conditions without decaying.

2. Existed a relative scarcity of precious metals among humans and, since procuring them involved much difficulty and little output, their available quantity usually varied in small amounts.

The relative stability in the amount available of those precious metals ensured that, if local conditions did not change, humans could repeat the bartering patterns without significant changes over time. Therefore, the *prices* of products and services in a quasi-stable bartering environment would remain the same.

[4.19]

Medieval humans, not experts in foreseeing the consequences of their actions and still with a primitive conception about the world, assumed wrongly that if they collected a large amount of precious metals, then they would command an ability to acquire a correspondingly large amount of products and services. Therefrom, within the «western» civilization ensued a race for obtaining precious metals while disregarding all other productive processes.

[4.20]

Furthermore, by this time became widespread the notion that hoarding the *standardized bartering commodity* –the precious metals– equaled to «hoarding the capacity to purchase whatever available for sale whenever one wanted». Thereon, using a concept called «wealth», hoarding the *standardized bartering commodity* equaled to «hoarding the future assets themselves». Enshrined by the faulty capitalistic theories, the metaphysical concept of «value» further propped the misconception of «wealth».

Due to this, people shifted from the notion of «hoarding precious metals for later bartering» into «hoarding the *value* inherent or within the precious metals».

Accordingly, using a horse as example, the notion changed from «I store this silver or gold coin for later exchanging it for a horse» into «I store this silver or gold coin for storing a *value* equivalent to the *value* of a horse».

[4.21]

Several things happened sequentially:

1. The race for obtaining large amounts of precious metals succeeded in bringing large amounts of those materials into circulation within the «western» civilization. Most of those precious metals arrived as the product of plundering the american continent through colonial invasions –from slave-based colonial enterprises which took the natural resources of the subdued people.

    Variations in the price of the bartered items happened due to that. The precious metals became less scarce while the availability of the rest of the products and services augmented at a slower pace. Therefore, the population could and did pay more precious metals in exchange for the same amount of items, and the sellers increased their prices merely to maintain the previous pattern of exchanges; thus happened a so-called *inflation*.

2. The scale of the operations of many single persons and organizations reached a size where the amount of precious

metals used for exchange resulted too large for practical and safe handling through great distances and brief but fast sequences of operations.

3. Some participants in commercial exchanges, including state-organizations and almighty religious organizations, hoarded precious metals so successfully that another scarcity ensued. This scarcity made much more acute by the then-expanding commercial activities, those gradually including new products and services, plus new and more raw assets available, as the «western» medieval world extended and incorporated new continents.

[4.22]

The limited availability of precious metals –which purportedly stored the metaphysical «value»– hindered the hasty expansion of exchange operations.

In this context a new type of service providers arose: those individuals and organizations that would store precious metals for a fee, so their owners would not need to carry them around while doing operations; those service providers herein denominated *storage establishments*. Hence, when depositing coins of precious metal, the owner of the coins would receive a paper-made payment promise called *promissory note* for that amount, issued by these new service providers.

These new service providers habitually called *goldsmiths* in historical records because originally they engaged in producing handicrafts made of gold and silver, but the term *goldsmith* not used here further since those individuals and organizations henceforth focused on another activity not related to their original specialization.

[4.23]

Instead of carrying a heavy mass of precious metals and perhaps getting robbed, the owner of the coins would carry and exchange promissory notes; and the storage establishment which issued each promissory note would deliver the specified amount of coins to anyone who presented the respective paper. In other words, each promissory note lacked a fixed, hard-coded owner; whoever held the paper became the legitimate «owner» of whatever coins written there.

Eventually, became a standard practice to redeem the coins of each promissory note in parcels. For example:

1. Someone could redeem 5 coins from a promissory note for 22 coins, at that event the storage establishment would make a note on the same paper stating the withdrawal of 5 coins of precious metal.

2. The same person could afterwards exchange the same promissory note now redeemable for 17 coins, as if it constituted the 17 coins, and the recipient of the paper could then present that same paper at the storage establishment to effectively obtain the aforementioned coins of precious metal.

Anyone could receive and exchange a promissory note without ever visiting a storage establishment, or opening an account in one of those.

[4.24]

The establishments specialized in storing precious metals became a close-knit cartel which, as intended, fostered and established procedures for commercial exchanges convenient for the interests of its members. Then as now, the main excuse focused on «safety».

Subsequently, the storage establishments also promoted the usage of personal payment promises called *checks*. A *check* consisted of a branded preprinted paper with spaces in which the customer could write an arbitrary quantity of coins of precious metal (either gold or silver) and a beneficiary to whom the storage establishment which ultimately collected the paper should deliver that handwritten quantity.

Henceforth, a customer would receive a number of preprinted papers, then in one of those write a name of a beneficiary and whatever quantity of coins, certify the paper with its own personal signature, and deliver the preprinted paper instead of the corresponding amount of coins –and so forth for the rest of the papers. Thereby the customer did not need to carry precious metals but only the bunch of preprinted papers furnished by his/her hired storage establishment. However, the usage of checks happened most frequently in large transactions, while for small transactions people continued using actual coins of precious metal (because receiving a check entailed a trip to a storage establishment, and usually those latter charged a fee for using their papers). The storage establishments touted the usage of these personal payments promises as a «proof» of a supposed «confidence» the storage establishment endorsed into the customer, supposedly due to the usual prosperity of that same customer.

Thereupon, a customer could fill a preprinted paper to pay for products and services, and the seller who received the preprinted paper would go to his/her own hired storage establishment and give or hand over the paper-made check to the clerk. Afterwards, the storage establishments would communicate to each other and verify that the person who paid using the check in fact deposited enough coins to deliver as written in the paper, and upon certainty the storage establishment which received the paper-made check would deliver the corresponding coins of precious metal to the person who gave it or handed it over. If lacked an account with the cartel, the recipient of a check could return it directly to the issuing storage establishment.

The storage establishments claimed that they would perform the whole and aggregated operations of exchange of their customers in a private and secure fashion. Accordingly, the storage establishments would periodically make the sums of what they owed to each other at each transaction, and then transfer among them only the positive or negative differences due, instead of whole amounts of precious metals. Therefrom, the storage establishments also pretended material and energetic efficiency.

[4.25]

Summarizing, by using two types of payment promises called *promissory notes* and *checks*, the usage of actual precious metals became circumvented; and this practice established the foundation of the capitalistic fraud and massive stealing scheme which ensued.

The promissory notes became fully standardized and renamed as *banknotes*. Once standardized those payment promises, instead of ordinarily delivering precious metals, the storage establishments would preferably deliver paper-made banknotes; and only if the customer explicitly requested it, the storage establishment would deliver the actual precious metals.

[4.26]

The storage establishments would deliver anyone's deposits if requested, but aimed all their propaganda towards dissuading the customers from doing so and implemented transaction settings strongly favorable to the usage of payment promises which produced a factual cost for those customers who still desired to use actual tools of exchange, just as still happens at the time of this writing. Thus, sundry marketing and propagandistic campaigns touted the usage of the storage establishments' payment promises as fashionable and modern.

Nowadays, any modern «storage establishment» offers rewards, discounts, prizes, and so on for those customers who use payment promises instead of actual money. Instead of papers, the customers now carry plastic cards with electronic chips and/or cellphones for issuing electronic records as payment promises.

[4.27]

The urge for a rapid expansion of the quantity of operations of exchange, coupled with a scarcity of precious metals, constituted an ideal environment for the start of the fraud and massive stealing scheme by the cartel of storage establishments; hence, constituted the environment adequate for the birth of the largest criminal venture in human history called *capitalism*.

In order to protect themselves from getting caught in the crime, the storage establishments promoted a «sacred secrecy» of both their operations and the amount of precious metals deposited by each customer, just as still happens at the time of this writing.

Nowadays, the «banking secrecy» promoted by the capitalistic criminals constitutes a cornerstone of their criminal venture, one they will defend until jail or death.

[4.28]

With all transactions and actual holdings of precious metals cloaked, each storage establishment could pretend it held more precious metals than it did in reality. Same as happens at the time of this writing. The scheme works because the customers do not establish a complete exchange of information among them, ordinarily because the customers do not know all each other and lack the means to do so, thus nobody may notice.

In this hotbed happened the birth of the capitalistic «credit».

[4.29]

Hereinafter the former storage establishments referred as *banks*. The reader will find useful to repeat or parse anew the foundation of the fraud in present tense: With all transactions and actual holdings of money cloaked, each bank can pretend it holds more money than it does in reality.

A capitalistic «credit» consists of a loan furnished by a bank. Purportedly the loan always consisted of precious metals furnished to a customer for temporal usage; this constitutes a blatant lie in the capitalistic fraud as described in subsequent sections. The customer who takes a loan hereinafter denominated *borrower.*

As usual in the code of lies and misrepresentations in the crime called *capitalism*, «credit» or «monetary credit» in most cases does not result «monetary», and the word «credit» in this context constitutes a plagiarism from its original meaning related to the concept of *trust.*

[4.30]

Thus, the banks acted as lenders to furnish loans to borrowers. The loans usually involved something called «interest» which consists of a fee proportional to the quantity borrowed; here, in order to keep the straightforward denomination of concepts and to abandon the code of lies and misrepresentations, the «interest» referred simply as *proportional cost of the loan.*

Of course, the banks charged for other types of «services» before furnishing a loan, examples include: «cost of *opening* a *credit*», «cost of researching the customer's activities», and other similar «services». The costs not tied to a proportion of a capitalistic loan's magnitude, herein better characterized as *fixed costs of the loan.*

To make the process even more cumbersome, in many cases the banks made the *proportional costs of the loans* dependent of several fickle variables. Furthermore, in many cases the *proportional cost of the loan* consists of a recurrent amount which the borrower must pay periodically while it does not return the initially borrowed quantity –and, of course, the magnitude of that recurrent amount can also vary depending on fickle variables.

[4.31]

The capitalistic propaganda provided a rationalization for the loans scheme as follows:

1. The bank lends the precious metals that other customers deposited for custody. These customers may receive a fee for depositing their assets and making them available for lending.
2. The bank charges a fee proportional to the quantity borrowed for—

a) Creating a stock of precious metals used to compensate for the loses incurred due to those customers who did not return the precious metals lent to them.

b) Compensating for the decrease of usefulness of the precious metals for exchange purposes. This because any increase in the average prices of products and services would render the returned precious metals less useful for exchange. Additionally, the retarded theorists who developed the capitalistic doctrine furnished a construct about a «variable value of money over time», the capitalistic thieves merely incorporated it into their speech.

[4.32]

After only a superficial examination the loans scheme would appear presumably honest; however, two facts set the final stage for the commission of the criminal activity:

a) Each bank can readily and safely pretend to hold more precious metals than it actually does, as described in section [4.28].

b) When «delivering» precious metals, each bank will preferably deliver only a piece of paper as *payment promise*, as described in sections [4.23] to [4.25].

Thereupon banks started lending precious metals they did not hold and started charging fees for doing it; banks keep doing a modernized version of this fraud in the XXI century, using money instead of precious metals.

Hence, in this way banks pretend to «lend» money they lack and, moreover, banks charge fees for «lending» that nonexistent money –now the banks use money instead of precious metals.

The consequences of this criminal activity described in subsequent sections.

[4.33]

At the beginning of the criminal venture called *capitalism*, as done at the time of this writing, each bank performs some statistical forecasts for estimating how many actual tools of exchange it must hold.

Accordingly, each bank forecasts how many actual tools of exchange its customers will request during any given time period. Thereby, when any customer requests the delivery of actual tools of exchange –at the beginning of the capitalistic crime, those coins of precious metal– the bank will actually deliver them physically, and the customer will not notice that the bank regularly lends nonexistent tools of exchange: either nonexistent coins of precious metal, or nonexistent money.

The cartel of banks habitually tracks the general mood of the collectivity of customers as part of a permanent effort aimed to prevent any disruptive event. In situations outside the consensus forecast of the banks or beyond their ability to influence and control the population, when the customers start withdrawing their tools of exchange massively, banks simply stop delivering them, typically without further explanation and/or using intense propagandistic campaigns to compel those customers to stop withdrawing.

Nowadays, in failed democratic regimes the practice of lending nonexistent money stands legalized by the traitors that captured the state-organization; and, of course, nowhere in the world any mention of this legalized practice stands included in mandatory education.

[4.34]

The criminal venture called *capitalism* became even more complex when failed democracies gradually ceased to require banks from actually holding any real asset –any real coins of precious metal. Eventually, the capitalistic criminal venture ceased to use at least some precious metals as backup and began a fully unrestrained money-printing pyramid.

The following sections include more details, enough for understanding why and how the criminal venture called *capitalism* thrived and blossomed for so long.

A Nurturing Cradle for Criminals

[4.35]

Section [4.21] serves as introduction for what follows.

The criminal venture called *capitalism* started growing massively during the XVIII and XIX centuries, in several stages, at the time of the rapid expansion of the modern «western» civilization. Such expansion of the modern «western» civilization happened due to—

a) The newly available unmatched technological resources which made possible new –also unmatched– production processes.

b) The fact that humans already fairly chartered the world oceans, and professional sailors already knew mature navigation techniques.

Therefrom, happened a new race for the expansion of production processes and for the introduction of new foreign products into the «western» civilization's commercial exchanges, into what «westerners» called «world markets» –into the exchange spaces belonging to their self-centered world-view.

However, this happened without ever considering «non-westerners» as equal humans, and while other civilizations stood in relatively weak and vulnerable developmental stages for deterring, repelling, neutralizing, or counterattacking «western» imperialism.

[4.36]

Thus, «westerners» expanded their civilization in search of profits and habitable zones, usually in detriment of foreign peoples. For their expansion, «westerners»—

α. Focused primarily on capturing land and any other material resources to use them as input in their industrial and commercial processes.

β. Enslaved the population of the zones used for expansion, or gradually exterminated it, or displaced it into areas less propitious for human living, or forced it into other artificially disadvantaged situations on a permanent basis, or any combination of these options, with the corresponding loss of life and either the destruction or degradation of the civilizations of those who survived.

[4.37]

In this civilization of little or none fraternity, with a self-assumed entitlement over every foreign society, not surprisingly an organized criminal venture, namely *capitalism*, fostered the wave of expansion in order to cheat all the other participants in the «western» commercial environment. In this context, seemed not extraordinary to cheat and steal from those who routinely killed, subjugated, and inflicted unmeasurable suffering to other people just for profit.

[4.38]

The self-assumed «western» entitlement over every foreign society nowadays results less prominently noticeable, mainly because most of the zones suitable for a relatively easy invasion already stand invaded, and «westerners» already either completely exterminated or reduced to a nadir most native populations in the places where they thrived. (Although some other racially-destructive systematic practices happened, like the Apartheid in South Africa.) In this regard, inside almost every «western» nation still dwell many individuals with identities rooted in racism and a sense of entitlement mixed with racial or national (tribal) pride. Nowadays, most individuals usually regard those expressions of self-assumed *supremacy* as pertaining to either «right» or «far-right» political positions.

[4.39]

Capitalistic criminals like to claim, in yet another lie, that their «organizational» capabilities constituted an indispensable instrument and essential foundation for the expansion of the «western» civilization. Hence, in their endless lies, the capitalistic criminals assign to themselves a post of «indispensable patrons of development»; while, in fact, the criminals merely spotted the opportunity to massively steal and earn dishonestly a massive amount of undue profits. The expansion of the «western» civilization would happened anyway –with or without the capitalistic criminals– given the «western» imperialistic culture, since the essential advantage of that civilization consisted in the nascent scientific and technical systematic research which produced a stream of new technological capabilities which in turn made feasible new faster, larger, more efficient, more complex productive processes.

[4.40]

The quintessence of the «western» civilization of the last three centuries consists in applying systematic scientific and technological research into the destruction of other human groups. Not capitalism, and certainly not democracy.

The «western» civilization of the last three centuries constitutes yet another instance of the classic human intra-species depredation described in [2.12] and subsequent sections. Precisely this failure to evolve into a mature civilization opened the opportunity for more backwards and destructive ways of life to compete with the «westerners» as fake «human-welfare providers», such as the fascist societies rooted in Russia and China.

Stealing from Hard-Working People

[4.41]

Recall the tale of the orange juice with Molly, John, and Sally from section [3.128], or otherwise re-read it.

[4.42]

An auxiliary tale, part two.

Say that Molly, John, and Sally live in a caribbean island during the XXVIII century –a future «banana republic». Within the island the general population uses standardized coins of some precious metal, which Molly, John, and Sally start using as a means to make asynchronous the exchange of products and services among them, as follows:

1. Molly and John share a single coin for the exchange of one banana per one orange. Therefore, the agreed price for each banana equals one coin, and the agreed price for each orange likewise equals one coin.

2. The price of producing squeezed juice from one orange equals three coins –remember, three oranges. Therefrom, the orange-juice industry requires three coins, but these three coins proceed through a slightly longer route, as here delineated:

   α. Start with John holding the three coins.

   β. John exchanges the three coins for the juice with Sally.

   γ. Sally exchanges the three coins for three oranges with Molly.

   δ. Molly exchanges the three coins for three bananas with John.

Clearly, the operation of the nascent juice industry requires a desire from Molly to acquire three bananas per cycle.

Once the three industrious islanders agreed to perform this exchange using a tool of exchange to convey data, they can—

1. Defer the actual delivery of their products and services.

2. Route those actual deliveries of products and services in more ways, in many cases skipping nodes. The buyer does not need to carry with itself all the assortment of assets and products, and/or provide all the services the seller could require;

furthermore, in a myriad of real-world cases doing so results either plainly impossible or highly inefficient.

3. During each exchange, leave undefined the possible subsequent bartering operations for the party that receives the tool of exchange. Now the party that receives the tool of exchange must independently imagine possibilities not tied to any specific type of asset, product, or service received. However, because of that deferred and unsettled future, those imagined possibilities now substantially more remote to realization and such realization more susceptible to unexpected events.

These new organizational capabilities furnish very convenient possibilities for the participants in the exchange; for instance, could happen any of the following:

- The season of oranges does not coincide with the season of bananas; therefrom, exchanging them synchronously –at once– would imply that a lot of the production of old fruit already spoiled, or its quality decreased.

- Molly and John simply cannot coordinate to harvest and deliver their fruits at the same time.

- Results more efficient that Sally visits Molly directly for acquiring the oranges, instead of John carrying the oranges from Molly's to his home, and then to Sally's.

- On some occasions Sally wants to obtain two bananas as profit, or one orange and one banana as profit, instead of two oranges; and she simply cannot convey expediently that much information during bartering, as she would turn her offer into: «I deliver juice from one orange in exchange for three oranges, or in exchange for one orange plus two bananas, or in exchange for two oranges plus one banana.»

  Here showcased two products in a very simple scenario and Sally already needs to speak a lot and explicitly consider those additional possibilities, if she wants to add some useful flexibility to the exchange.

Thereby, Molly may just store the coins received from both John and Sally, until the season of bananas arrives, or until she wants a banana. Likewise, Sally may store the two coins obtained as profit from producing juice for John, until the respective seasons of oranges and bananas arrive, or until she wants oranges or bananas.

Until here, everything in the islanders' commercial and industrial environment appears honest and fair, although inchoate. Then of course, with so much ongoing prosperity on the island, the capitalistic criminals intervene; this related in the next parts of the tale.

§

[4.43]

The organizational capabilities available because of the usage of tools of exchange made feasible the operation of complex productive cooperative systems and complex social arrangements within a commercial environment. Noting that a productive cooperative system may furnish products, or services, or both.

Such enhancement happened as a *byproduct* since, presumably, primitive individuals envisioned the formation of neither complex cooperative systems nor complex social arrangements when they started using tools of exchange –standardized bartering commodities– but rather they strived to solve immediate and already pressing problems.

For example: The islanders in the auxiliary tale so far neither attempt nor envision the creation of complex productive cooperative systems. Their transition from direct bartering into bartering using a tool of exchange happened to satisfy more direct and immediate goals.

[4.44]

Worth noting here again: The tools of exchange –namely, standardized bartering commodities and money– serve merely to pass data from one place to another, although this data stands unmarked and subject to subjective interpretation. The complete explanation about a complete, basic commercial exchange recorded in chapter [5].

Illustratively, the reader can observe how the islanders in the second part of the auxiliary tale use coins merely to pass data.

[4.45]

Carefully acknowledge the following:

1. Each new steady supply of any type of item –asset, product, or service– introduced into a commercial environment and successfully exchanged, alters the customary routes and circuits transited by the available tools of exchange, or creates new

routes and circuits, or both. Designate the provider of this new steady supply as *new supplier*.

2. Whoever routinely buys the new items, at each exchange cycle must hold in his/her domain a larger amount of tools of exchange than before: those utilized to pay for his/her old customary expenses, plus those utilized to pay for the new items. Designate this buyer as *new happy buyer*.

3. Accordingly, the new happy buyer also must increase its income in order to offset its now enlarged expenses. This participant must therefore produce more and exchange also this increased production for obtaining the newly additional indispensable tools of exchange for his/her bigger budget at each exchange cycle.

   If relative prices in the exchange keep stable –the income from selling one banana still affords buying one orange–, then somehow the customers of the new happy buyer must obtain an additional quantity of tools of exchange for paying for the increased production during the *first cycle* of the modified exchange, thereby starting the cycle or circuit of those new tools of exchange. Those customers thenceforward form a commercial circuit with the *new supplier* who furnishes the new steady supply of point 1 –whenever the *new supplier* buys something, the tools of exchange must reach the customers of the *new happy buyer*, thereat the cycle completes.

   Alternatively, all the relative prices in the exchange must decrease –the income from selling one banana still affords buying one orange, but now both cost 25 cents– so the purchasing power of any given amount of tools of exchange results bigger –a single coin now affords 4 bananas or 4 oranges. Nevertheless, the coordinated decrease of prices usually does not happen because involves a highly cumbersome reorganization, as illustrated in section [4.46].

4. To solve what stated in point 3, the most easy and on most occasions the solely practicable solution consists in introducing more tools of exchange into the exchange circuit –more of the standardized bartering commodity, or more money. This can happen by two ways, these often simultaneous:

α.   Some individuals previously held hoarded tools of exchange in their domains –some people accumulated «monetary savings»–, or produce pristine new tools of exchange, and they utilize those to buy the *first output* of the recently increased production furnished by the *new happy buyer* described in points 2 and 3. Alternatively, or as complement, the same *new happy buyer* can produce new tools of exchange, or can utilize any previously hoarded quantity of those.

β.   A participant external to the customary or stable exchange circuit furnishes new tools of exchange –delivers either money or a quantity of a standardized bartering commodity– in exchange for some production of the participants inside the stable exchange circuit. Thereupon the participants inside the stable exchange circuit now can proceed to use those new tools of exchange for their increased operations.

Notice again the word *external*, as this on-time buyer or non-habitual participant does not play any role in a customary or stable exchange circuit.

The auxiliary tale of the orange juice with Molly, John, and Sally serves to illustrate and easily convey the ideas stated in this section. Recall the tale or otherwise re-read the corresponding sections.

[4.46]

An auxiliary tale, part three.

Another participant named Paul devoted himself to mining. Upon success, Paul exchanged a coin of a precious metal with Molly in exchange for an orange. From that time on, Molly used the coin together with John for exchanging one orange per one banana: one morning Molly received a banana and gave John the coin, instead of an orange; thereby both would remember that she owed him one orange; and during the afternoon John went to Molly's to redeem the coin and get the corresponding orange.

And so the operation repeated customarily: Molly would give John the coin during the morning, and during the afternoon John would return the coin to Molly, every day. Therefrom the exchange circuit of this single coin lasted one day and comprised two participants.

In this situation Sally made the offer of squeezing and delivering the juice of one orange in exchange for three oranges. Initially the exchange proceeded directly by John delivering the oranges to Sally and waiting until she squeezed the juice of one. However, eventually John and Sally resolved to use coins of precious metal for their exchange, since using those would provide the flexibility described in the second part of the auxiliary tale.

Then a problem of feasibility arose: only one coin circulated back and forth among Molly and John.

John still wanted to eat at least one orange from time to time, besides drinking orange juice; but even in the case he resolved to convert all his purchases of oranges into Sally's juice, the feasibility problem would remain.

For making the operation feasible, John and Sally could enact any of the only two possible paths:

- *Option 1.*

  Convince Molly to decrease the price of one orange from one coin into 25 cents, with the promise that also the bananas would cost now 25 cents each and, since Molly only wanted to eat one banana per day, the exchange cycle would rearrange as follows:

  i. The first day Sally would buy three oranges from Molly, using the 75 cents John would pay her that day. Also, the first day John would buy one orange from Molly, that orange the one which John wanted to eat directly. Therefore, the first day Molly would deliver four oranges and would receive 100 cents (one coin).

  ii. The first day and the next three days Molly would buy one banana per day, as usual, and therefore would pay John 25 cents per day.

  Molly of course refused to this cumbersome deal since she would not earn anything from it and, by any measure, an arithmetic operation of division involves much more difficult procedures than the arithmetic operations of addition and subtraction she used to do. Besides the problem of splitting the coin in four parts.

- ■   *Option 2.*
   Wait until Paul the miner offered for exchange another three coins of precious metal, and John would then exchange with him three bananas for three shiny polished new coins. Afterwards, John would pay those three coins to Sally, who would in turn exchange them with Molly for three oranges, and everything else proceeds as already described during four days.

   This option neither requires Molly's explicit approval, nor requires her to reduce the well-known price per orange, nor requires anyone to perform that difficult arithmetic operation of division. Moreover, this option does not require anyone to fully understand the exchange cycle. As long as Molly keeps buying one banana daily, she will notice little more than a bulge of sales every four days.

Notice that John can choose to buy the spare single orange at any of the four days, and nothing significant changes in the exchange cycle. Molly can also parcel the delivery of oranges to Sally, thereby delivering one orange per day during three consecutive days, and also in this case nothing significant changes in the exchange cycle.

Of course, perhaps John hoarded some coins of precious metal previous to Sally's offer of orange juice, in which case he would immediately select the second aforementioned option for securing orange juice, namely, just pay three coins to Sally. However, in any case Molly's rate of purchase of bananas conditions John's long-term rate of purchase of orange juice, and any surplus coins she may just store for herself.

For example, if John held six spare coins when receiving the orange juice offer, he could immediately exchange them for the juice of two oranges, Molly would receive those six coins subsequently and would simply store them until needed. Molly would need to deliver only three of those new six coins, since John would stop purchasing a daily orange from her three of every four days, because John would start saving coins again for buying orange juice from Sally. And three spare coins would remain in Molly's domain for an indefinite time.

§

[4.47]

In a real-world primitive commercial environment –such as where the capitalistic criminals started their mass fraud, cheating, and stealing operations– securing the agreement of all the participants for reducing prices in a coordinated fashion ordinarily results plainly impossible, because usually—

- The participants in the exchange neither share any actual membership into anything, nor they know all each other.
- The involved participants find either impossible or impractical to physically split the standardized bartering commodities.
- Many participants in the exchange do not obtain any profit from the increased complexity while those seek to fulfill only short-term and immediate interests –otherwise a formal societal cooperative system would exist there.

Thus, in inchoate commercial environments the only feasible solution for augmenting the quantity of exchange operations consists in introducing new additional tools of exchange.

[4.48]

Two capitalistic theft instances, the most easy and straightforward, happen when either the quantity or the magnitude of the available operations of commercial exchange becomes larger in a primitive commercial environment, and thereat for the execution of those new or larger available operations the participants indispensably need a bigger amount of circulating tools of exchange as described in section [4.45].

Recall or re-read the description of the capitalistic loans scheme recorded in sections [4.32] and [4.33], it serves as indispensable foundation for understanding what follows.

[4.49]

The said capitalistic theft instances happen at two different events:

a) New assets and products constructed by natural processes become ready for commercial exchange. This added quantity of assets and products not usually within the target commercial environment, in this sense they completely «new» for the usual operations of exchange.

The new assets and products constructed by natural processes may not constitute novelties, may those consist of something already known. The items brought into existence by natural processes comprise land, edible products, raw materials, and anything the Earth can afford which humans can use as either a benefit or an advantage.

b) New assets, products, and services artificially fabricated or performed become ready for commercial exchange. Also in this instance the output not usually within the target commercial circuits, in this sense it completely «new» for the usual operations of exchange.

The new artificial assets, products, and services may constitute technological innovations at first, but usually they consist of augmented productive outputs of those previously available.

[4.50]

Thus, the capitalistic main crime materialized centuries ago: When a participant lacked tools of exchange –coins of precious metal– with which the participant wanted to buy any newly available asset, product, or service of those described in section [4.49], a capitalistic bank lent him some non-existent coins of precious metal.

And with that action the cartel of capitalistic banks entered full-time into the world of crime.

[4.51]

When the capitalistic bank lent those non-existent coins of precious metal to the participant of the exchange –when the bank cheated the customer– it also introduced a fake tool of exchange embodied as a *payment promise*, as described in sections [4.22] to [4.25]. Specifically, instead of introducing coins of precious metal into the commercial exchange, the bank introduced pieces of paper.

[4.52]

An auxiliary tale, part four.

In time a port town grew nearby to the place where Molly, Sally, and John lived, and at this town regularly docked merchant ships arriving from a place called «Old World».

Sally and John started to sell their products in a weekly downtown marketplace, and on average from that commercial activity each obtained a profit equal to seven coins of precious metal each week.

Highly industrious, Sally and John each one independently asked the captains of the merchant ships if they would buy their merchandise and resell it in that remote «Old World». Sally also heard about a technological innovation called *pasteurization* and understood that she could use that technique to bottle juice inside glass containers.

To each one, every captain replied that they would buy only a quantity of merchandise that would fully load a ship. This because for the captains of merchant ships transporting and selling small amounts of any product constituted a waste of time and effort, and in general provided little or no profit.

Hence, Sally and John started, each one, to devise a way to sell a full cargo of product. John noticed that he needed the product of 50 parcels of land like the one in his domain. Meanwhile, Sally noticed that she needed a large squeezing and bottling facility for she to command the capacity to produce that much quantity of juice in a short time.

John resolved to buy the land of those 50 parcels –reselling other people's bananas would involve unstable commercial relationships with partners prone to deliver low quality bananas. Likewise, Sally resolved to buy all the tools necessary for building the required industrial facility. But none of them held a quantity of coins enough to do so: in both cases they needed about 1,000 coins of precious metal.

Thereupon, Sally and John started saving the profit of their weekly sales at the downtown marketplace. They knew that they would spend approximately 3 years of work collecting the necessary coins.

However, during those 3 years a precious-metals storage establishment (like the ones described in this chapter) appeared in the town, and all the islanders started accepting its written payment promises for coins of precious metal. A crook called Morgan «owned» the storage establishment.

Morgan saw Sally and John toiling every week in their endeavor to build undoubtedly profitable businesses, and there he saw his opportunity for stealing. An appearance of «neutrality» served as an essential facade for Morgan's business, therefore he could not get seen publicly partaking in activities beyond storing (or claiming to store) coins of precious metal and issuing written payment promises for those.

Hence, Morgan resolved to involve someone else as accomplice, someone who would show its face publicly for their deeds but at the same time would never become a threat for Morgan itself. Consequently, Morgan recruited someone eager to quickly obtain riches and prone to magical thinking; that individual named Adam.

Thereat, Morgan wrote two paper-blocks of payment promises amounting each block to 1,000 coins of precious metal in favor of Adam. Morgan did not hold such amount of coins in his vault, but he knew that as long as most of the islanders did not ask for the delivery of their stored coins, nobody would notice.

As profit for Morgan, he would charge annually 15% of the total amount of coins to Adam, until Adam reimbursed all of them. Besides, Morgan secretly obtained some «shares» of the newly created corporation by Adam; thereby Morgan secured a perpetual right to a periodical distribution of profits.

Adam used the first group of payment promises for 1,000 coins to buy the land that John previously foresaw as basis for his business. Some land tenants asked for cash, for physical coins, to which after much resistance Adam agreed. Morgan could deliver cash for those cases, again as long as most of the islanders did not request the delivery of their stored coins; accordingly, Morgan delivered coins belonging to someone else, presenting those as belonging to Adam.

Adam used the second group of payment promises for 1,000 coins to buy the equipment that Sally previously envisioned for her industrial facility. Again using the same tactics as in the previous case: deliver painstakingly coins to anyone who asks for them, but deliver mostly the almost-costless paper-made payment promises.

For ensuring that nobody knew that fraud and stealing happened, Morgan promoted something which he called «banking secrecy», upon which he would never reveal how many coins stored for each islander.

Thereafter, Adam started the businesses which Sally and John envisioned and supplied the demand of orange juice and bananas to the «Old World». The commercial overtaking by Adam factually prevented Sally and John from starting profitable businesses.

People started asking how Adam did to become so *wealthy* in a short period of time, how he could gather so fast that large amount of coins; and for answering this question both Morgan and Adam started referring to Adam as an «investor», as someone who purportedly «acquired his coins somewhere else, deposited them at Morgan's business, and then Morgan issued payment promises for that stored coins».

Disappointed by the fate of their first businesses, both Sally and John looked for new opportunities. John thereupon started saving coins for buying land plots which produced mangoes, while Sally focused on saving coins for building a facility to bottle palm oil. However, yet again, Morgan and Adam noticed them toiling for new goals, sent a scout to check upon which profitable businesses John and Sally directed themselves, and afterwards repeated their now well-known and developed stealing scheme.

This completes the auxiliary tale.

§

[4.53]

This last part of the auxiliary tale intends to showcase in very simple terms the traditional method by which the capitalistic criminals steal both assets and opportunities from everybody else. This behavior, now made much more sophisticated in the real human world, continues at the time of this writing and will continue until the destruction of the capitalistic criminal scheme.

[4.54]

Without producing and exchanging anything, the capitalistic criminals steal resources from the whole society as a unit. By rigging a core societal function for cheating everyone else, these criminals take for themselves resources from every kind illegitimately, without holding any entitlement for doing so, without the people's actual (socially acknowledged) *social contract* allowing for it. Does not matter that such crime happens in front of everybody.

[4.55]

The capitalistic criminals and their accomplices routinely search for and track pioneering people and pioneering businesses, because they know that they can always steal the opportunities built by those pioneers by, in sequence:

1. Quickly emitting payment promises and distributing *currency* –payment promises mixed with tools of exchange– among themselves.

2. Using the aforementioned *currency* to immediately build overly large enterprises that satisfy the demand for those new products and services. The large enterprises therefore usually reach lower production costs by building mass-production

processes and quickly positioning their offerings (sales-mix) by enacting massive marketing campaigns; the smaller pioneers cannot compete with those lower production costs and exorbitant initial expenses.

Consequently, capitalistic criminals and their accomplices called «investors» routinely search for and track technological innovations, and actively promote both the expansion of the exchange space and the introduction of new products regardless of their actual usefulness for human welfare.

The innovators and explorers do the hard work, and the criminals get all or the largest part of the profits.

The Modern Criminal Scheme of Capitalism

[4.56]

Since its origin, the capitalistic fraud used *standardized bartering commodities* as bait, with some intermittent periods of halt, until the decade of 1970, when capitalistic countries officially abandoned the so-called «gold standard».

Before that, in diverse time periods, the capitalistic criminals claimed and promoted the idea that the coins and bills circulating in capitalistic countries constituted «representatives» of *standardized bartering commodities* (physical assets) stored somewhere; thus, those coins and bills constituted the successors of the *promissory notes* described in sections [4.22] and [4.23]. The last of such lies happened after the Second World War, until the aforementioned decade of 1970.

Hence, according to the propaganda, every circulating coin and bill corresponded to a fixed amount of a precious metal stored in some «super secure vault» managed by a coordinating institution specialized in «monetary reserves» called *central bank* –or other similar name.

Those coins and bills (standardized *promissory notes* rebranded as *banknotes*) that the criminals presented as «money» constituted in fact merely payment promises over the supposedly stored assets, as done since the beginning of the capitalistic fraud.

The Pyramid of Payment Promises

[4.57]

After that decade of 1970, the coins and bills which circulate physically in commercial exchanges within the capitalistic criminal operation constitute actual money, whose usage the state-organizations enforce by law; mixed of course with lots of payment promises made over non-existent money.

The social order which exists after the decade of 1970 constitutes a culmination of the institutionalization and legalization of the capitalistic crime; thereat:

1. *Central banks* detached from democratic control, and protected by law, issue variable amounts of money which then they transfer to capitalistic *commercial banks*, state-organizations, and capitalistic corporations controlled by the world elite.

   The criminals who operate *central banks* habitually call such distribution a «technical operation», typically cloaked with accounting schemes referred as «debt», «injection of liquidity», «bonds purchase», and others akin.

2. *Commercial banks* upon receiving each parcel of money furnished by a *central bank* can legally create more payment promises, which they call money, in the same way they used to do when giving paper-made *checks* instead of coins of precious metal. There, the money furnished by the *central bank* plays the role that the coins of precious metal used to do.

Nowadays, when a customer goes to a capitalistic commercial bank and withdraws coins and bills, those coins and bills constitute the ones that the *central bank* furnished to the *commercial bank*; and the payment promises created by the commercial bank circulate as checks, electronic «transfers» of money, electronic payment promises issued using «debit» and «credit» plastic cards or using cellphones, and so forth.

Afterwards, the *commercial banks* only make the sums of what they owe to each other, and then transfer among themselves only the positive or negative due differences, just as described in the last paragraph of section [4.24]; and, as always, for the vast majority of payment operations and «monetary deposits» the capitalistic commercial banks never held the corresponding money.

[4.58]

Yet again, the people of democratic countries neither agreed to nor voted in favor of allocating the emission and distribution of money outside the institutions of the state-organization; such approval never happened.

In other words, nobody voted in favor of the bankers; the people of democratic countries never agreed to give the capitalistic criminals the right to issue money.

[4.59]

Over time, in an attempt to stabilize the fraud, as an institutionalized criminal syndicate, the criminals and their lackeys successfully promoted the creation of several supranational «international banks», such as the «International Monetary Fund».

State-organizations receive money pooled at those «autonomous banks» within a variety of conditions. Hence, for example, the state-organization of a *third-world* country will receive money with different contractual conditions and in different quantities than the United States of America, or any country within the European Union.

This latter distribution of money to state-organizations usually functions as a disciplinary tool applied to non-compliant members of the syndicate. In many cases, the traitors to democracy within failed democratic regimes do their utmost efforts to conceal and/or divert the attention from the terms agreed for receiving money.

[4.60]

Of course, by the time of this writing all the criminal scheme stands legalized by the traitors to democracy.

Direct Distribution of Money and Payment Promises Among the World Elites: «Financial Markets»

[4.61]

In this context, currently a very small elite controls the largest capitalistic corporations at a planetary scale.

Those capitalistic corporations typically receive money and payment promises furnished by the *commercial banks* within privileged and exclusive schemes, usually disguised with the aforesaid terms of «debt emission», «credit», or «bonds purchase».

[4.62]

The privileged and exclusive schemes used by the capitalistic corporations for receiving money most frequently happen within the interactions that the criminals call «financial markets». Thereupon, capitalistic corporations secure *proportional costs of the loans* or «interest rates», through «financial markets» and other privileged and exclusive schemes, usually much smaller or negligible when compared with the costs that ordinary citizens must pay when borrowing from commercial banks. Likewise, the quantities of money and payment promises available at «financial markets» surpass by several orders of magnitude the quantities available to ordinary citizens who must hire commercial banks and who neither fulfill the requirements nor command enough resources for effectively participating in «financial markets». Thereby, combined with the usage of the methods described in section [4.55] by capitalistic corporations, the «financial markets» cement the structural advantages and perpetuation of the plutocratic world elite.

In other words:

- The businesses built by ordinary citizens cannot effectively participate in the privileged schemes of the «financial markets» because of their small size and small amount of resources available, besides their lack of criminal connections with the corresponding elite.

- At the same time, the capitalistic corporations ordinarily either capture or obtain a large share of any new commercial opportunity available that could produce the required large-scale profits for effectively entering and participating in «financial markets». The capitalistic corporations achieve this goal by searching for and tracking technological innovations, pioneering people, and pioneering businesses and, whenever spotting one opportunity created by those latter, immediately starting large scale operations using low *proportional costs of the loans* and extremely large quantities of money and payment promises available only in «financial markets».

If a pioneer or innovator does not «cooperate» and yields both a shared «ownership» and profits, some copycat will.

The capitalistic «financial markets» constitute the backbone of the plutocratic world order.

[4.63]

After the abandonment of the «gold standard» in the decade of 1970, the capitalistic scheme of fraud and stealing degenerated into an interplay where the criminals need to emit more and more money for keeping the criminal scheme running, just for averting an organizational collapse.

[4.64]

The massive emission of money without actually using it for real commercial exchanges aggrandized a kind of parallel fantastic commercial world detached from reality within the capitalistic «financial markets». Thereat, within those «financial markets» ordinarily—

+ Circulate amounts of money and payment promises several orders of magnitude greater than the money and payment promises used for those commercial operations with actual assets, products, and services which sustain societies.

+ Mid-size and even small-size commercial enterprises frequently result regarded as super-giant entities by the standards used by the magical thinking.

+ The perceived magnitude of many commercial enterprises of all sizes varies or fluctuates in a fast-paced roller-coaster fashion which also does not correspond to reality.

[4.65]

The capitalistic criminal scheme stumbled so out-of-control during the first two decades of the XXI century, that the *central banks* resorted to emitting and directly distributing money in extraordinarily large quantities to both capitalistic corporations within the criminal gang and to compliant state-organizations. So large quantities that some larger-than-usual sectors of the population noticed. Such instance of criminality frequently branded by the criminals themselves as «quantitative easing».

Again, the criminals and traitors to democracy publicized highly demagogic excuses like «this constitutes a technical operation for the common welfare», «the corporations know better what to do with very large quantities of money», «for distributing wealth first someone must create it, and the corporations outperform everyone else in creating it», «we will *stimulate* the *economy* or, this constitutes a *stimulus* package, and this will create new jobs», «these corporations play a fundamental role in the performance of the *economy*, therefore by helping those we help everybody», and so on. Cynical lies that only in the current completely failed democracies passed without consequences.

With the practice of «quantitative easing» the criminal operation reached a new extent, where massively robbing resources from societies happened in an almost straightforward way. Henceforward, obtaining lower and exclusive *proportional costs of the loans* or «interest rates» becomes secondary for maintaining a plutocratic position; now the main goal consists in obtaining money furnished directly by the *central bank* which legally holds the exclusive right to issue money without democratic accountability and democratic control.

[4.66]

The criminals already distributed among themselves quantities of money so large that, even if societal cooperative systems proscribe the usage of payment promises, the criminals can continue operating comfortably for decades by using their monetary reserves.

The distribution of money under the brand «quantitative easing» lasted several years, once finished, the criminals can just claim that it «constituted an extraordinary measure», then wait a few more years for most individuals to shift their attention elsewhere, and restart or repeat the distribution of money using another name.

Electronic Money

[4.67]

Apparently, much of the money issued and distributed through «quantitative easing» (and even before that), due to its massive nature, never became actually printed or coined, and remains in commercial banks as «authorized electronic records» upon which the same commercial banks issue payment promises which they present as either «money» or «monetary deposits».

Thus, «electronic money» does not constitute money at all, but consists solely of *«authorized electronic records»* issued by a central bank *mixed with electronic payment promises* issued by commercial banks; the sum of both quantities *recorded as a single entry* in an electronic database for each customer of a capitalistic commercial bank.

By implementing the usage of «electronic money» as a complete and mandatory replacement of cash, the opportunity to expand the issuance of payment promises by capitalistic banks becomes unlimited, for the cartel of commercial banks will find no need to demonstrate to the public any holdings of actual money. And, in this way, the enhanced fraud of the «electronic money» sets the foundation for the full privatization of the issuance of tools of exchange into the plutocratic mafia which controls the capitalistic commercial banks.

Hence, the «electronic money» sets the foundation for a steeper decline of democracy in the XXI century.

[4.68]

Fraud constitutes a peculiar form of robbery which the capitalistic criminals mastered and developed. These prominent fraudsters and con-artists learned to steal without the victims understanding the cause of their misery.

[4.69]

Many excuses attempt and attempted the capitalistic criminals to conceal, dilute, and justify their crimes. Some of those excuses include claiming that they «provide a service» by issuing fake money privately. Others include claiming that they lend, partially, some cash with the consent of their customers and, thereupon, claim that they issue payment promises partially backed by some actual cash. Even other excuses assert that «anyone can ask money borrowed, and the borrower can search for the lowest *interest rate* (proportional cost of the loan), and there will exist a low interest rate because of competition among banks»; this excuse comprises several lies in a single statement:

a) The capitalistic criminals always formed a cartel, does not exist true commercial competition among them, but rigged practices.

b) In any case, the capitalistic criminal that lends keeps in secret the nature of its operations. Therefore, does not need to charge all the customers the same cost of borrowing (proportional plus fixed costs of the loan) nor needs to disclose any partnership with its «customers» or accomplices.

c) The capitalistic criminal still commits a blatant fraud and steals from the society by emitting a payment promise without holding money to fulfill it, and presenting it as «money» or its equivalent.

d) Any ordinary customer or businessperson lacks effective access to the capitalistic «financial markets» and therefore obtains more expensive and smaller loans. Furthermore, the *proportional costs of the loans* for ordinary customers in some *third-world* countries reach ridiculously high magnitudes not related to any commercial factor beyond the capitalistic desire to squeeze and enslave the population.

And in yet another gross display of cynicism by «playing stupid», the criminals assert that the payment promises –for example, the electronic records in a bank account for which they lack the corresponding amount of coins and bills– that they delivered instead of actual money, constitute in fact «money» because they just chose to call them «money» according to their doctrine.

In section [4.65] already described the excuses which the criminals proclaim for directly distributing massive amounts of money among themselves through «quantitative easing» and similar operations.

[4.70]

And while all this happened, the retarded theorists that served and backed the capitalistic criminals just aggrandized their structure of magical thinking for justifying the crime.

For grasping the magnitude of the magical thinking, just look into the vast literature about «financial markets», see how every prestigious and modern book of *economics* includes a «variable value of money over time» as a fundamental tenet.

Hereat, *economics* constitutes a fully failed discipline.

Alternative Courses of Action

[4.71]

As already mentioned in section [2.26], even lacking the fundamental knowledge for organizing mature and sustainable commercial exchanges, enacting any of several feasible options would produced a different outcome, instead of committing fraud and massively stealing from everybody. However, the capitalistic criminals –the bankers and their associates– chose to steal, they engaged in that course of action deliberately and understanding its consequences.

[4.72]

In an honest societal environment, upon the shortage or scarcity of coins made of precious metal used for bartering, the participants of the exchange could established a new social contract which adopted and maintained another type of tools of exchange. For example, two basic options:

a) Issuance of money by the state-organization, detached from any physical asset. (This option at the time of this writing happens detached from democratic control, thereat the capitalistic criminals distribute the money among themselves, and furthermore they mix it with a lot of payment promises.)

b) Establishment of another type of standardized bartering commodity to either replace or supplement gold and silver.

The state-organization could attended those operations, without resorting to fraud, without resorting to stealing.

[4.73]

In the case of the issuance of money exclusively by the state-organization, in truly democratic regimes the social contract would proscribed the emission and circulation of payment promises. And thereupon, a truly democratic state-organization would used all the tools of exchange introduced into the exchange space in expenses aimed to the public welfare –in expenses for infrastructure, basic scientific research, social services, and so forth.

Because, worth highlighting again, every piece of *currency* –money, or standardized bartering commodities, or payment promises– introduced into an exchange space, results in a product or service taken from *someone* within the society.

[4.74]

Yet, the capitalistic criminals never wanted honesty or fairness, they always wanted and want to steal both resources of every kind, and opportunities from everyone else. They deserve jail sentences.

The Alliance of the Plutocratic Criminals with Parasitic Factions

[4.75]

As previously described in section [3.171], the members of the parasitic psychopathic subspecies carry and develop a methodological propensity towards authoritarianism.

In authoritarian cultures, someone or a class of individuals can «bear» an exclusive right to occupy privileged positions within a society; and those privileged individuals «bear» the right, they do not «receive» it –in this aspect, the social contract of the society thus created corresponds to the authoritarian culture. These privileged positions can reside within the state-organization or within a rigid social structure. Typically, those who «hold more rights» in an authoritarian world do not owe accountability for their actions to anyone of the lower castes and subordinate ranks in the authoritarian ladder.

[4.76]

Therefrom, kings and feudal lords could legitimately extract a profit from their vassals and did not owe them any accountability for it. And authoritarian individuals did not regard the extraction of such profit as *stealing*, nor regarded concealing the destiny of everybody's pseudo-taxes as *unfair* or *unjust*.

[4.77]

Likewise, individuals with a deeply ingrained authoritarian culture cognitively apprehend the fact that the capitalistic criminals hold privileged positions from where they routinely exploit and steal from everyone else, not as an act of *social parasitism* and actual *stealing*, but as *the rightful exercise of privileges by a superior class*.

[4.78]

In this context, the parasitic psychopathic subspecies just accommodated itself when the plutocratic capitalistic criminals displaced the old kings and feudal lords. And, as happened before with kings and lords, the factions of the parasitic psychopathic subspecies offered their services in exchange for privileged positions for themselves where they could keep pretending they «own» humankind.

The Failure of the Capitalistic «Market Theories»

[4.79]

Failed theorists developed the capitalistic doctrine just in time for the criminals to use it, neither a few centuries earlier nor later than needed for stealing. Most components of the capitalistic doctrine proceed from an evolution of magical thinking. The capitalistic magical thinking includes the usage of objects as containers of metaphysical entities and the conversion of statistical correlations into metaphysical entities –recorded in [3.111] and subsequent sections.

[4.80]

The most basic and pervasive errors of the capitalistic doctrine arise from the concepts of «value» and «market price». The capitalistic theorists failed in the first paragraphs of their books; they made a whole building over bricks of falsehoods.

[4.81]

When the criminals known as bankers reviewed the conceptual buildings and theses furnished by those astray theorists, surely they laughed until tiredness. Noticing the unmatched opportunity, the criminals used all their available pawns and propagandistic means to promote the failed theories, and thereby henceforward the criminals use the capitalistic theories as a doctrine.

[4.82]

Howbeit, the greatest feat of the criminals known as bankers consisted in identifying the profile of the (breed of) retarded humans that embraced such failed theories, and systematically promoting them to upper organizational ranks both in their own criminal enterprises and in general human societies.

The aforesaid systematic promotion of retarded humans constitutes an organizational policy essential and indispensable for the long-term survival of the criminal venture called *capitalism* –without it, capitalism would ceased to exist.

[4.83]

Over time, the failures of the magical-thinking theories became largely intertwined with deliberated lies, as the criminal venture grew in complexity. Humans with a conscience readily notice the capitalistic falsehoods, but those humans lacking a conscience and fully indoctrinated with the capitalistic lies may never acknowledge what follows.

Thus, here a few more failures and lies of the capitalistic doctrine:

[4.84]

1. Lie: *A «free market» consists of the unfettered exchange of assets, products, and services; people can remain constrained by national borders, only banks can legitimately emit money –the main tool of exchange–, and withal it constitutes a «free market».*

   An actual «free market» would consist of an unfettered exchange of everything, this would include unrestricted transit of people. In an actual «free market» any individual would go wherever desired for exchanging its assets, products, and services, including selling personal labor –the labor a service.

   Furthermore, in an actual «free market» everyone would use whatever tool of exchange each one wanted, with neither restrictions nor exclusive privileges for anyone; therefore, anyone would use whatever «money» as desired, not only the money and payment promises disguised as money furnished by capitalistic criminals, whose usage enforces the state-organization. An actual «free market» consists in an anarchical exchange, and such case may exist only within small semi-organized bands of primitive people, within a small group of friends, and similar proto-societies.

   [4.85]

2. Lie: *«Free market» implies capitalism.*

   This constitutes a naked lie, an irrational leap just memorized by the repetition of propaganda.

   [4.86]

3. Failure: *An unfettered exchange of assets, products, and services constitutes a stable and «self-regulating» set of activities. «Markets self-regulate» –especially «free markets» do it– and this «self-regulation» produces an intrinsic long-term organizational stability.*

   This failure arises mainly from the magical thinking that regards human behavior as a «system» –recall sections [3.132] and [3.143]. Therewith:

α. As already said, an unfettered or unrestrained exchange would imply anarchy, and ordinarily this does not happen in modern societies where a social construct called state-organization exists; in these modern societies the stipulations and terms for exchanging assets, products, and services proceed regulated by a *social contract* –remember sections [2.32] and [2.34]. Capitalistic economists either stand completely unaware of this fact or they lie cynically: they may call either «unfettered exchange» or «free market» to a state-sanctioned activity. The abuse in the usage of the concept of *freedom* found fertile conditions in some historical and current psychological traumas due to the fight against authoritarianism.

β. Commercial competition leads participants to the formation of large-scale processes as a means to increase the efficiency of those, and thereby command an ability to displace and wipe competitors by offering lower prices than smaller enterprises could achieve; consequently reducing the number of participants in the exchange. Therefrom, the very behavioral interactions of unrestrained and unregulated competition lead to the destruction of the incentives for low prices –and the associated efficiency– in manufacturers and providers; this latter stage usually leads to the formation of oligopolistic gangs and industrial cartels, and ultimately leads to the formation of monopolies. Several times this already happened and always capitalistic economists find or invent some excuses and rationalizations for these events. Thus, «market economy», as capitalistic publicists call it, does not constitute the «natural order of things», and certainly does not «self-regulate».

[4.87]

4. Failure: *The participants in an exchange of assets, products, and services behave rationally, if not individually then the whole aggregated mass does.*

This failure happens purely because of the retardation of capitalistic economists; no need to know about advanced analysis of human behavior to notice that humans do not behave rationally in many circumstances, whether individually or aggregated as a whole; it does not matter that the outcome of their actions or the surrounding events may either directly or indirectly affect their welfare. For the long explanation about why humans do not behave rationally, just re-read chapter [3]. Furthermore, doctrines implanted successfully in large populations produce correspondingly large-scale biases in human behavior analyzed as an aggregate –more about this in [7.62] and subsequent sections. For example, in the XX and XXI centuries hitherto ordinarily, repeatedly, and conspicuously happens the distribution of propaganda favorable to the consumption of articles and services with a combination of these qualities:

α.   Unneeded.

β.   Unhealthy.

γ.   Environmentally destructive.

δ.   Unreasonably costly.

ε.   Inefficient.

στ. Dysfunctional for the proclaimed purpose.

And almost equally ordinarily, repeatedly, and conspicuously those propagandistic campaigns succeed.

To make things worse, many participants in commercial exchanges during the XX and XXI centuries cared and care only about their short-term survival. Focusing each one only on its own short-term survival ratcheted up the massive consumption of resources and the destruction of the Earth (as described in section [2.24]), thereby those practices jeopardized the survival of humankind and created a fast-progressing scarcity due to which the welfare of humankind gradually decreases –nevertheless due to deficiencies in their *executive functions* many humans experience great difficulties just to recognize the gradual diminution of living standards. The human self-destruction does not qualify as rational behavior by the participants of a commercial exchange.

[4.88]

5. Failure and lie: *The increase of the efficiency, diversity, and scale of production processes enhances and secures the aggregated human welfare in a «free market» social setting.*

    This one started as a theoretical failure but, upon the outstanding real-world failure for it to happen, became a cynical lie. Typically, capitalistic criminals and their aides will claim something like: «in order to *distribute wealth* first results indispensable to create it» (as already recorded in section [4.65]), of course such mythical «distribution» never happens. In their magical thinking, capitalistic economists add apples plus bananas plus everything else they find; and using such magical constructs they created an esoteric algebraic output called «gross domestic product» whereby they claim to «measure» the productive activity of any country; this kind of mistakes will pass into one of the most shameful chapters of human history. From there, capitalistic propagandists usually claim that a larger «gross domestic product» of a country reflects an increased welfare of the population; in this case, besides their magical thinking, the liars deliberately ignore the never-happening mythical «distribution of wealth».

    Actually, an unfettered exchange of assets, products, and services does not automatically produce a full coverage of the participants with the products and services indispensable for a living within standards deemed as *welfare*; does not matter whether the group of participants in the exchange command the means to physically achieve it. This trend overtly evident when machines displace human labor in productive processes simply because humans cannot outperform the efficiency and precision of a modern machine; and therefrom the former craftsmen and craftswomen tend to become marginalized or excluded from the unfettered exchange. The more advances technology, more people become redundant in an unfettered exchange; may they attempt to service the privileged ones that control the production processes, but this latter ones also neither need nor want so many superfluous services. For example, a single person does not need a thousand massagists.

Exist accessible historical records about the displacement of human labor by machines since the First Industrial Revolution. However, here again the capitalistic propagandists managed to shift away the attention of most people. Furthermore, the successive emergence of other new industries during approximately two centuries at least partially cushioned the displacement of human labor by machines, these new industries requiring new labor willingly supplied by the displaced persons.

Thus, for example, many of the made-redundant persons from the agricultural revolution found opportunities for labor in the nascent metal-mechanic revolution. In time the same metal-mechanic industries improved their technology, introduced automated labor, and thereupon tended to reduce the necessary human labor for any given output. Thereat, happened another wave of laborers displaced by technologically improved processes.

In this context, when the emergence of new initially–labor-intensive industries ceased at the mid of the XX century, the capitalistic mafia focused by all means into a wasteful consumption-based social behavior: those items previously made to endure changed into either disposable or short-lived articles, and the general population received massive amounts of propaganda promoting behavioral patters focused on «buy, use or consume, discard, buy again everything». During the last two decades of the XX century the decrease of quality became remarkable and manifest in everything: automobiles, washing machines, hand tools, clothing, and the interior decoration of a house, to name a few; the increase in both the rate of consumption of resources and the rate of environmental destruction happened accordingly. Hence, at the end of the XX century any ordinary affluent individual routinely bought a new automobile every one or two years and discarded the old one, while not-so-affluent humans habitually spent a sizeable share of their income in buying and discarding clothing according to the publicized (and artificially created) fashion of the season. This industrial shift into *production for discard* employed another share of displaced humans.

One desperate attempt to keep employing people displaced by technologically improved processes happened at the beginning of the XXI century with the failed promotion of a «services economy». Another desperate attempt to employ redundant people happens at the time of this writing with a professed shift from fossil fuels into renewable sources of energy and ecologically sustainable processes.

The criminal capitalistic money-printing pyramid –which started at the decade of 1970, as described in [4.56] and subsequent sections– further and strongly fostered the capitalistic urge to keep the expansion of consumption and waste. Thus, first and foremost the criminals promoted the expansion of consumption and waste for upholding and feeding their operation of massive stealing. And likewise the criminals fake an interest in human and planetary welfare by means of promoting ecologically sustainable processes, merely to keep their criminal venture running.

The massive *production for discard* promoted by the capitalistic criminals since the second half of the XX century until the end of the first two decades of the XXI century, with everybody also noticing the human demographic explosion of that time, amounted to a sort of «extinction party» for humankind.

[4.89]

6.   Lies:

   a.   *The organizations that do not belong to the state-organization enact more efficient, honest, and socially-constructive practices than the aforementioned state-organization, in a «free market» social setting.*

   β.   *The state-organization by its own inherent nature tends to corruption and inefficiency; the state-organization's corruption and inefficiency result proportional to its size and available resources.*

The criminals say the first lie referring to organizations which do not belong to the state-organization (particular cooperative systems) both *for-profit* and *not for-profit*. In the framework of the human exploitation described in [6.40] and subsequent sections, *for-profit* organizations consist of those which strive to produce a monetary income for their «owners», while *not for-profit* organizations do not produce a monetary income for any entitled humans or «superior entities». Hence, typically the criminals pay for a lot of *not for-profit* «non-governmental organizations» which pretend to champion some purely socially-constructive cause or goal –contrasted with striving purely for monetary profit, in this mythology regarded as «individualistic» and therefrom not directly socially-constructive. The criminals establish and support those *not for-profit* organizations for obtaining favorable publicity by distributing charitable crumbs, and for using those organizations as institutional cover for their agents and the activities and intentions of these latter. Of course, when actual fights for democracy, for the advancement of humankind, and against authoritarianism happen then other, usually grassroots, actually democratic and humanitarian organizations do the work, frequently using scarce material resources –those latter organizations built and operated by persons truly aiming to enhance, protect, and strengthen the common welfare.

The criminals typically use the second lie to justify the transference of functions from the state-organization into private control, far away from democratic control, public accountability, and transparency. In this context, the criminals used the second lie to promote laws separating the emission of money from democratic control, thereby cementing the legalized and institutionalized protection for massively stealing; this constitutes another abject failure of «western» democratic regimes. In some other instances, the criminals, when they deem convenient, promote «decentralized institutions» in order to protect, hide, and conceal their own socially-harmful activities by purchasing the will of the public servants who now work isolated both from any real accountability and from the democratically managed command chain.

The organizations that do not belong to the state-organization very frequently enact the same dysfunctional and socially-destructive practices supposedly inextirpable from the same state-organization, as explained next:

α. The state-organization of a democratic regime can and must stand subject to public supervision and socially-organized accountability; but private organizations do not owe accountability and transparency to the public. Thus, private organizations in many (or most) cases merely hide their malfeasances if not caught by law-enforcement agents. From systematically deceiving their customers, to cheating gas emissions' controls for engines, the examples abound.

β. The same failures of organizational design that happen in the state-organization, also happen in private organizations. For instance, the proclaimed and mythical flexibility of *for-profit* organizations with thousands of members –nowadays *transnational corporations*– simply does not exist, and anyone within those organizations can observe it.

γ. Typically, private organizations and individual citizens actively promote and sponsor the corruption within the state-organization, the inverse case rarely happens –except in fascist regimes. In fact, in *representative democracies* the elected representatives of the people stand in a position of structural disadvantage towards *for-profit* organizations, and the *for-profit* organizations typically –either legally or illegally, directly or indirectly– pay amounts of money to public representatives for these latter to enact a lot of dishonest and treacherous activities in their favor; anyone who lived in a *representative democracy* knows it first-hand. This structural disadvantage happens because typically the individuals engaged purely in *for-profit* organizations accumulated resources and revenues which the elected representatives cannot sustainably obtain due to the very short tenures they enjoy in public posts earning limited wages, after which they must again focus their time and effort on winning an election and securing a personal income. In many cases, a group of individuals who a few weeks before strived to avoid unemployment, suddenly find themselves managing the massive budget and assets of the state-organization. This problem addressed further in [7.67] and subsequent sections.

In several countries, traitors to their corresponding homelands used both lies as excuse for transferring large state enterprises into the control and domain of particular citizens, usually by means of fraudulent payment schemes known as *debt for shares*, during the last decade of the XX century. A typical fraudulent payment described in the following sequence:

α. The traitors within the state-organization give a loan to a future oligarch.

β. The future oligarch uses the loan to buy a large state enterprise –at this stage typically the traitors within the state-organization obtain their booty or share of profits, usually covertly.

γ. The new oligarch uses some profits of the newly acquired monopolistic or oligopolistic enterprise for paying the loan over a few subsequent years.

Frequently, within a single contractual scheme, the traitors linked the loan directly to the purchase of the large state enterprise.

Differing from the typical private-sponsored corruption in democratic countries, in fascist and totalitarian regimes the state-organization intervenes into *for-profit* organizations for securing obedience and compliance to the desires of the ruling fascist faction –thus, it consists of state-enforced corruption. In these cases the operational source of this specific kind of socially-harmful and dishonest practices typically stands where the ruling fascist faction stands: can reside solely inside the state-organization but more commonly resides in several fascist organizations; and certainly the size of the state-organization does not cause those practices, likewise those practices do not constitute an inherent feature of a state-organization. Fascism addressed further in sections [7.8] to [7.11].

In any type of organization or cooperative system, ordinarily some individuals will attempt to steal, underperform, and form gangs for their own benefit if left unchecked.

Capitalistic criminals and retarded theorists likewise blame the supposed intrinsic inefficiency of the state-organization to a «lack of competition in business»; this blunder addressed next.

[4.90]

7. Failure: *In a «free market» social setting, for-profit organizations will conduct themselves with efficiency, since they perform driven by a desire to constantly maximize their profit, and due to the competition processes those which do not perform efficiently will disappear.*

    Like the failure described in section [4.86], this failure arises mainly from the magical thinking that regards the aggregated human behavior as a quite simple «system», where humans would behave quasi-mechanistically or like automatons; not surprisingly such theory does not correspond to reality.

    The destruction of competitors as described in the same section [4.86] completely offsets or counterbalances the claim of this failure, wherefrom happens merely a private accumulation of resources using prices much higher than the production costs by the *winners* of the competition. Furthermore, typically the *winners* focus on safeguarding their *feeding spot*, usually by:

    α. Preventing and precluding the incorporation of new participants into the industries and distribution channels which the *winners* regard as their commercial realm –by threatening, ostracizing, or actively punishing those who do business with newcomers, by occupying all the physical means available, by active defamation, or by otherwise hampering any new or potential competitor.

    β. Blocking the emergence of new technologies which they do not control or simply do not understand –typically by enacting and supporting backward, expensive, or access-restricted technical standards and regulations.

    The socially-harmful practices aimed to safeguarding *feeding spots* happen extensively in many commercial environments of every kind, the participants in an exchange space neither need to stand in oligopolistic positions nor actively join industrial or commercial cartels as an indispensable prerequisite to engage in these practices; and actually a myriad of small commercial establishments engage in them. Oligopolistic positions and industrial or commercial cartels do not constitute an indispensable instrumentality for safeguarding *feeding spots* and attempting to *freeze* the status-quo. Hence, for example, even relatively small commercial environments stand plagued by participants who seek to increase their profits using both socially-harmful practices and antisocial usually-undisclosed verbal accords (known as *gentlemen's agreements*); from small-scale electric-equipment resellers to taxi drivers and so on, many individuals just seek to «accommodate themselves» and keep everything static afterwards. Thus, in mediocre societies and mediocre social environments, the claimed efficiency of commercial organizations never happens, and those encompass a very large share of the human world.

Therefore, commercial competition and competitive conditions neither cause nor effect an increase of efficiency in cooperative systems. Humans can choose to increase that efficiency, and such choice remains a volitional one that many reject.

[4.91]

8.   Lie: *The emission of money should stand allocated in mature, professional, specialized individuals, detached from democratic control, or «autonomous» from democratic processes; because functionaries of the state-organization tend to behave dishonestly and, worse, they tend to fulfill the urges of the people that chose them. Fulfilling the urges of the people constitutes something called «populism», and that practice should get wiped from the democratic landscape. If democratic representatives control the emission of money, then calamitous events ensue.*

In this lie the capitalistic criminals and their propagandists used as arguments the failures of the *representative democracy*, and managed to mingle those failures into falsehoods made into their favor. Furthermore, detaching a fundamental societal choice from democratic control arguing «imbecility» from the voters highly pleases and satisfies the fascist formations which aid the capitalistic criminals. The aforesaid sequestered control pleases the fascists because scores of them dream of living in a sort of distorted authoritarian «kindergarten» which requires top-down management by «strong individuals» for maintaining «order».

In this context, some failures of the current *representative democracy* –further described in [7.47] and subsequent sections– happen as follows:

α. Once elected and in functions, typically a *democratic* representative stands beyond any effective and efficient control from the people. And, in many cases, after selling their will or by their own initiative, the representatives become traitors to the cooperative system.

β. Typically, happen fast-paced propaganda-infested electoral procedures where at best the democratic processes degenerate into a frivolous personal popularity contest (hence, wins the most personable candidate, not the most competent candidate coupled with the best project for the cooperative system); therefrom in many cases incompetent representatives reach high posts within the cooperative system. Such incompetent representatives frequently make a lot of far-reaching consequences-bearing mistakes, and typically due to deficiencies in the *executive functions* of their brain they make a lot of myopic choices. What stated here, coupled with the usual absence of effective and efficient control by the people, in many cases produces disastrous consequences.

γ. Some traitors that reach high public offices or posts through democratic processes typically twist *representative democracy* into a mockery of itself; and sometimes these traitors perform actions and enact policies contrary to the interests of the capitalistic criminals. Thereat, a quarrel of criminals within positions of privilege typically happens in the context of a state-organization captured by a gang or faction not subservient to the capitalistic criminals. Both the *independent* traitors and the capitalistic criminals typically resort to manipulate the population using all the means at their disposal and relying on the retardation of many citizens. For example, some prototypical fight may happen as follows:

   i.   The *independent* traitors publicize a future trial and either tacitly or expressly request «popular support» for it –or they use another circus-like procedure, like a «congressional hearing»– to decide whether the judicial system should process and condemn some well-known former state-functionary subservient to the capitalistic criminals. The farce goes as «express your support or approval for enacting already existing laws with this one known 100% guilty».

ii. The capitalistic criminals blame the *independent* traitors as «populists», arguing that such show happens geared towards lynching their pawn, merely to divert the attention from the dishonest activities of the same *independent* traitors.

If the quarrel becomes too expensive, the capitalistic criminals can always end buying the will of some or most of the *independent* traitors. A proposal for reforming democracy recorded in the last chapter of this document.

The obvious purpose of detaching and isolating the emission of money consists in fulfilling the desire of the capitalistic criminals to continue their stealing activities in a large scale without accountability, and without competitors in crime; which largely happened successfully now during centuries.

Controlling the emission of money and distributing the newly minted money within the criminal gang constitutes one of the cornerstones of the organized crime venture called *capitalism*, as recorded in [4.56] and subsequent sections.

[4.92]

9. Lie: *In a capitalistic «free market», honest competent hard-working individuals will thrive and succeed. Those who innovate and develop solutions, and then bring them into a commercial exchange, will prevail in a capitalistic «free market».*

Many naive people thought this lie resulted true, and thereupon experienced dearly loses. This lie already explained extensively in [4.41] and subsequent sections.

This lie also serves for blaming the hard-working individuals for their own poverty, as «if you really worked *hard*, you would not live in poverty, look at these individuals in those newspapers who made a fortune before they reached the age of 30».

[4.93]

10. Lie: *If exists less or almost no state-organization, the society enjoys more freedom in which each citizen can obtain in the most effective and efficient way the resources and social arrangements convenient for its personal development. In contrast, the state-organization oppresses the individuals, hinders personal initiative, produces a diminution of creativity, and thereby causes the diminution of the general prosperity.*

This lie relies on the deficiency of *executive functions* in many humans. There a patent abuse of the concept of *freedom* and, like the lie recorded in section [4.86], the abuse relies on the psychological trauma due to the fight against state-sanctioned fascism and totalitarianism –thus, in the fight against the products of authoritarian people. As stated before, complete *freedom* would imply anarchy; general or widespread prosperity, and the full expression of *personal initiative* do not happen when the individuals need to divert a lot of time and attention into securing basic living environments, as would happen with anarchy.

Individuals in a society usually behave, or their peers expect them to behave, according to a formal and/or informal *social contract* –recall [2.30] and subsequent sections. *Formal* social contracts exist explicitly codified, but not necessarily externally written. Also, humans may expressly communicate *informal* social contracts at some times, and at other times *informal* social contracts spread implicitly within the people's shared culture or shared mind-set. At any given time a society may create, store, and transmit social contracts by all those three means: formal codified, informal explicit, and informal implicit; notwithstanding if the social contracts differ in some aspects. A *social contract* prescribes, among other provisions:

α. The space for action for each individual within the society.

β. The type of activities each individual should perform volitionally and independently.

γ. The type of activities allocated for organized or concerted social action –plus the method used to perform them.

δ. A set of individual duties and rights.

In other words, among other content, the *social contract* prescribes a *degree of freedom* or *margin of personal action* for each individual (as already recorded in section [2.34]) and, at the same time, prescribes social rights for each individual. In modern societies the core of the formal *social contract* stands codified in the document called *Constitution*.

Therefrom, the state-organization operates where the social contract prescribes its activities; such activities typically comprise those routinary affairs where stability and predictability constitute paramount operational requisites for the social welfare. Accordingly, in societies with democratic freedoms typically the state-organization neither prohibits nor significantly impedes the exercise of creativity and fruitful *personal initiative* within the exchange space.

Some versions of this lie state that «bureaucratic regulations stifle creativity and *personal initiative* because they burden the citizens who must comply with them». However, in this case, any cumbersome procedures at the state-organization stem from a defective design of the respective organizational branch; therewith, cumbersome procedures do not constitute an inherent feature of the state-organization itself. If any procedures prescribed by law happen cumbersomely, including those which the citizens ought to perform autonomously, the solution consists in streamlining the implementation of those procedures and, if necessary, also the legal framework.

Furthermore, the law will always prescribe some regulations within the exchange space, precisely because enacting those regulations secures the most effective and efficient way for each citizen to obtain the resources and social arrangements convenient for its personal development. Instances of this comprise food quality assurance, mandatory minimum content for elementary educational curricula, safety compliance, and so forth. Would constitute a very inefficient and ineffective societal cooperative system that one where, for example, each citizen needed to arrange for itself a precise quality control of the food purchased, or needed to check the hazards in every building which enters; all those activities would entail a decreased quality of life for each citizen who would spend much more resources and time doing simple things.

The absence of the state-organization by no means guarantees nor anyhow fosters efficiency and effectiveness in those fields or industries readily suitable for oligopolistic or monopolistic activities.

The capitalistic criminals use this lie as a protective measure against any lawful regulation of their monetary cartel and criminal enterprises, and against any scrutiny that would expose the criminal scheme used to massively steal from everybody. Thus, the capitalistic criminals and their lackeys lie once and again claiming: «Do not lawfully regulate us, do not even dare to interfere with our activities, because that hinders social progress and diminishes the welfare of the people. Furthermore, the best state *economic policy* consists in lacking an *economic policy* at all.»

The state-organization of an independent society does not constitute some sort of external entity which commands itself and behaves by its own will; rather, the state-organization constitutes a concrete expression of the societal culture –this described further in [7.13] and subsequent sections.

Only when a fracture happens in the societal shared culture or shared mind-set, and one of the factions captures the state-organization, then the captured state-organization becomes alien to the excluded social group and conflict ensues. These cases produce extremely pernicious consequences especially when a fascist social layer captures the state-organization whereupon frequently ensue widespread oppression, targeted deprivation of rights, selective expulsions from workplaces, deportations, incarcerations, assassination campaigns, child-abduction campaigns for «reeducation», and alike.[4] Hence, in such cases ensue variable-intensity and targeted genocidal efforts by the fascists who typically seek to «uproot the malign and corruptive elements from the society».

---

4   Such atrocities happened –and still happen– not only in the eurasian continent; remember the fascist dictatorships in Mesoamerica and South America during the second half of the XX century.

Summary

[4.94]

From now on, a civilized world will take no more bullshit from liars proclaiming «the invisible hand of the market», or proclaiming «the market's self-regulation», or stating that «*free* market economy constitutes the natural outcome of human behavior», or about a non-existing «widespread rationality of the market participants».

Furthermore, no cultivated human will consider true that a «*free* market» consists of an unrestricted exchange of (fake or real) money, assets, products, and services excluding unrestricted transit of people: this double standard constitutes an essential foundation of the system of domination built around the capitalistic crime syndicate.

[4.95]

Every payment promise not backed by money constitutes an instance of fraud and theft from the society as a whole.

[4.96]

Beyond directly stealing by issuing payment promises, the capitalistic criminals steal the opportunities built by pioneers and explorers.

[4.97]

The capitalistic criminals promoted massive *production for discard* practices during the second half of the XX century which depleted the Earth's natural resources, and caused grave long-term ecological damage.

[4.98]

The cornerstones of the organized crime venture called *capitalism* consist in:

1. Payment promises.
2. Banking secrecy: secrecy about transactions; secrecy about the amount of money hoarded, or its actual absence.
3. A brainwashing *economic* doctrine disseminated by failed educational institutions and widespread propaganda.
4. Issuance of money –tools of exchange– captured by the criminal gangsters for their own benefit, thereupon: alien to democratic control, detached from public accountability, full of dishonest practices.

[4.99]

The capitalistic «financial markets» constitute the backbone of the plutocratic world order, where the world elite can obtain very large quantities of money and payment promises in exclusive and preferential conditions with which that elite can outmatch any competitor in business. However, obtaining massive amounts of money directly distributed from *central banks* into capitalistic corporations became the primary method for maintaining a plutocratic position at the beginning of the XXI century.

At the same time, the size of the «measurements» within the aforementioned «financial markets» showcases how far reached the magical thinking embraced by retarded theorists, showcases how far these latter detached from reality.

[4.100]

No superior human cooperative system will emerge from the evolution of the criminal venture called *capitalism*.

5

Fundamental Concepts of Commerce

[5.1]

THE ACTUAL KNOWLEDGE required to describe the fundamental interactions of a mature commercial exchange results relatively small, when compared with those ideological structures built upon magical thinking that prevailed before. At the same time, the absence of magical thinking precludes the possibility of making gross simplifications.

[5.2]

Remember the definitions of *exchange space*, *tool of exchange*, *standardized bartering commodity*, and *money* recorded in sections [4.7] to [4.10]. The reader may find useful to review those concepts again.

[5.3]

A commercial exchange happens upon reaching social accords, and can happen either synchronously or asynchronously. In the following sections explained these two scenarios.

In this chapter, the tools of exchange alternatively called *external data conveyors*, since the participants in a commercial exchange use them to carry data externally to their bodies.

Synchronous Exchange

[5.4]

As part of the development of the interdependence and exchange among hominids, the human brain developed through evolution a psychological structure resembling an index –which can remain implicit and completely in the unconsciousness. The individual uses this index to evaluate or assess what, among the items and capacities in its domain, would regard as suitable for transference or performance in exchange for certain items and capacities in the domain of another individual, and thereby obtain a favorable net outcome.

In other words, the individual uses an internal index for evaluating or assessing which of its assets, products, and services would transfer or perform in exchange for a given collection of assets, products, and services which another individual can provide.

Hence, the index operates solely in the brain of each individual hominid, and that hominid in particular must assess which of its items and capacities and in which amount would provide or produce in exchange for receiving certain items and capacities in certain amounts, whatever the hominid regards as adequate to satisfy its basic psychological needs and, in general, the goals of any living organism.

This index of *convenience* gets formed at each individual transaction (or exchange) inside the hominid's brain to compare what provides or produces with what receives. The index of *convenience* does not constitute a static structure and accepts as input –as items and capacities suitable for exchange– almost anything that the hominid may find available.

[5.5]

Therefore, a *Homo sapiens* individual does not require tools of exchange and neither requires to express numerically the *convenience* of the items and capacities which receives compared with the items and capacities that transfers or performs. An individual can perform a barter.

[5.6]

Without using *external data conveyors* (tools of exchange), a group of entities can perform an operation of synchronous exchange: each participant agrees to receive a first group of items and capacities and to deliver a second group of items and capacities in a single operation –the same operation. Each entity can deliver or receive or both.

Each entity may lack access to all the other participants; therefrom each participant may, constrained by isolation, exchange agreements with only a subset of all the universe of players and likewise obtain a particular perspective of what can receive from that subset.

The items and capacities exchanged of course may vary in nature, there neither required that they «compensate» each other in some way, nor needed any sort of «balance» –someone can deliver nothing, or receive nothing, as example. Moreover, each participant can deliver more items and capacities and receive the same compared with other participant who delivers items and capacities of the same nature in a lesser quantity; there not required any of the participants not knowing about this difference, for it to happen.

In this synchronous exchange the sole-necessary organizational structure consists in the agreement or commitment of each participant to perform the exchange.

[5.7]

Hence, the participants in the exchange first commit to do it: «I agree giving to you, set (or subset) of people, these items and capacities if you agree to deliver me those items and capacities.» These individual commitments must then compensate or balance each of the individual commitments from the other participants. When all the participants achieve this compensation or balance, the situation may get labeled as *general agreement reached* (a *social pact*, or a transient *social contract*), and usually its execution ensues –happens the transference and performance of those agreed upon items and capacities.

[5.8]

Relevant features to highlight here: they did not use any sort of *external data conveyors* (tools of exchange); without using some (any) public index each participant performed a particular operation of *convenience assessment*, if the participant performed any, to gauge or estimate (an operation of divination or guessing always provides an input, recall section [3.45]) if what the participant receives compared with what the participant delivers, together with the collateral effects, produces a result conforming to the participant's objectives.

[5.9]

If in this synchronous exchange existed a *convenience index*, what would share? Which would constitute the common trait or common characteristic? A tridimensional array can get built with the data from the exchange, as follows:

- First axis: A participant i in the exchange.
- Second axis: A participant j in the exchange.
  Both i and j from 1 to n. Where n the number (the sum, the quantity) of participants in the exchange.
- Third axis: An item k, with items labeled from 1 to m. Where m the number (the sum, the quantity) of items and capacities perceived by the participants.
- Each spot (i, j, k) associated to two numbers, namely: the price $p_{i,j,k}$ for each unit of the exchanged item or capacity, and the amount transferred $q_{i,j,k}$ (the number of units transferred).
  If the participant i transfers to the participant j a quantity $q_{i,j,k}$ of items or capacities labeled k, then the participant will attach a positive sign to $q_{i,j,k}$ (marking it as a positive number). In the complementary stand, if the participant j receives from the participant i a quantity $q_{i,j,k}$, of items or capacities labeled k, then the participant j must attach to that quantity a negative sign. Therefore, for every i, every j, and every k: $q_{i,j,k} = -q_{j,i,k}$.
  Notice that for every type of items or capacities labeled k in the exchange, $p_{i,j,k} = p_{j,i,k}$ for any given pair i, j.
- Further, in a synchronous exchange –hence, in a completed social exchange– for every (any) participant i:

$$\sum_{j=1}^{n} \sum_{k=1}^{m} \left(q_{i,j,k} \cdot p_{i,j,k} \right) = 0$$

Each participant comes out from the exchange with the same amount of *tools of exchange* with which went in. There shown a fundamental relationship in the exchange: The *tools of exchange* constitute solely tools for executing the exchange, they neither add nor subtract anything to the environment. Expressed differently: The *money* constitutes solely a tool for the operation of exchange, it does not constitute an item to exchange. (In a healthy cooperative system, it works that way.)

And remember that not everybody may command an ability to access all the other participants, or that any participant may lack a chance to exchange items or capacities –or even just to communicate– with all the other participants. Thereupon, for each participant i a binary or boolean vector can get built to describe the subset of participants with whom i can exchange. As example, if a participant i can perform exchanges only with participants tagged with numbers 2 and 3 respectively, then the boolean vector results:

$$b_i = \left(b_{i,1}, b_{i,2}, b_{i,3}, \dots, b_{i,n}\right) = \left(0,1,1,\dots,0\right)$$

[5.10]

In the synchronous exchange, with or without *external data conveyors* (tools of exchange) involved, each transaction peer-to-peer of each item or capacity essentially consists of the quantity, the direction, and the price of the item or capacity.

Typically, the quantity, the direction, and the price will get negotiated and bargained all together at each transaction and, consequently, they result interdependent among them in each individual transaction. Therefore, anyone can notice with certainty that, even in a synchronous exchange, prices share nothing.

[5.11]

If for each participant the *convenience index* for each item or capacity gets expressed numerically using *external data conveyors* (tools of exchange), such numeric index in tools of exchange will differ according to the participant's uniqueness and according to the quantity of tools of exchange available to that participant. There does not exist any relationship which links a tool of exchange to the organizational interactions as if constituting a system. Similarly, there does not exist a «market price structure».

[5.12]

Those antecedents greatly facilitate the description of the parasitic and predatory effect of islands or subsets with a higher concentration of money, with a limited amount of exchangeable items through the subset's boundaries, and the corresponding effects over the whole exchange space.

The framework stands as follows:

α. In a boundary gets allowed the transit solely of money and certain merchandises; this boundary delimits an island within the exchange space.

β. A subset of the participants inside the island provide the full exchange space with a product or service for which they charge large compensations. Meanwhile, for the members of the island manufacturing such product or service entails a very low cost. For example, the members of the island may manufacture «financial services», or may perform any other parasitic scheme.

Then can live within the island individuals performing ordinary tasks receiving a disproportionately large income for their labor compared with the rest of the exchange space.

The aforementioned practices constitute the essence of the «capitalistic neoliberal globalization» and the colonial activities of transnational corporations. These interactions also comprise part of the parasitic scheme with which the current core of the capitalist fraud (the capitalistic structures in the United States of America) accumulates and expends disproportionate amounts of resources of all kinds. The rest of the siphoning of resources made by just emitting money and payment promises, as already described in [4.56] and subsequent sections.

Asynchronous Exchange

[5.13]

An asynchronous exchange simply consists of a deferred synchronous exchange, where the participants reach and enact the peer-to-peer agreements scattered within a set of successive time lapses. Excluding the difference of temporal concurrency, all the qualities of a synchronous exchange remain the same in an asynchronous exchange.

[5.14]

The synchronous exchange does not constitute the cause of the existence of tools of exchange –since, as previously noticed, a set of individuals can execute a synchronous exchange without using *external data conveyors*. The tools of exchange exist solely to make possible the asynchronous exchange.

[5.15]

The asynchronous exchange happens due to the fact that, in a vast majority of cases, all the individuals who participate in the exchange (of articles and services) cannot possibly build a *general agreement* during a single time interval, ordinarily because of societal temporal behaviors.

[5.16]

For example, in a cooperative system with unfixed and changing boundaries new participants in the exchange will get accepted dynamically. Typically, in that case the tool of exchange consists of a physical asset withdrawn from its originally intended function and thereafter used solely (or mainly) as a tool of exchange. Thereby the asset becomes a *standardized bartering commodity* as defined in section [4.9].

Occasionally the holder of the primitive tool of exchange «redeems» it by using it as an ordinary asset. Typically, the «redemption» happens by consuming it in the case of edible *standardized bartering commodities*, or by using metals for structural and/or ornamental purposes in the case of coins. These primitive cases not addressed here further.

[5.17]

At the end of an asynchronous exchange among a fixed set of participants, each participant must finish the exchange holding the same amount of tools of exchange with which the participant started, same as in a synchronous exchange –because an asynchronous exchange simply consists of a deferred synchronous exchange, as already said.

Within a cooperative system, the asynchronous exchange can happen by cycles, where each cycle concludes when the participants equalize or balance their tools of exchange.

[5.18]

Nevertheless, in a traditional society the asynchronous exchange never ends –for it started incidentally and grew without design–, so the tools of exchange just get recycled in a continuous perpetual way. And therefrom typically no-one must compulsorily perform a balance or a periodic equalization of the tools of exchange in its domain.

The Amount of Tools of Exchange

[5.19]

In a synchronous exchange each participant needs neither a minimum nor maximum amount of tools of exchange because these result redundant.

In contrast, at the beginning of an asynchronous exchange every participant must hold in its domain an amount of tools of exchange equal to the largest deficit that the participant may undertake during the course of that cycle or instance of asynchronous exchange. This amount of tools of exchange will enable the participant to reach agreements and perform exchanges where delivers the referred tools of exchange, before reaching agreements and performing exchanges to receive back the same quantity of tools of exchange. Though, in any ordinary society, for any given participant such amount of indispensable tools of exchange typically varies among temporal periods of equal length.

6

Asynchronous Exchange in the Context of a State

[6.1]

HEREINAFTER explained how to build a social arrangement which comprises a stable, fair, mature, and prosperous commercial exchange.

The ongoing endless asynchronous exchange must conclude, thereat the criminal venture called capitalism ceases to exist. That simple.

[6.2]

Every modern society defines a space and environment for performing commercial exchanges using an explicit *population-wide social contract* –remember section [2.32]. In that same *social contract* the people must specify the regulations for the asynchronous exchange inside that defined exchange space.

[6.3]

Particular cooperative systems or *particular organizations* consist of those not subsets of the state-organization, whether focused on profitable commercial activities, or focused on enhancing the social welfare, or focused on any other purpose –as already defined in section [2.31]. In this social arrangement, the distinction *for-profit* and *not-for-profit* for particular organizations lacks both meaning and foundation because henceforward no outsider will *milk* productive organizations, as explained in [6.40] and subsequent sections.

In a mature asynchronous exchange, the state-organization performs both the role of arbiter and participant.

[6.4]

First explained the behavioral interactions related to the participation of single individuals, afterwards the explanation expands to include particular cooperative systems as participants in the commercial exchange. This sequence because of the convenience of first explaining certain concepts.

The Conclusion of the Exchange Cycle

[6.5]

As explained before, money constitutes solely a tool of exchange (an organizational tool), does not store anything within, and does not constitute an asset or a merchandise. At the end of each cycle of asynchronous exchange, each participant must finish with the same amount of money with which entered into that specific cycle; such retained money at the conclusion of the cycle neither confers nor grants any claim over assets, products, or services.

[6.6]

Since the state-organization performs the role of arbiter, the same state-organization must allot money to each participant at the beginning of each exchange cycle, and must verify that each participant finishes the cycle with that same amount of money.

Moreover, the amount of money that a participant must hold at the beginning of each cycle of asynchronous exchange in order to fully perform his/her operations of exchange, constitutes a choice relative to the structure of the overall cooperative system.

Therefore, the quantity of money allotted by the state-organization to each participant constitutes an amount that the people through the social contract must regulate.

[6.7]

The act, performed by a participant in the exchange, of adjusting the quantity of money in its domain so that such quantity equals the quantity of money obtained at the beginning of the exchange cycle, herein denominated *monetary equalization*.

[6.8]

The conclusion of the asynchronous exchange can happen *simultaneously* (or *concurrently*) for all the participants in the exchange. Thus, everybody can make a *monetary equalization* at the same time, and start a new exchange cycle also at that same time.

[6.9]

Nevertheless, finishing the asynchronous exchange simultaneously for all the participants involves three undesirable effects:

1. The state-organization must build (and presumably keep idle most time) a large operational capacity since, every conclusion of the cycle, must at-once:

   a) Supervise that each participant in the asynchronous exchange retains or holds the same amount of money with which started that cycle.

   b) In the cases where such compliance did not happen, enact the corresponding administrative procedures described in [6.23] and subsequent sections.

   The simultaneous attention of many cases, which will create a peak of activity for the state-organization, very easily can degenerate into an administrative jungle.

2. During a close temporal vicinity before the time of simultaneous conclusion the participants in the exchange will tend to massively diminish the quantity and magnitude of their commercial exchanges, as they focus on making only small purchasing and selling operations in order to adjust the quantity of money they hold, and thereby reach the intended monetary equalization goal.

3. Numerous participants will rarely, if ever, reach a full agreement simultaneously; this due to the fact that, with numerous participants –say, 1,000,000– results very complicated a precise balancing of offered products and services with those demanded at a single period of time.

   Thus, in a simultaneous conclusion of the exchange ordinarily more people will end holding amounts of money different from those amounts with which each started the cycle, when compared with the *flexible stepped conclusion of the exchange cycle* described in the next sections of this document.

The last two described effects may, in many cases, produce a race for monetary equalization days or weeks before the simultaneous conclusion of the exchange cycle.

Thus, a simultaneous conclusion of the exchange cycle may develop into an awkward organizational scheme in a real world setting.

[6.10]

As a second preliminary approach, the cooperative system's social contract could provide a framework for a *stepped conclusion of the exchange cycle*, as follows:

Each participant obtains assigned a different periodic day for the conclusion of his/her exchange cycle and its corresponding monetary equalization, where the temporal duration of each participant's exchange cycle equals a predefined length –the same amount of days from start to end, for everyone.

For example, if the exchange cycle lasts one calendar year, a participant A may perform a monetary equalization every May 1st, while a participant B may perform a monetary equalization every September 19th, and so forth for everyone else.

[6.11]

However, a participant should not obtain an immutable day for its monetary equalization, which cannot volitionally modify or relocate.

A rigid stepped conclusion of the exchange cycle promotes a systemic fragmentation of the participants in the exchange, because each participant finds easier to perform operations of exchange with those participants scheduled for monetary equalization in the temporal vicinity of his/her own monetary equalization day. Therefrom, a rigid stepped conclusion of the exchange cycle creates incentives and conditions for the formation of commercial cliques based upon the vicinity of rigidly allotted monetary equalization days.

Hence, a stepped conclusion of the exchange cycle requires flexibility: The social organization must allow each participant to make a monetary equalization any day, or within a chosen temporal window, before a predefined maximum temporal duration of the exchange cycle (before a predefined temporal ceiling), and on that event the exchange cycle of the participant restarts.

This enables any participant to adjust its exchange cycle in any way needed upon anticipated commercial operations.

Fortunately, by using modern electronic data technologies a society can accomplish all this with relative easiness.

[6.12]

For clarity:

+ *Simultaneous conclusion of the exchange cycle*: When everybody performs a monetary equalization the same day –at the same time.

+ *Stepped conclusion of the exchange cycle*: When each participant starts and ends its own exchange cycle by performing its own monetary equalization on an individually assigned day, with the same amount of days from start to end for everyone. Those individually assigned days scattered through a time period.

+ *Flexible stepped conclusion of the exchange cycle*: When, at each cycle, each participant volitionally chooses a day or temporal window for performing a monetary equalization, provided that the time interval between that new monetary equalization and the last performed monetary equalization does not exceed the maximum temporal duration of the exchange cycle as defined in the social contract. Thereupon, at each individualized cycle the participant can volitionally change the specific day or temporal window at which it will perform its own monetary equalization.

Remember that in all cases each participant ends holding the same amount of money with which started the cycle.

[6.13]

Therefore, all other things equal, cooperative systems should prefer and enact a *flexible stepped conclusion of the exchange cycle*.

[6.14]

One conservative way to establish a flexible stepped asynchronous exchange consists in enacting the following sequence:

1. Set the organizational framework for a flexible stepped conclusion of the exchange cycle.

2. Start the asynchronous exchange assigning all the participants the same periodic day for monetary equalization. In other words, start with a simultaneous (concurrent) conclusion of the exchange cycle.

3. Observe the participants flock into desired and convenient days or temporal windows for monetary equalization.

For example, if in the social contract the people specified a maximum temporal duration of the exchange cycle equal to one year, and the initially-simultaneous conclusion of the exchange cycle happens at the last day of the calendar year, when most people performs diverse types of celebrations; then perhaps most individuals will result not interested in changing their date of monetary equalization, and they will spend their last spare money purchasing stuff useful for celebrating. But, in contrast, the sellers of such partying stuff will result highly interested in changing the date of their monetary equalization into another day.

[6.15]

Using modern electronic devices, the tools of exchange can consist of electronic records in a database managed by the state-organization; thereby precluding the possibility of both physical loses and the covert hoarding of tools of exchange.

The electronic records in an electronic database used for an asynchronous exchange do not constitute money; and happens no need to keep a list of each individual commercial operation that any participant performed, but only a single numeric entry for each participant –although, of course, keeping a list of each individual transaction would add some useful redundancy to the database.

Likewise, if an electronic database does not stand available, the asynchronous exchange can proceed using written *payment orders* that the participants would at a later time submit to an arbiter for that entity to either add or deduct from the corresponding accounts in a centralized ledger.[5]

Using money –physical coins and bills– in an asynchronous exchange also results possible. Though in this case the conclusion of the exchange cycle must happen simultaneously for all the participants. At that single conclusion time, the coins and bills used for the previous cycle must become superseded by new coins and bills marked

---

5   Notice that a *payment order* differs from a capitalistic *check*; because the arbiter will reject any payment order for which the emitter lacks sufficient tools of exchange. In contrast, capitalistic banks can emit checks –in favor of a customer– for which they lack the corresponding amounts of money. By using a capitalistic check, a participant can accomplish a commercial operation using fake (non-existent) tools of exchange created by the bank.

specifically for usage during the next cycle; in this way precluding the possibility of covertly hoarding money from one cycle through the next.

[6.16]

For easiness of understanding, considering that the term *tool of exchange* may constitute a novelty for most readers –and considering also the absence of a proper adjective for *tool of exchange*–, regardless of whether the tools of exchange consist of either electronic records or actual money, in this chapter those called *money*, but the reader should remember the distinction.

[6.17]

A participant in the asynchronous exchange can purchase something and pay for it in parcels through several exchange cycles.

Notice that purchasing something and paying for it in parcels constitutes neither monetary borrowing nor a rent over assets.

An Easy Monetary Equalization

[6.18]

In a flexible stepped conclusion of the exchange cycle, a participant does not need to exactly or accurately reach the target amount of money at the end of the exchange cycle, just needs to *pass through the target* during the temporal window selected by the same participant.

Thereat, the arbiter of the exchange will parcel in two the transaction which crosses the monetary target. Hence, in sequence:

1. The arbiter will adjust the size of the portion which belongs to the ending cycle to actually reach the intended monetary target of the participant at the end of that cycle.

2. By accounting methods, the arbiter finishes the cycle of the participant; thus, assigns a new quantity of tools of exchange to the participant for their usage during the next cycle. As already commented in section [6.15], all this operation may just consist in updating an electronic database.

3. Therewith, the second and remaining portion of the last transaction will pass directly into the starting cycle as either the first deposit or the first deduction of the account, according to the type of transaction.

If the money assigned to a participant for the starting cycle does not suffice for the deduction of the second portion of the transaction, then the arbiter will reject the transaction and keep the participant in the old exchange cycle.

Moreover, if the participant does not make any suitable transaction for ending its cycle during the corresponding temporal window, then the arbiter will process the unaccomplished monetary equalization as recorded in [6.23] and subsequent sections.

[6.19]

Next, recorded two examples for easiness of understanding.

[6.20]

Completion of the Cycle by Receiving a Payment

Sally's great-granddaughter runs a small agricultural business, and the maximum exchange cycle –as required by law– lasts one calendar year plus one calendar month.

She selects the whole month of November as the temporal window for her conclusion of the exchange cycle; usually at the beginning of the month she holds almost no money, and during that month most of her customers pay for already commissioned production, thereby she replenishes her monetary reserve during November.

Say that Sally's great-granddaughter obtained allocated $500 000 by the arbiter of the exchange at the beginning of the exchange cycle, and that by the beginning of November she holds only $50 000. Happily, she starts receiving payments, until reaching $450 000 on her account by mid-month. Then appears a customer who pays her $75 000.

Thereat, the arbiter of the exchange will do the following, in sequence:

1. Split the transaction for $75 000 in two: one for $50 000 and another for $25 000.
2. Add the $50 000 to the $450 000 and conclude the exchange cycle of hard-working Sally's great-granddaughter.
3. Start a new exchange cycle for Sally's great-granddaughter, and thus allocate a new quantity of tools of exchange to her. She may obtain again $500 000, or she may obtain another amount –this described further in section [6.27] .

Say that she obtains $600 000 for the new exchange cycle.

4. Add the carried $25 000 to the freshly allocated $600 000 and consequently set her electronic account at $625 000.

Sally's great-granddaughter did nothing special, she just continued her normal activities, she will merely notice in the electronic records that a new exchange cycle just started for her, and she will see $625 000 on her account.

[6.21]

Completion of the Cycle by Making an Expense

During the next year, Sally's great-granddaughter obtains a lot of success in her business, and by the beginning of November she holds a much larger monetary reserve than her monetary target.

Therefore, she resolves to make some expenditures in new research equipment which she can utilize for developing new products, with the immediate goal of reaching her monetary target.

Say that Sally's great-granddaughter starts making large expenditures at the beginning of November, and by mid-month she reaches a reserve of $700 000. Then she resolves to pay $150 000 for the last piece of research equipment. Recall that she received allocated $600 000 at the start of the exchange cycle.

Thereat, the arbiter of the exchange will do the following, in sequence:

1. Split the transaction for $150 000 in two: one for $100 000 and another for $50 000.
2. Subtract $100 000 from the remaining $700 000 and conclude the exchange cycle of Sally's great-granddaughter.
3. Start a new exchange cycle for Sally's great-granddaughter, and thus allocate a new quantity of tools of exchange to her.
    Say that she obtains $800 000 for this new exchange cycle.
4. Subtract the remaining $50 000 from to the freshly allocated $800 000 and consequently set her account at $750 000.

Here again, Sally's great-granddaughter did nothing special, she just continued her normal activities while passing from one cycle into the next.

[6.22]

Thus, all the transition from one exchange cycle into another can happen fully automated by electronic means.

Corrective Actions Upon an Unaccomplished Monetary Equalization

[6.23]

If at the end of its asynchronous exchange cycle a participant retains more money than with which it started the cycle, then the state-organization must confiscate an amount equal to that accumulated in excess, and the state-organization must immediately make that money available to the participants in the exchange; either by merely spreading it among the participants, or by performing purchasing operations. If the exchange finishes simultaneously for all the participants, then the arbiter will discard the amount confiscated.

Additionally, the transgressor must receive a punishment to dissuade further disruptive behavior. In this regard, any pecuniary penalty –any fine– obtained from a participant, the state-organization can handle as an income within its own particular exchange cycle. Every fine must equal the sum of:

1. The expenses incurred by the state-organization because of the transgression.
2. A quantity proportional to the magnitude of the monetary fault.
3. Another quantity adjusted according to the particular conditions of the case.

In the case of money accumulated in excess by a participant, the state-organization can deduct a fine at the beginning of the participant's new exchange cycle, or otherwise can confiscate assets from the participant and sell those to pay the corresponding fine.

[6.24]

Conversely, if at the end of its exchange cycle a participant retains a smaller amount of money than with which it started the asynchronous exchange, the state-organization must fix the monetary discrepancy with charge to the participant. For this purpose the state-organization can confiscate assets in the participant's domain and sell them among the other participants in the exchange for collecting the missing money. Also in this case, when selling the confiscated assets, the state-organization can charge a pecuniary penalty.

If the participant lacked assets with which pay the debt with the cooperative system, then the societal cooperative system must oblige such participant to labor under the command of other human, or under the command of a productive organization different from any other to which previously belonged to, until the participant rehabilitates itself by paying the missing money and associated fine. Afterwards the state-organization can assign tools of exchange again to the participant –can allot money again to the person. An obvious escape from monetary rehabilitation consists in someone else paying the missing money and associated fine.

Thereupon, during the next exchange cycle or cycles the participant at fault must obtain its own welfare through labor under the command of a human acting as coach, or under the command of a productive organization, until furnishing the missing money and pecuniary penalty to the state-organization.

In a stepped asynchronous exchange someone else will hold the missing money, therefore that missing money results recoverable. However, if the exchange finishes simultaneously for all the participants, then the arbiter must write-off the missing money; in this latter case the associated pecuniary penalty must equal the quantity of missing money plus the corresponding fine.

[6.25]

The human or productive organization that takes an individual under its command for rehabilitation, herein denominated *monetary tutor*, must also manage the monetary expenses of such individual by using the own monetary tutor's money to pay for those. The aforementioned management because the human temporarily expelled from the asynchronous exchange lacks its own money.

This organizational setting creates the conditions for a new type of state-sponsored productive organizations, where people that cannot go anywhere else, or neither obtain a job nor create a place anywhere else, can find a productive occupation.

In any case, particular cooperative systems should not accept laborers in rehabilitation beyond a small percentage defined as ceiling, even those supplied by state-sponsored organizations acting as monetary tutors. Here proposed a maximum of 5% of the total workforce as laborers in rehabilitation, aiming to prevent both systematic abuses and the easy formation of bands of antisocial or predatory individuals.

Thus, by assigning monetary tutors and coaching individuals into a stable way of life, anyone can go into a monetary ruin, and get out of it.

[6.26]

To keep the stepped asynchronous exchange running smoothly, when a participant (or participants) becomes indebted with the cooperative system by an amount larger than that recoverable through one cycle of tutored labor, then the state-organization can retain some money obtained as income (from services provided, taxes, and so on) equal this money to the amount that the indebted individual (or individuals) will still need to repay after each cycle of tutored labor. And afterwards the state-organization can gradually make expenditures using that money, by the same quantities and at the same rate that the indebted individual or individuals should repay the money owed.

Hence, the state-organization can retain the surplus of money that circulates within the stepped asynchronous exchange and release it gradually, for the purpose of simplifying the monetary equalization of the regular participants.

The Quantity of Money Allocated to Each Adult Citizen

[6.27]

Adult citizens should place assets as guaranty for receiving money allocated by the societal cooperative system. Accordingly, the arbiter of the exchange should assign a quantity of money to each individual equal to or smaller than the largest of the following:

+ The monetary income expected in the case of selling all the assets which the participant placed as guaranty for the money received. A participant can also place assets as liability in favor of someone else. The assets committed therefore banned from sale. The social contract or another subsidiary regulation directly controlled by the people must define explicitly which types of assets a participant can place as guaranty –review [7.105] and subsequent sections for the proposal of direct democracy.

+ The monetary income from tutored labor during one exchange cycle, at the lowest legal wage.

In any case, assigning money according to an expected income –from a contract, for example– offers a favorable condition for fraud.

How to allocate money to a particular organization explained in [6.64] and subsequent sections.

[6.28]

Of course, the cooperative system must enact preventive measures and arrange organizational pathways whose effects tend to minimize the amount of money that any given individual may lose during one exchange cycle. The following specifications provide such effects:

- Establish a relatively small maximum cycle length. For example, six months for a fast exchange, one year for a regular one, and never two years or more.

- Actively intervene when someone unequivocally experiences hard times. Specifically, when someone suddenly loses its habitual source of income or an event disrupts the normal course of actions, the person may apply for unemployment benefits or social-welfare support, but must immediately return a fraction of the now-presumably-oversized amount of money previously allocated.

Savings

[6.29]

Accumulating material resources constitutes one of the practices useful for the survival of organisms, as recorded in section [2.2]. Here included a further description about how such accumulation of material resources happens.

[6.30]

All elements not belonging to an active living organism or self-keeping organization, or physical assets, or materials existent in the physical –aka real– world, tend to decay as time passes due to a series of ordinary phenomena until they reach a basal, in many cases useless state (for humans) within the environment.

For example, materials transit into states of minimal energy, substances either decompose or mix with others, microorganisms thrive bringing organic materials into basal states thereby collecting energy and material products. Therefrom metals rust, buildings fall, vessels leak, food rots, and so on.

Even in the case of metals that do not rust easily, like gold, these require devices and storage facilities suitable for their accumulation and safekeeping, and those devices and storage facilities do require maintenance.

Therefore, does not exist something akin to «maintenance-free savings» nor exist «savings unbound from maintenance»: All things stored or accumulated require direct and/or indirect maintenance and, in some cases, periodic replacement.

[6.31]

Furthermore, if a participant accumulates large amounts of tools of exchange as savings, and then during a relatively short time interval attempts to use all those tools of exchange for purchasing assets, products, or services, then such practice fosters instability of prices because it alters the habitual balance of offer and demand. In this way, a participant who holds very large amounts of tools of exchange can manipulate the prices of any targeted group of items according to its interests. Such antisocial practices usually produce deleterious effects in cooperative systems.

Likewise, a participant who accumulated very large amounts of tools of exchange can easily eliminate any small competitor by offering prices lower than the production costs until the competitor disappears.

In contrast, if all the participants accumulate their savings as assets or products, then any antisocial individual who accumulated large amounts of any kind may at most manipulate the prices of the specific items stored, and at such event any damage to the regular activities of the cooperative system happens mostly circumscribed to those sectors.

[6.32]

In a stable, fair, and prosperous exchange space, each participant must accumulate its own profits as assets (not as money) and in this circumstance each participant must enact or otherwise furnish the maintenance of its own savings.

For example, the participants in the exchange may purchase gold and silver bars, accumulate refined fuel, accumulate tools and spare parts for machinery, accumulate raw materials, and so forth.

Will arise a series of commercial establishments specialized in «solutions for saving in assets», and the arbiter of the commercial exchange must perform a special supervision to ensure that these warehouses keep an amount of assets equal to that declared to their customers –because, of course, the criminals called bankers will attempt to hide there. The people through the social contract must ban those warehouses from engaging in any other activity additional to safekeeping material assets, and from issuing any kind of exchangeable certificates over stored assets.

Anyone who dares to use rights over assets or uses anything else as a payment promise, or transfers the ownership of any kind of debt, must spend a lengthy term in jail without parole.

[6.33]

Storing real savings and affording their maintenance should discourage individuals from hoarding –and by extension, from earning– profits disproportionately larger than what they need for real life.

Although people will still hoard fixed (Earth-bound) nonperishable assets, such as parcels of land, usually cooperative systems charge recurrent taxes for them; these taxes due to the fact that the cooperative system also requires an income akin to maintenance in order to keep running the state-organization and thereby secure the continuance of the cooperative system from which it arises. If the state-organization collapsed and the cooperative system dissolved, the «proprietor» of such assets would need to undertake the defense of those by itself. Thus, even in the case of fixed nonperishable assets, the depredation among humans makes indispensable a recurrent expense for their maintenance.

Insurance for Assets

[6.34]

Anyone can engage in the private business of providing «monetary insurance for damaged or lost assets», though the insurance-providing organizations presumably will find convenient to refine their cash-flow statistical forecasts and pay large insured amounts in parcels through several exchange cycles.

Destroying Circuits of Unproductive Transference of Money

[6.35]

The sole –and large– disadvantage of a stepped conclusion of an exchange cycle compared with a simultaneous conclusion, consists in the possibility of establishing circuits of transference of money as a way to hoard money among a group of participants.

The circuits of transference of money would also serve to inflate any supposed income of a participant during any given exchange cycle; therefrom, allocating a quantity of money proportional to the income obtained by a participant during any previous exchange cycle would constitute an ideal condition for criminal activities. In section [6.27] already discarded the possibility of using someone's income as input data for the process of allocation of money.

Hence, a stepped asynchronous exchange requires an organizational framework aimed to destroy circuits of unproductive transference of money.

[6.36]

Hoarding money within a circuit or cartel of participants can happen as follows:

1. Some participant A earns more money than what spends.
2. Participant A buys a fake service or product from participant B and thereby transfers its surplus of money to B. The exchange cycle of participant B finishes at a time later than the cycle of A.
3. The exchange cycle of A finishes with the participant reporting no money hoarded.
4. Participant B buys a fake service or product from participant A, thereby returning the hoarded money to A.
5. The exchange cycle of B finishes with the participant reporting no money hoarded.
6. Participants A and B repeat the routine of fraud.

This sequence illustrates how simple the fraud can happen, although most real-life cheaters would try to make it meshed and entangled when attempting to disguise it. Besides or instead of using fake services or products, the criminals could also merely inflate ordinary prices of any items –compared with the prices they would bargain if they exchanged outside the criminal cartel.

[6.37]

Charging ordinary taxes constitutes the most straightforward way to hinder and turn unprofitable the practice of hoarding money through circuits of unproductive transference of money.

For every transference of money, the participant that delivers it must pay a quantity equal to 15% of the amount transferred, as tax on monetary expenses. No exceptions for *charitable expenses*, nor for *tax-deductible expenses*. If anyone wants to make a tax-exempt donation, then stick to the real world: donate a physical item, or perform a real service, or allocate money for expenses as described in [6.39]; otherwise pay taxes.

In contemporary societies, ordinary commercial operations –those which exchange actual products and services– usually obtain a profitability of 15% or more, and currently in many jurisdictions particular cooperative systems collect taxes on behalf of the state-organization equal to about 15% (or more) of the monetary-flow of every commercial operation. Thus, collecting 15% (or more) of the magnitude of every commercial operation already happens and proceeds in an organizationally sustainable fashion.

In any case, the people through the social contract can specify a larger tax on monetary expenses.

[6.38]

A 20% tax on monetary expenses would produce a faster depletion of the unproductively hoarded money. With a 20% tax, any aspiring criminals at the fifth year of their «enterprise» would retain only approximately 40% of the unproductively hoarded money, whilst with a 15% tax they would retain approximately 50% of the same original amount. The following graph serves for comparison.

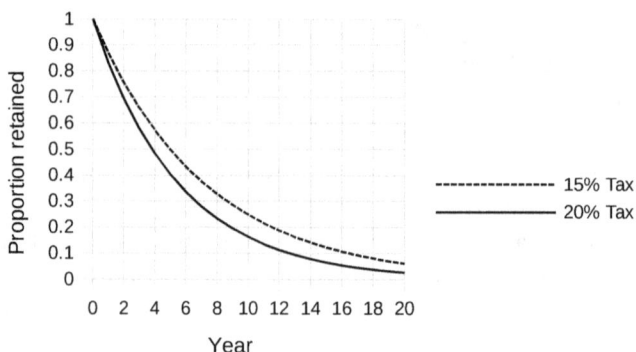

Figure 3. Tax on unproductive monetary expenses.

Family Expenses

[6.39]

The usage of electronic data devices provides also a very convenient solution for household needs. Thus, using electronic data devices an individual who obtains a monetary income could easily distribute money for family expenses through any kind of authentication mechanism given to family members who routinely make purchases. And thereby such money distributed does not account as a transference subject to taxes. Naturally, both partners in a matrimony could pool their income.

For example, a housekeeping partner could receive a card with an electronic chip, and use this card as authentication mechanism to make monetary expenses which deduct from the account of the income-receiving partner; the same for the offspring.

Regime of Domain Over Assets

[6.40]

Capitalistic theories about money, commercial exchanges, and production processes spring from magical thinking. In contrast, the modern conceptions about property proceed from a long sequence of authoritarian culture, which started upon the emergence of the first civilizations. In the «western» civilization, the last two links of this authoritarian culture and associated conceptions about property consist of those conceptual constructs about property corresponding to the Middle Ages, and those corresponding to the modern criminal venture called *capitalism*. Meanwhile, some civilizations which play toxic, backwards, and peripheral roles for the advancement of humanity –like the autocratic Middle-East countries, and fascist Russia– still carry even more primitive authoritarian constructs.

In the context described in [4.35] and subsequent sections, medieval privileged social classes crafted the modern conceptions about property as an adaptation of the previous authoritarian culture. This happened when those privileged social classes transited into an environment of human exploitation where resulted indispensable to dismiss enslaved workers while at the same time new industries required new subordinated labor.

From this deliberated transformation of human exploitation processes arose both the modern conception of individual granted *freedom* and the modern conceptions about property.

Recall from section [2.34] the exaggeration of the perceived freedom in modern democratic societies, such exaggeration became implanted in the shared culture at the aforementioned transformation of human exploitation processes.

[6.41]

The transition of regimes of slavery and bondage into granted *freedom* and (at least some) private property in many instances happened primarily due to a desire of the privileged and ruling humans to increase their income by means of increasing the productivity of feudal agricultural enterprises –like manors– and other basic industries such as mining.

In this subset of cases, the ruling humans aspired to increase the productivity of those feudal industries in their domain, and the profits thereof obtained, for—

α. Acquiring much of the output of the incipiently-modern, nascent industries without diminishing their living standards. Accordingly, due to a desire to increase their welfare and luxury.

β. Retaining their status as elite, which now stood under the threat of becoming fully obsolete, especially when competitors in foreign countries could achieve greater productive outputs at lower costs, which would leave them in a vulnerable position.

The managed transition from slavery and bondage into granted *freedom* and private property produced a basal increase of productivity because wage-based laborers perform more efficiently, even without the immediate introduction of significant technological improvements. Wage-based laborers perform more efficiently than slaves and bounded laborers chiefly because they obtain a materially unfixed reward for their work which they can now spend volitionally; thus, not only the increased welfare due to the control of their own destinies contributes, but also an enhanced satisfaction of their basic psychological needs.

Likewise, if given the opportunity, many autonomous peasants excel for the purpose of retaining a portion of the increased output for themselves, thereby increasing their welfare. Hence, in many formerly-rigid agricultural instances, old feudal lords transformed into landlords and thereafter focused on leasing the land.

Furthermore, the rise of the capitalistic stealing scheme shifted the essential organizational mechanisms for retaining a privileged position from direct physical control into indirect stealing. The aforementioned agricultural elites experienced the effects of this shift by the gradual erosion of their social standing, and merely reacted to those events.

[6.42]

In [7.49] and subsequent sections described further such transformation of the human exploitation processes, the passage into regimes of individual granted *freedom*, and the largely faked democracy in «western» countries. In this chapter, in the immediately subsequent sections described the current human exploitation processes directed to obtain material profits.

[6.43]

As described in section [5.12], inside the exchange space built upon the criminal venture called *capitalism*, exist a series of «prosperity islands» or nations favored by the current world-wide commerce.

Within these «prosperity islands», millions of humans who produce and provide relatively few raw materials, products, and services routinely squander disproportionally large amounts of those and, therefrom, squander large amounts of the Earth's natural resources. The most obvious example of this type of squandering consists of the United States of America from the second half of the XX century until at least the time of this writing; as mentioned in section [1.1].

The fully authoritarian counterpart of this squandering of resources consists of fascist Russia. The fascist russians embrace a much more straightforward centuries-old brutal imperialism through which they target other people for destruction, exploitation, and displacement in order to accumulate natural resources; in this regard, the russians behave either indifferent or averse to any concept of humankind. Serve the fascist russians as comparison, although the origin and patterns of their socially-harmful behavior differ in many aspects.

[6.44]

The accumulation of income inside «prosperity islands» happens through the application of modern imperial-domination schemes which originated in the organizational mechanisms of colonial exploitation developed by european nations and applied upon all the countries invaded by rapacious european encroachers. Hence, the accumulation of income inside «prosperity islands» constitutes the continuation and evolution of a centuries-old status-quo. In this refurbished status-quo the capitalistic banks and associated corporations play a fundamental and essential role, usually in collusion with local supporting elites.

[6.45]

As introduced in section [4.36], the practices enacted by europeans for advancing their colonial expansion typically comprised three main tactics regarding the fate of the non-european people, broadly:

α.   Straightforward genocides. For example, the european invaders in North America, Australia, and Argentina.

β.   Regimes of either explicit or factual slavery and bondage upon the subjugated people, combined with the extraction of natural resources and mostly agricultural products. These regimes geared towards obtaining the maximum amount of profits from the territory and the enslaved labor; and in many cases the invaders merely took what they wanted and left the rest as stock or reserve of human and material resources ready to take and exploit when needed. For example, the european invaders in Central and South America.

γ.   Regimes of artificial disadvantages towards the colonized, geared towards extracting profits from those subdued while driving them into pauperism. For example, the british colonial regime in India and the Apartheid in South Africa.

Usually the european invaders combined genocide, slavery, bondage, and systemic racism in diverse scales, intensities, and styles. Since genocidal endeavors erased the corresponding victims from any commercial exchange, thereafter only the social arrangements of slavery, bondage, and artificial disadvantages –which in time evolved into granted *freedom* and faked inclusivity– played a role in the historical outcome of the «western» civilization.

Within the «western» civilization never happened any relevant accountability because of the genocide and exploitation of several nations. For example, hitherto rarely some country furnished a compensation to the descendants of enslaved and exploited people, or returned stolen objects to their ancestral owners; practically no european voluntarily vacated an invaded land. Instead, in some «western» countries from time to time happen efforts to either justify or deny the history colonialism and genocide.

[6.46]

The regimes of colonial dominion and exploitation constituted an expansion of the authoritarian social relationships established within ordinary societies in the european Later Middle Ages, typical of the political schemes of monarchies and fiefdoms.

In the case of the fiefdoms, authoritarian individuals consider that the land and its inhabitants belong to the *feudal lord*, as property and vassals; and that all the utilities obtained in that region belong to the «proprietor» of those lands, who also constitutes the «proprietor» of the labor of those humans –of either full-time or just partial-time tributary compulsory labor. In this social arrangement, the fiefdom constitutes a type of regime of simple slavery.

Organizationally, the fiefdom constitutes a human cooperative system, wherefrom became further popularized a mind-set postulate which causes people to regard as normal and socially acceptable that a human or group of humans legitimately appropriate for themselves the profits from a human cooperative system. The aforesaid mind-set postulate typically supports or sets the predominant cognitive pattern for outcomes favorable to humans regarded as «privileged» or «entitled» by other auxiliary parts of the culture. These cultural patterns already described in [4.75] and subsequent sections for the case of the parasitic psychopathic subspecies.

[6.47]

In this way, many humans regard the depredation and exploitation of entire nations as «legitimate» because some «entitled» humans hold the «rights» of exploitation of those cooperative systems.

With the rise of the industrial and commercial expansion at the beginning of the modern times, as recorded in sections [6.40] and [6.41], the involved humans transformed the notion of «legitimate rights» of exploitation and depredation of whole cooperative systems to fit in the context of mercantile organizations. Those mercantile organizations thereafter explicitly called *capitalistic corporations*.

[6.48]

In all cases, expressly in the fiefdom, the colony, and the corporation, the defenders of the status-quo assert as argument –using the social contract as foundation– that some «entitled» humans:

1. Hold the «rights» over the assets of the cooperative system.
2. Hold an exclusive «right» to make arbitrary choices over that cooperative system.

In other words, the defenders of the status-quo proclaim that the assets of any given human cooperative system, and the cooperative system itself, belong to the personal domain of «entitled» individuals, and that those individuals can arrange and decide upon the cooperative system and its assets as they want.

And therefrom, in a leap, those same defenders of the status-quo assert that the «entitled» humans can obtain for themselves the profits generated using assets within a cooperative system.

[6.49]

The regime of corporate property associated to the criminal venture called *capitalism* constitutes the last refuge of slavery in modern societies and thus, by far, the most retrograde and anachronistic element of such unfair social arrangement. Hence, forward-going humans must implacably eradicate the capitalistic regime of corporate property, with the same ruthlessness with which their ancestors deprived monarchs from centuries-old command posts and privileges.

In the conception of the autocrats, a human cooperative system results «*my* kingdom», «*my* fiefdom», «*my* corporation»; but no more.

[6.50]

Certain humans solved such ancient problem by previous efforts, and probably different humans solved it several times again and again, though people did not recognize the solution or lacked the capacity to comprehend it; now in what follows the solution stated again.

[6.51]

Circa 110 years ago, in a region called *Morelos* approximately 40 kilometers south from the mexican capital, mexican peasants assembled an armed uprising against yet another fundamentally colonial social scheme where many of them lived factually enslaved by quasi-colonial enterprises and those who either escaped or avoided enslavement lived in autochthonous communities dealing with a constant loss of land in favor of those quasi-colonial enterprises.

The scheme against these peasants constituted only a subset of the whole quasi-colony, where several types of subjugation and exploitation methods coexisted against the almost illiterate population.

The case further noteworthy because:

a)   Formally, mexicans achieved independence from their former colonial invaders one century before those events.

b)   The people that promoted, maintained, and profited from a fundamentally colonial social scheme consisted largely of the descendants of the former colonial invaders, those who even at the time of this writing espouse a systemic racism and pretended supremacy against whatever they may call «native-american», «indian», or «indigenous».

As always, the historical records of the era contain data consistent with a full support and collaboration of the members of the parasitic psychopathic subspecies with the traitors and their authoritarian project.

[6.52]

Accordingly, at the dawn of the XX century, about one century after formally attaining the national independence, mexicans fully repeated a traditional colonial way of life and they themselves worsened it with:

- Capitalistic practices, along with the control and extraction of mineral resources by foreign capitalistic corporations.
- Large, expensive, and explicit efforts to copy a facade of a european culture.

- Relinquishment of national territory instead of spending resources to keep or develop it and perhaps losing a war, like happened with the northern more-than-half of the territory lost.
- Faster, more effective ethnic cleansing –genocidal– campaigns within the country.

In the vision of the traitors, all these modifications constituted «enhancements». Against that mixture of the worst of everything the aforementioned malnourished peasants assembled their uprising, in the context of the mexican «revolution» of those years.

[6.53]

The peasants, or at least some of them, understood clearly the root cause of their local problems; they understood the essence of their exploitation. Specifically, the peasants understood that the neo-colonial elites always claimed the productive assets and the obtained output as their property –in this case the assets mostly land.

Thereupon, in an act of intellectual brilliance the peasants, with some few individuals who aided them, synthesized the solution in a single slogan:

«The land belongs to those who work it with their own hands.»

I will translate this peasant brilliance into general organizational terms, just adding the implicit productive output in the peasant version:

The assets and output of a cooperative system belong to those humans who actually work in it.

[6.54]

The solution could not become visible to the apprehension of the mind in more simple and straightforward terms.

To those peasants I owe the understanding of how to eliminate a cornerstone of centuries or thousands of years of destructive human exploitation. Most of them perished by a brutal assassination campaign and a scorched-earth policy.

[6.55]

Yet, incapable of thinking in productive terms, mexicans—

α. Established a «communal» property of land assigned to tribal communities: one static world outlasted another inhumane.

β. Repeated the slogan like parrots during decades without understanding its underlying meaning, and one century later a vast majority of mexicans completely forgot those words.

[6.56]

The variability of the human *executive functions* and the distinct sets of available mental functions for each individual, render unfeasible to directly establish something akin to equality among all the *Homo sapiens* individuals within the organizations (human cooperative systems) inside the exchange space.

Instead, herein proposed a transformation without immediately disrupting the traditional organizational ways of the *Homo sapiens*. This transformation particularly aimed to draw humans lacking a conscience with them perceiving a minimal organizational shift and thus skipping large indoctrination efforts directed towards those individuals.

Therefrom, the individuals entitled as «owners» of current organizations must write a *particular organizational social contract* that will supersede any legal «incorporation act» –recall section [2.32]– and, likewise, will supersede any legal title or claim of «ownership». The individuals entitled as «owners» must write such particular social contract according to their interests, but excluding any concept of *ownership*.

Consequently, the particular social contract will not contain the concepts of *shareholder, stockholder, corporate shares, corporate ownership*, and every other akin. Yet, the particular organizational social contract can include, for example:

- That only the members of the «dynastic family» or «control group» can occupy and perform the command posts, and/or that they can inherit those same posts to their own kin.
- That the distribution of the organization's profits proceeds in a way disproportionately favorable to the «dynastic» workers.
- That only those «dynastic» workers can modify the particular social contract (as long as its reformed content complies with the population-wide social contract).

[6.57]

Thenceforth will not exist any *shareholders* or alike positions, and nobody –no one– will ever sell or buy the «ownership» of a human cooperative system in a structured exchange space as the so-called «stock exchanges» as if exchanging indentured laborers or slaves; and only those who work or toil in an organization will hold a legitimate right to receive profits distributed by the organization.

[6.58]

Human organizations belong to those who directly labor in them; the sole exception consists of the state-organization which belongs to every citizen, and in that case the citizens ordinarily must perform civic duties and furnish material income that contribute to the welfare of the social organization.

For this regime of domain over particular cooperative systems (and the corresponding assets) to function, of course, the societal cooperative system must eliminate any fissure which antisocial and parasitic individuals may employ. Specifically, the people through the social contract must restrict the maximum number of organizations to which any given participant of the exchange can belong or hold a membership into and receive profits from.

Here proposed that an individual can participate in maximum 12 (twelve) human organizations and receive something from those. For example, assuming an extremely hard-working individual who devotes twelve hours of its day to toil, and that yet performs any substantial activity in each organization, the person should –out of usual human performance– devote at least one hour daily to each organization. Therefrom, 12 (twelve) memberships results a fair and reasonable limit for a very tireless human. In any case, anyone can easily verify in real-world settings that nobody –no human– can simultaneously belong to more than 12 (twelve) human organizations and still proclaim that performs any relevant activity in each one of those.

The state-organization must maintain a publicly accessible and searchable database enumerating the organizational affiliations of each citizen.

Lease of Assets

[6.59]

The social contract must include an organizational constraint regarding the lending of assets in the asynchronous-exchange space, which complements the just described regime of domain over assets and cooperative systems:

A participant in the asynchronous exchange can lend an asset to another participant, but the rent or cost of this lease must consist of a fixed amount or a fixed compensation of any kind; in no case the lender will lawfully subtract from the borrower a toll or an income related with any activity that the borrower performs employing the lent asset. The same rule must apply for any lent item regardless of whether the participants consider it an asset or not.

[6.60]

In other words: The people through the social contract must categorically prohibit to obtain an income from the work performed by a human utilizing assets or items in the domain of an individual or group of individuals different to the one that performs the work.

Therefrom, the compensation –monetary or any other– paid for a lent item cannot vary contractually using as input any «index» or numerical variable. Thus, if a lender wants to modify the compensation demanded for lending an item, then it must wait until the current contract finishes, and the borrower will not stand obliged to accept any new modified contract.

[6.61]

Likewise, the people through the social contract must prohibit usury or the practice of charging a compensation for lending money (as if the money constituted an asset); and those who dare to do it must spend time in jail without parole.

Notice that the prohibition of usury neither directly stems from nor equals the prohibition of obtaining an income related with any activity that a borrower performs employing a lent asset.

[6.62]

And remember that, according to section [6.32], a lender cannot transfer the ownership of any kind of debt –monetary, in physical deliverables, or in services– into another individual and therefore cannot exchange the title of a debt, or lent item, as a payment promise.

[6.63]

The elimination of these three pernicious activities –extracting a rent from the work done using lent assets, usury, and transferring the ownership of debts– completes the destruction of a cornerstone of feudal, colonial, and capitalistic corporate schemes; and will certainly produce a more prosperous and fair human world.

Allocating Tools of Exchange to Subsidiary Cooperative Systems

[6.64]

As a prerequisite for becoming member of a human organization inside the exchange space, a human must reside within the respective societal cooperative system and, of course, must regularly furnish the corresponding contributions to the latter.

[6.65]

In this context, when formally establishing and starting a particular cooperative system, the founders may—

a) Pay collectively for specific organizational expenses, as an electronic *crowdfunding* using money from their personal allotments. The seller will see multiple inputs.

Additionally, each founder can list the private organization as a *monetary dependent* –as with family expenses– and thereby can authorize the organization to make periodic expenditures from its personal account up to a predefined ceiling.

b) Place personal assets as guaranty in favor of the organization, for this latter to obtain money allocated to itself.

c) Transfer personal assets into the private organization; then the organization may directly use those assets as guaranty to obtain money allocated to itself.

Of course, once the organization generates some profits and accumulates those as assets, the organization may use those same assets as guaranty to obtain larger allocations of money.

[6.66]

The members of the organization, without exceptions or privileges, will answer for whatever deficit, or surplus, of money incurred by the organization at the end of each exchange cycle whenever it lacks resources to pay for such deficit and corresponding pecuniary penalty. Thereat, the members of a broken or insolvent organization will answer for the outstanding monetary liabilities by an amount proportional to the personal income –monetary, or in assets, or any other– transferred to each one of them since the beginning of the organization's activities or, alternatively, during the last five years before the disaster.

The participants in the exchange should find the requirement of proportional solidarity upon failure as an incentive for joining only private organizations which perform transparent accounting practices. Likewise, people should refrain from joining organizations commanded by unreliable or incompetent individuals, as they themselves may end up paying a share of the costs of the wreckage.

Moreover, the requirement of proportional solidarity upon failure constitutes an indispensable provision for—

- Avoiding abusive social contracts where the commanders or the «dynastic» workers transfer all the liabilities upon the members of lower ranks.
- Preventing low-rank individuals from avoiding accountability for their own actions, no matter if those happened within the context of a command chain –commands they chose to enact.

[6.67]

The choice-making and accounting procedures of a particular cooperative system must exist codified in its social contract or in auxiliary organizational documents, and all the current and prospective members of the organization must hold an updated copy of these latter. Besides, the main accounting variables of the organization must stand available to any member at any time without an explicit request.

Therefore, the necessary data for assessing the quality, nature, and effectiveness of the organizational conditions and performance must stand available to any member of a private organization.

[6.68]

The shared organizational accountability upon failure, together with mandatory internal transparency, should promote an increased participation of all the members in the organizational choices.

In an advanced society results unsustainable and unacceptable to—

α. Hold into someone else for that person to make the correct choices regarding one's life in normal circumstances.

β. Evade accountability for one's own actions under the excuse that those arose from «orders received».

Every person must answer for each «order» enacted: Each person physically commands its own directed corporal actions, hence *following* or enacting an «order» constitutes an act arising from an intrinsic, inalienable volition and, consequently, performing an «order received» qualifies as a personal choice which entails accountability.

One must answer for one's own choices, does not matter if one chose to *follow* «orders» –does not matter if one chose to perform organizational instructions.

If someone attempts to enslave or direct a person by coercion, and the person does not agree, a fight for freedom always ensues; in this case again *following* «orders» constitutes a volitional act, just as fighting for freedom constitutes another one; the person chooses its own path.

This explicit shift in personal accountability will also prop and strengthen the social environment which arises from the reform of democracy proposed in the last chapter of this document.

Trade with Foreign Cooperative Systems

[6.69]

Most ordinary activities of a human society happen within the spatial limits of the corresponding cooperative system. The state-organization which arises from a society regularly acts within the aforesaid limits, as the social contract prescribes it –extraterritorial legal state activities usually comprise only those related with defense and diplomatic purposes. Therefrom, the state-organization must control the transit through the limits of the societal cooperative system as part of its basic functions.

[6.70]

The limits of a terrestrial societal cooperative system consist of:

- Terrestrial-surface geographic limits (including oceans), in many cases adjacent to other societal cooperative systems. These form a perimeter which serves as basis for calculating the other limits.
- Spatial limits, either legal or just factual, at the Earth's outer crust; the societal activities cease anywhere from the outermost layer until some kilometers downward in direction of the Earth's center.
- Spatial limits at the Earth's atmosphere, also either legal or just factual, upwards from the surface.

Typically, the outmost legal limits of the exchange space coincide, or almost coincide, with the spatial limits of the whole societal cooperative system which contains it.

[6.71]

Accordingly, at the limits of the societal cooperative system the state-organization must act as the sole and exclusive intermediary for the transit of resources to and from the asynchronous-exchange space, particularly in operations of commercial exchange with other cooperative systems. Such function of intermediary sometimes consists simply in checking the items that traverse the borders.

[6.72]

For preventing traitors from succeeding, and for thwarting any colonial attempt, the only resources that citizens and legal residents may extract from the societal cooperative system consist of:

- Those items destined to sale operations –in terms described in the immediately subsequent sections.
- Personal-usage items that travelers may transport as part of their luggage, typically already explicitly regulated by modern legal frameworks. Additionally, household items when a citizen temporarily emigrates from the societal cooperative system, and the items required in special events and for adventures.
- All the items in the personal domain of an individual who renounces the citizenship and exits through the border.

Must stand categorically banned to extract any other resource from the societal cooperative system.

[6.73]

The state-organization must establish minimum compensations for items sold abroad, or otherwise sold and delivered to foreign customers. Of course, must stand banned the extraction of resources scarce within the societal cooperative system, except in those individually examined cases where causes of strategic partnership, defense, or warfare justify it; the population-wide social contract must include procedures for these cases.

The citizens may find additionally useful to prescribe jail terms for the transgressors of these organizational dispositions.

[6.74]

For achieving minimum compensations for resources extracted, the state-organization must require, as counterpart, maximum compensations for resources imported into the societal cooperative system. Otherwise, someone could recurrently purchase abroad some product or service at an artificially inflated price, thus producing a loss for the societal cooperative system.

Therefrom, the state-organization must establish both:

- Minimum compensations that an exporter (seller) must obtain for resources extracted from the societal cooperative system, this in the form of minimum selling prices in local currency. These minimum compensations must equal the highest of the following:

  + The production costs plus a 20% profit margin –or another profit margin established by the people in the social contract for this purpose.

  + The average selling price for those items in the local exchange space plus a 20% additional cost.

  Thereat, a seller must publicly offer by retail –in small quantities– inside the local exchange space those same items that may export, with a selling price lower than the price offered to the exterior.

- Maximum compensations that an importer (buyer) may pay for resources introduced to the societal cooperative system, this in the form of maximum purchasing prices in local currency. When an analog or equal item exists readily available for sale in the inner exchange space, the maximum compensation which an importer may pay for the foreign item must equal 70% of the local average price –or another margin established in the population-wide social contract for this purpose. If the foreign item lacks a local counterpart then will proceed what described in section [6.76].

The merchants must obtain the payment of a foreign buyer before extracting physical items, or otherwise become accountable for any loss.

[6.75]

Therefore, for arithmetic purposes, the state-organization must calculate and establish monetary exchange rates between the money in the asynchronous exchange and several brands of foreign money –in current times two or three brands of foreign money would suffice. For setting these reference exchange rates the prices of a group of selected items can serve for comparison; those selected items as standardized as possible, and statistically significant percentages of the foreign populations must regularly exchange them.

More items that fulfill the requisites will produce a better average –but never forget that such ratio just constitutes an approximation to a very simplified reality.

[6.76]

If the foreign item lacked a counterpart or equivalent available for sale in the inner exchange space, and therefore the state-organization lacked an indigenous benchmark for setting maximum compensations for imported products, then the state-organization must:

1. Publish the description of the item in a searchable database available to all the citizens as described in section [6.81].

2. Forward the description of the item to every public research organization. The research organizations specialized in the field must answer with:

    i. A technical study detailing an approximate cost of—
       + Developing such product or service.
       + Establishing a minimal production chain for it.
    ii. A general description about how to reach the aforesaid goals.

    Public research organizations must neither produce nor distribute complete «recipes», but only the indispensable basic knowledge for achieving industrial goals; and thereupon the citizens and private organizations must develop and hone their own technology. Research organizations must likewise publish these documents in the database described in section [6.81].

    If the basic knowledge indispensable for the development and production of the foreign item comprised confidential data or non-publicly-available know-how, then the public research organizations must refrain from detailing and disclosing such advantageous knowledge, and instead must clearly indicate which information omitted and establish a non-exclusive selling or licensing price for it as part of an advisory service.

3. Conduct research in those foreign lands where someone manufactures or performs such item, and retrieve data about:
   i. Its production costs, to the extent possible.
   ii. The average selling prices of the item within those foreign exchange spaces.
   All public research organizations must also receive this data.

Then the maximum price for a non-locally available foreign product or service will equal the average foreign selling price.

If the foreign item results a rarity or a unique piece and for that reason the state-organization cannot determine an average selling price, then the buyer will write an explanatory document stating why this product affords a useful outcome for the societal cooperative system; and a specialized council will either approve or deny such purchase, after which the resolution also will become available to all the citizens in the aforementioned public database.

Notice that such purchases proceed independently of those made as part of foreign travel expenses for exploration, leisure, or recreation; these latter contemplated in section [6.86].

[6.77]

The people through the social contract must prohibit the individual citizens from extracting the tools of exchange of the asynchronous exchange from the boundaries of the societal cooperative system and, conversely, must stand banned the entrance and circulation of foreign tools of exchange.

In this context, the state-organization must act as intermediary to receive payments in foreign money for products sold in the exterior. The seller then leaves deposited (in the state-organization) the income received, and may thereupon exercise two options:

1. Use that foreign money for purchases in the exterior, while fulfilling the foreign-commerce regulations. Then import those items into the societal cooperative system.

2. Wait until another participant in the asynchronous exchange wants to purchase and import foreign articles using foreign money. Then the participant who left deposited foreign money in the state-organization will receive in exchange the money (of the asynchronous exchange) which the second participant delivers in exchange for foreign items purchased.

[6.78]

The population-wide social contract or some other ordinance directly controlled by the people must specify the maximum amount of foreign currency that a participant can leave deposited in the state-organization. Here proposed a maximum of foreign money equal –using the arithmetic *exchange rate*– to a quarter of the societal money allocated to the participant of the asynchronous exchange.

The members of a private organization within the exchange space will share the accountability for foreign money in the case that the organization cannot fulfill its commitments with the societal cooperative system, in the same way as with the money of the asynchronous exchange, as already described in section [6.66].

[6.79]

Then the members of the cooperative system can enact two internal mechanisms for an agile exchange with the exterior:

1. An exporter and an importer together, or a group of those, can communicate the state-organization that they want to balance the sales of the first with the purchases of the second, according to the regulations of minimum and maximum compensations. This case yields as advantage that the seller neither needs to join a *waiting list* nor exposes its profits to any unnecessary, undesirable event while waiting to obtain the income from the sale.

2. In the case that a seller (exporter), for obtaining the income from the sale, chooses to wait until another participant desires to execute foreign purchases; then the state-organization can sell the foreign money by public auction and by small parcels among the participants of the asynchronous exchange.

    Using electronic data devices, for example, an internet website can perform an automated and impartial auction process, where each buyer:

    α. Selects the classification of the items which wants to acquire, inputs the corresponding quantity and purchasing price, and thereat obtains clearance related to the maximum compensations for imports.

    β. Once authorized the import, places a bid for the requested foreign money previous to the closing time of the auction;

the bids and amounts must stand publicly visible thus enabling anyone to observe them. A bid must not imply a lower exchange rate than the one calculated by the state-organization as described in section [6.75], and should not exist a minimum amount for each bid.

The state-organization will continue to hold the foreign money. Must proceed an auction for each individual export operation that deposited foreign money.

Each bid must consist in a maximum price that the bidder wishes to pay for a specific amount of foreign money; and all the buyers at any single auction must acquire the foreign money at the same price per unit –at the same exchange rate. Therefore, an automated balancing can proceed as follows:

α.   Allocate the lot among bids starting with the higher ones, until allocating all the foreign money available.

β.   Sell the foreign money at the price of the last assigned bid, namely, the lowest one.

The buyer of each parcel of money then assumes the accountability for any variation of foreign prices.

[6.80]

If the average prices of foreign articles increase to such extent that the deposited foreign money results certainly insufficient for acquiring items that compensate for those extracted (according to the arithmetic exchange rates), then the exporter may choose one of two paths:

1.   Wait until the foreign average prices decrease, thus requesting that the state-organization *freezes* the deposited foreign money, and remain banned from performing exchanges with the exterior while that happens.

2.   Discharge the liability because of the failure and loss by:

α.   Paying a pecuniary punishment –a fine– twice the production cost or twice the average selling price of the lost items, whatever higher.

β.   Forfeiting the foreign money in favor of the state-organization.

γ.   Remaining banned from performing exchanges with the exterior during 5 years. Here assumed 5 years of punishment as enough to discourage unnecessary boldness.

This organizational regulation will—

1. Encourage the participants to plan beforehand and then perform foreign sales and purchases at once.

2. Strongly discourage doing business with unstable foreign cooperative systems, for which cases the sellers will need to set large prices to allocate large quantities of collected foreign money as a hedge.

3. Constitute an incentive to accept assets as payment –like precious metals– or foreign money from sources well-known as stable, instead of accepting money from precarious exchange spaces.

[6.81]

Finally, the state-organization must—

+ Establish a specialized department engaged in analyzing and approving (or denying) foreign marketing and promotional expenses, since those may produce profitable returns, or involve a squander of resources, or both.

+ Publish all the data and decisions concerning foreign commerce in a publicly searchable database available to all the citizens without delay and without explicit request. This data includes the details of each transaction. Thereby, any vigilant citizen or group of citizens can quickly identify any anomaly.

By using electronic data equipment humans can very efficiently accomplish these tasks. More about transparency of the state-organization recorded in [7.132] and subsequent sections.

[6.82]

No dispositions made for cycling purchases and sales of foreign items in foreign lands, since those would enable anyone to speculate with foreign items in foreign lands –and, yet again, seek to make a living without producing anything useful.

In the same regard, no dispositions made for allowing the establishment of «foreign branches» of particular cooperative systems from the asynchronous exchange; this constitutes a particularly relevant organizational vacuum since the asynchronous exchange here proposed aims to end –or push towards the end of– a millennial culture of human exploitation.

If a societal cooperative system performing an asynchronous exchange finds another akin, then a fusion or integration should ensue. A proposal for that recorded in [7.162] and subsequent sections.

In other words: *We* will not colonize *them*, and *they* will not colonize *us*. Rather, we can integrate into a single society as equal humans.

[6.83]

The informational framework indispensable for standardizing minimum and maximum prices of foreign items already exists well-developed in countries with modern tax and customs regulations. Specifically, already exist detailed industrial classifications.

[6.84]

The organizational mechanism for foreign commercial exchanges secures a balance of payments and precludes the existence of any debt in foreign money in which the participants of the exchange space could otherwise incur.

Consistently, the social contract must categorically forbid the state-organization from borrowing any type of foreign tools of exchange; and if any traitor within the state-organization commits its society in such scheme, then the ensuing judicial procedure must nullify those agreements and the traitor must spend time in jail.

[6.85]

Outstandingly, the mechanism for foreign commercial exchanges compels to an organic growth within the societal cooperative system: the citizens must produce articles and services desirable to foreign buyers, and there exists neither foreign «investment» nor foreign organizations that may arrive to «rescue» inept people. More about the organic growth recorded in [6.103] and subsequent sections.

Foreign Travel for Exploration, Leisure, or Recreation

[6.86]

A societal cooperative system cannot feasibly ensure the payment of adequate maximum compensations for expenses during foreign trips for exploration, leisure, or recreation, since many of those may involve activities outside any regular or functioning foreign cooperative system.

For that reason, in my opinion, the best option consists in allowing, for each citizen and its monetary dependents, a yearly expenditure of an amount of foreign money equal –using the arithmetic exchange rate– to the maximum of the following two options:

α. A percentage of the last annual contribution paid as taxes.

β. A fixed minimum amount determined by the people in the social contract.

Then each citizen and its monetary dependents (each family) can spend that amount of money in foreign lands without accountability.

The Procurement, Basic Preparation, and Distribution of Natural Resources

[6.87]

Only by securing an equal access, without minimum purchasing amounts, to the underground natural resources available to the societal cooperative system, the participants of the exchange space can efficiently, fairly, and thriftily use those in real-world settings.

Furthermore, the cooperative system must act to provide for itself the external resources necessary for operating and securing its survival –akin to a living organism, recall section [2.2]. Thereupon, ensuring an adequate and rational usage of basic material resources constitutes a basic function of the state-organization; this function of the utmost importance in the case of either scarce or non-renewable resources.

[6.88]

Mineral ores, fluids within underground layers and, in general, all kinds of mineral deposits in many cases exist in configurations where several participants cannot feasibly extract those simultaneously. And, even in those cases where several participants could reach the deposits simultaneously, such simultaneous extraction typically would produce highly inefficient outcomes. For example—

α. Would constitute a highly inefficient outcome to drill two or three competing wells for the same oil reservoir, considering the very high cost of drilling each. Moreover, the competitors must actually coordinate to perform simultaneously any technique for the enhancement of the output, otherwise they will leave behind quantities of a non-renewable resource.

β. Only a single organization can feasibly extract the mineral resources of an open pit –precisely because it consists of only one pit. If two or more organizations collaborate for extracting the minerals from a single pit, that collaboration entails a joint venture, since for all practical purposes the organizations would share all the major expenses and would perform joint logistics.

Therefore, usually only a single (privileged) organization extracts each mineral deposit. Such situation renders unfeasible to establish any true competition among a set of participants specialized in drilling geological layers, mining, and quarrying.

The aforesaid scarcity and restrictive configurations of mineral deposits happen in contrast with arable land, which usually exists widespread through large regions and stands readily accessible to any entity within those. Also in contrast with the components of air and water, which usually stand readily available for everyone.

[6.89]

To make things worse, private or particular organizations ordinarily strive for obtaining profits immediately because, due to their size and internal organizational interplay, they cannot afford to wait decades for obtaining profits.

Consequently, particular organizations typically make technical choices for extracting non-renewable mineral resources focusing on extracting only those resources which can yield immediate profits, even at the expense of leaving behind some (significant) quantities of those non-renewable and, frequently, rendering them practically irrecoverable, by that means causing irreparable or now-unavoidable damage to the welfare of the societal cooperative system.

[6.90]

Moreover, in the case of mineral resources close to the surface, their extraction frequently involves an extensive modification of the landscape and thereby either serious alterations to or destruction of ecosystems. Meanwhile, in the case of underground minerals, their processing at the surface frequently also involves the usage of large quantities of resources with the corresponding modification of the local landscape and the generation of long-term toxic waste.

[6.91]

Due to the massive nature of such deposits, delegating to the exchange space the procurement of mineral resources, their preparation into basic compounds, and the subsequent distribution of those—

α. Produces a useless accumulation of resources in a few individuals.

β. Entails that the state-organization loses a capability for strategic initiatives –including the loss of strategic knowledge.

γ. Produces enduring commercial circumstances favorable to cartels, oligopolies, and factual monopolies which serve as foundation and stronghold for assembling oligarchies.

In many cases, the very act of delegating such activities to the exchange space creates the corresponding oligopolies and factual monopolies.

Delegating to particular citizens the procurement of mineral resources, their preparation into basic compounds, and the subsequent distribution of those, always produces a subversion of the democratic social order and the ultimate formation of oligarchies and plutocracies –such oligarchic regimes akin to a colony built within.

The people, through a democratically managed state-organization, must manage, control, and regulate the mineral resources. Accordingly, the state-organization must perform all the activities related to the extraction, basic preparation, and distribution of those underground resources classified in the social contract as suitable for civilian use.

[6.92]

Several participants in the exchange space could attempt to compete for providing equipment to the state-organization. Nevertheless, this setting can function only in the case that those industrial participants incursion and acquire customers in many other commercial environments, such that the state-organization constitutes neither their sole nor most (potential or actual) profitable customer. Hence, the social contract must specify that no particular organization or individual can obtain more than 20% of its income from sales to the state-organization –or other percentage adjusted by the people.

Otherwise, the state-organization must produce the unique or specialized equipment required for activities reserved for itself.

[6.93]

Obviously, the state-organization must routinely publish in real-time all the bookkeeping data about these activities as part of its organizational transparency and accountability to the people, as described further in [7.132] and subsequent sections.

[6.94]

Auction mechanisms similar to the one described for selling foreign money can serve for selling scarce natural resources among the participants in the exchange space.

If, for instance, the participants in the exchange space can acquire some natural resources cheaper outside the societal cooperative system and then import those, then the state-organization can just save its own available natural resources for times of greater necessity.

The Construction, Operation, and Maintenance of Infrastructure

[6.95]

In general, the state-organization must perform all commercial activities in every context where, due to a limited physical space available, only one entity can perform these efficiently, safely, and orderly.

These activities typically comprise the construction, operation, and maintenance of physical infrastructure, therefrom including:

- Static networks for the distribution of fluids –comprising water and flowing hydrocarbons– using pipes, channels, or any other construction adhered to the Earth's crust.
- Water dams and other water reservoirs.
- Facilities for generating and distributing electric energy.
- Roads, including highways.
- Trains and railways.
- Fixed telecommunication networks.
- Navigational ports. These include maritime, large aeronautical, and any other facility where ships either dock or land.

The facilities for collected superficial water and energy for self-consumption within private lands do not constitute infrastructure.

Faking or pretending the establishment of an exchange space in those activities just leads to the formation of—

α. Cartels, oligopolies, and pervasive, giant monopolies.

β. Parasitic toll-based or tribute-based schemes like those described in entry *d*) of section [2.6].

And, consequently, the democratic social order results soon or later factually subverted.

[6.96]

Furthermore, the physical infrastructure usually supplies services and products critical for the operation of the whole societal cooperative system. The state-organization therefore cannot relinquish accountability for the correct, efficient, and optimal performance of the infrastructure which, in most cases, should operate quietly in the background.

Circulation of Wasted Materials

[6.97]

Recycling and reusing materials temporarily prolongs human life on Earth and, at the time of this writing, humans must enact drastic measures just to make feasible and secure such extension of life during another thousand years. This civilizational interplay and associated material dynamics will continue indefinitely merely because of the nature described by the thermodynamic entropy; at least until humans find or devise a mechanism or tool that sustainably reverts the increase of entropy in the universe or, also as a temporal alternative, humans may find or devise a way to obtain resources from the Solar System while continuously relocating the generated garbage outside of Earth.

Thereat:

α. Current human ways of life always utilize a (typically variable) quantity of material resources.

β. Recycling and reusing materials still does not reach a relevant quantity.

γ. Anyway, recycling and reusing materials will not reach a stable state using the current and foreseeable human technology combined with the current and foreseeable human ways of life.

[6.98]

Earth's ecosystems, in contrast, maintain a rate of consumption of resources –specifically, consumption of resources per unit of geological time– equal or very similar to the rate at which the planet's physical and chemical processes can transform, circulate, and reincorporate those resources into the Earth's crust. These harmonized rates produced a stable existence of living organisms over the planet's surface during hundreds of millions of years –the Earth sustained the aforesaid stable existence of living organisms before the expansion of the *Homo sapiens.*

In the case of terrestrial ecosystems, ignoring momentarily the giant distortions caused by the *Homo sapiens*, the stability will end upon the depletion of the planet's inner thermic energy, or when the incoming flux arriving from the star Sun either ceases or decreases to an insufficient power.

[6.99]

The collection and processing of wasted materials –yet another fundamental activity for the operation of a healthy societal cooperative system– can happen in mixed schemes where the state-organization sells recyclable or reusable wasted materials. Hence:

a) The state-organization must operate the collection of trash among the population, and must charge a fee for receiving it. The collection of trash by the state-organization provides a fundamental input for this organization to enact adjustments and modifications easily and immediately using all kinds of directly-gathered data; those actions indispensable in a world where managing and recycling wasted materials constitutes a critical function for the welfare and sustainability of the societal cooperative system.

b) The state-organization must build, operate, and manage all long-term waste dumps.

c) The state-organization can auction all recyclable or reusable wasted materials among the participants in the exchange space, for those latter to perform any further processing, and for those to reincorporate the wasted materials into productive processes within that same exchange space.

Furthermore, the state-organization must dismantle discarded *composite products* –which comprise machines and devices– until obtaining raw materials. Because of efficiency based on large-scale operations, the state-organization must achieve a lower unitary cost than any single participant of the exchange space who attempted to do the aforesaid task partially.

The requirement to dismantle discarded composite products also sets a foundation for:

α. Charging differential fees for collecting different types of trash.

β. Setting differential taxes for either manufacturing or importing different types of composite products, depending upon the cost of their subsequent dismantling. The cost of dismantling must comprise both fixed expenses from indispensable training, processing equipments, and facilities, and variable expenses from processing each unit of product.

The manufacturer or importer of any given product must—

1. Either commit to a single production quantity, or pay the fixed and variable expenses from dismantling a recurrent maximum output.

    For example, a manufacturer may agree to produce at most 1,000 pieces per month of any given product. Thereupon the manufacturer pays the state-organization the fixed expenses from dismantling those 1,000 pieces per month, and the variable expenses from dismantling every piece actually sold.

2. Calculate and provide an average *serviceableness time* of the product –the time interval during which any given product may serve its intended purpose.

    The state-organization can then use the serviceableness time of each product for making forecasts and thereby schedule its own operations.

3. Provide the necessary instructions for dismantling the product (after usage).

Then the state-organization must verify the received average serviceableness time and dismantling instructions, calculate the cost of such operation with the production committed, and charge a tax accordingly. Also, these instructions for dismantling and the associated taxes must stand publicly available as part of the state-organization's transparency and accountability.

Manufacturers should establish industrial associations where each member can commit production quantities of any given type of product, and share proportionally the fixed expenses associated to the dismantling of those.

In all cases, the auctions of collected materials must produce a profit for the state-organization. If the auction of a spare recyclable or reusable material does not reach such threshold of profitability, then the state-organization can—

α.   Raise the cost for receiving such type of discarded (wasted) materials.

β.   Set a tax for using new or pristine materials of that type, or increment it if already exists.

[6.100]

Notice that if someone sells a used item to another participant of the exchange space, and that second participant recycles or reuses the item or its materials, then the sold item does not account as wasted.

[6.101]

Charging fees for receiving trash results preferable to charging all costs to manufacturers because—

+   Fees charged to buyers constantly remind those latter of the fact that the industrial cycle of the products bought does not finish when they discard the objects.

+   Fosters personal accountability among citizens, fosters a mature behavior.

+   Provides an incentive for the population to recycle trash within the exchange space, instead of everybody automatically relying on the state-organization for everything.

[6.102]

The requirement of properly managing and disposing trash implies a minimal human quality threshold for the societal cooperative system. While large fines and even jail terms for littering may deter some humans, in general the population must manage and transfer trash appropriately without much police intervention; otherwise the scheme will prove unsustainable.

The Organic Growth

[6.103]

In the asynchronous-exchange space reinforced with the regime of domain over assets described in sections [6.53] to [6.60] does not exist «monetary credit». A participant can obtain borrowed assets from another participant and pay, or not pay, a fixed fee, and that constitutes the «credit» that can obtain from other participants in the asynchronous exchange.

If a participant holds in its domain real assets, then the participant can lend them; conversely, if a participant lacks assets to lend, then the participant cannot engage in lending: nobody can lend what lacks.

[6.104]

In combination with the organizational control of the boundaries described in [6.69] and subsequent sections, and the elimination of monopolistic and oligopolistic positions, this environment drives the participants of the asynchronous exchange into an *organic growth*: each actor –each doer– must perform a sustainable activity and execute a sequential growth; the velocity of its sequential growth depending upon the velocity at which recovers its expenses and obtains profits during each exchange cycle where participates.

In this civilization happen neither «explosions of investment» nor sudden out-of-nothing accumulations of assets by someone in the exchange space, and does not exist any quasi-magic blazing-fast road to material prosperity. Instead, everyone thrives by its own labor, and the loses caused by any misadventure result marginal and limited. For example, in this civilization exist neither «banks», nor «financial crises», nor «financial system», nor the misery engendered by those.

[6.105]

If a participant lacks enough resources for executing any given project, then it must involve other participants of the asynchronous exchange in order to accomplish its execution; this constitutes a true gregarious association, this the true essence of a cooperative system.

[6.106]

Hereon any reader should readily acknowledge that a viable alternative against the criminal venture called *capitalism* already stands available. Another world results possible and within reach.

Limits on the Concentration of Income

[6.107]

A participant in an exchange space may find or develop a way to sustainedly extract an income much larger than what spends and cumulatively hoard the surplus.

Extremely large superfluous incomes for a few participants of the exchange space and massively hoarding assets for no purpose produce deleterious outcomes for a society.

Therefore, the cooperative system must establish a mechanism to deter and dissuade participants from both extracting extremely large superfluous incomes and massively hoarding profits.

[6.108]

Two organizational regulations can hinder the concentration of income and the practice of hoarding extraordinarily large accumulated surpluses:

a) Hard limits in the amount of unused of assets that any participant in the exchange can hold. These limits usually applicable to the practice of hoarding extraordinarily large extensions of land and unused buildings, although the societal cooperative system may extend those limits into any other asset massively hoarded for no justified purpose.

b) A gradually-increasing *tax over profits* depending upon the individual profits reported compared with the sum of profits from all the participants during each fiscal period: as the share of total societal profits reported by a participant increases, so will the tax over profits paid.

A *tax over profits* consists in a tax calculated using as basis the income received by a participant during any given period of time minus the expenses paid specifically in order to perform the involved income-generating activities during that same period. Thus, ordinarily the tax over profits equals a percentage of the *profit margin* of the participant. Modern taxation codes normally define profusely which expenses under which circumstances constitute *expenses paid specifically in order to perform the involved income-generating activities* or *tax-deductible expenses*.

Usually accountants attempt to legally maximize the share of expenses labeled as tax-deductible. However, when dishonest practices happen typically the criminals apply many schemes for concealing profits, and regularly the societal tax-collecting service starts judicial procedures against those transgressors. Because of the widespread routines of tax fraud and fiscal evasion, using reported profits as scale to measure the individual concentration of income in many cases would either flatly fail or produce unstable and/or unreliable outputs. Notwithstanding the variable-quality and possibly-inconsistent input data, using the reported profits still will serve as a first and rough line of defense against the concentration of income –the ultimate barrier consists of the hard limits on accumulated unused assets.

Thereupon, the societal cooperative system can increase a tax over profits in such way that, when a participant obtains one thousandth of the total reported societal profits during a fiscal period, the participant will pay as tax the entirety of such profits. This shown in the following graph:

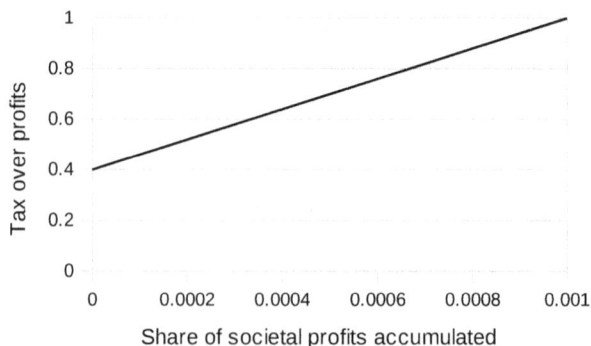

Figure 4. Incremental tax over profits as a participant accumulates a larger share of the total.

The people can perform a fine estimation of which percentage must constitute the threshold for a participant to transfer the entirety of its profits as tax; here the number one thousandth placed as example.

Additionally, this organizational regulation should promote a more equally distributed income among the members of productive organizations.

Supplementary Note
The Automation of Labor

[6.109]

As recorded in section [4.88], during the last three centuries, when the human labor necessary for attaining any given end decreased due to technological and technical improvements, several societal disarrays ensued and still ensue. Typically, many humans deem the progressive automation of labor as the fundamental cause of these societal disarrays; however, this accusation results completely false.

[6.110]

The fundamental causes of societal disarrays –for instance, massive unemployment– upon the introduction of technologically and technically improved production processes consist of:

a) Societal regimes of human exploitation which include the control of productive assets by a few privileged –those regimes described in [6.46] and subsequent sections.

b) Overpopulation of *habitable zones.* What constitutes a *habitable zone* described in section [2.5].

c) Human incompetence to develop and adapt science and technology.

[6.111]

Furthermore, several social groups –the parasitic psychopathic subspecies, capitalistic corporations, «state security agencies»– actively attempt to control any new scientific knowledge and technological improvement. Added to and leveraging the difficulties produced by the aforementioned fundamental causes, those predatory activities produce devastating consequences for an adequate incorporation of new scientific knowledge and new technologies by average humans, beyond behaving as directed users.

[6.112]

The automation of labor constitutes one of the greatest achievements of the human species, one that makes a difference in the destiny of humankind with long-range and wide-scope consequences. Humanity's dysfunctional social arrangements and a parasitic psychopathic subspecies prevent humans from truly enjoying the advantages of a widespread automation of labor; humans themselves turned one of their greatest achievements into a nightmare.

[6.113]

Introducing any kind of «universal basic income» into societies as a method to quell the symptoms of the failure would only make much worse the already mentioned fundamental causes, and would furnish paradisiac conditions for an already massive parasitic psychopathic subspecies.

Reducing individual working time in order to employ more persons, also will overshadow the fundamental causes of the failure, will merely defer their resolution while they worsen, and will promote yet another sort of sanctioned mediocrity; this does not foster the development of humanity.

As in many instances of life, here result nonviable any shortcuts for *hard work*, in this case the *hard work* consists in correcting human faults.

[6.114]

Therefrom, a societal cooperative system must agree on the proper strategies and frameworks for—

α. Fixing the aforementioned fundamental causes of disarrays upon the introduction of technological improvements.

β. Eliminating any attempted social control or manipulation, and performing judicial procedures against those who attempt it.

[6.115]

Outstandingly, every societal cooperative system must formulate developmental policies that best suit its own resources and conditions.

A strong *social services* department from the state-organization should act to provide assistance in reorganizing the lives of those in dire need –it should leave no-one behind. The scheme of tutored labor described in section [6.25] could operate as first instance when assisting a healthy adult.

The best policy consists in taking care of each other, in helping each other to grow, but the society itself must do that loosely, without active parenting by the state-organization. Each citizen must build its own personal destiny –this further addressed in [7.41] and subsequent sections.

[6.116]

Meanwhile, the members of any societal cooperative system must make mature choices for controlling and decreasing the nowadays rampant human overpopulation in a fair, honest, and civilized way. For achieving such maturity, humans must first understand and agree on which kind of world they want to live in.

Overpopulation renders futile all other measures.

7

A Reform for Democracy

[7.1]

A MORE EQUITABLE AND FAIR COOPERATIVE SYSTEM will comprise a true societal democracy as essential component. Societies could reform the modern failed *representative democracy* to reach a true democracy sufficient for and coherent with the improved commercial-exchange behavior. However, doing so requires an indispensable degree of maturity and cognitive capacities from the population that chooses to embark in the journey.

Those who can move forward because they steadfastly resolved to do whatever it takes to, must do it.

[7.2]

First and foremost everyone must understand *why democracy*: Why choose democracy as a way of life, as a way to organize a societal cooperative system; why choose democracy as a survival strategy, as a strategy for the expansion and prosperity of one's self, of one's family and kin, of one's species.

Why democracy and not any of the many variants of authoritarian forms of organization. Thus, why not enthrone a king, or a dictator, or a council of elderly or outstanding individuals, or a patriarch, or a matriarch, or a deity, or the sacred books written by a deity. Why not any of those authoritarian forms of organization, which so many primitive people used, still use, and adhere to.

Therefore, this choice explained in the following sections.

Authoritarian Misconceptions

[7.3]

One popular authoritarian misconception about humanity consists in considering the human species as a single whole, akin to a single organism. Partially as product of this misconception authoritarian individuals say about themselves «we constitute one». However, the human species does not constitute a single whole; the human species does not constitute something akin to a hive, where all individuals could work coordinated without considering personal interests and this would guarantee the survival of oneself or of one's own kin.

Natural hives as assembled by evolution arose because one of the members specializes in procreation –reproduction– while all the others remain sterile. The sterile members of the hive therefore result siblings from a single mother, and only the mother can procreate the next generation. Thereat, the sterile members of the hive specialize in providing all what the mother may need for her to produce both more of their siblings, and the members of the next generation. If the mother dies, the hive must either find or generate another, or otherwise the hive will perish.

In contrast, humans do not descend all from a single mother; if a human queen dies the reproductive capabilities of the people continue unaltered. In this context, a human population does not consist of siblings since—

α. A human female can produce at most a few offspring.

β. The offspring of each human female draw survival advantages from the partnership of the female with the male parent. Hence, females very frequently select uncompromised males to share the child-rearing tasks.

Therefore, working for the survival of everybody else does not guarantee the survival of one's own kin. Instead, working either solely or chiefly for the survival of everybody fosters the survival of those who give less resources to the whole while keeping advantageous resources for their own kin. Thus engaging in pretended communism produces the eventual disappearance of those who mistakenly regarded it as real.

When nominally all the members within an authoritarian social scheme stand entitled to the same, an individual can engage in obtaining unfair and illegitimate advantages alone, but more often this happens by joining a fascist formation or a fascist faction. Thereupon, the members of these fascist formations or factions collectively depredate the society –a society supposedly made of *equals*, of comrades. And frequently the fascists also depredate, exploit, or terminate the ones within their own ranks. The history of authoritarian regimes leaves no ambiguity about these events.

Section [7.10] contains a further description of the methods employed by the fascists within a captured human society, and in any society where they constitute the majority.

[7.4]

Another authoritarian misconception states: «Organization and order implies a command chain, a command chain implies a commander, therefore must exist a commander and all the others must obey. Either rule or obey, that constitutes the essence of organization and harmonious life.» This misconception arises from shortsighted mind-sets and/or very scanty *executive functions.*

An organization does not imply a command chain; rather, an organization implies a predefined method to make choices. In this context, a command chain constitutes one of the most simple and primitive options for making organizational choices.

Humans can exercise their creative capabilities and develop a myriad of organizational methods to make choices. From this creativity arose democracy.

[7.5]

An additional authoritarian misconception states: «The entitlement for emitting upper commands arises from holding a *higher position* in the world than everybody else. May this *higher position* consist in a divine nature, or some non-transferable, non-distributable, or non-developable capacity for the others, or any combination thereof.» Thus, individuals with an authoritarian word-view spend considerable amounts of energy and resources searching for someone «superior» and/or enthroning an individual into an assumed higher position.

The described authoritarian culture still permeates through nominally democratic societies which spend large amounts of energy and resources enthroning «democratic presidents» and keeping such aura of superiority.

This authoritarian misconception arises because authoritarian individuals refuse to engage in personal accountability. Hence, the misconception constitutes a rationalization for attempting to transfer the capacity to exercise volitional choices into someone else.

[7.6]

And another key authoritarian misconception states: «The effective performance of an organization requires the *unity* of its members; we *united* can do more and result stronger than *separated*. For achieving *unity* we must suppress or diminish our differences, we must become as *one*.» When authoritarian individuals talk about becoming «one» or «united» usually they refer to synchronizing their mind-set and thereby act at unison in many circumstances –especially in circumstances regarded as *adverse*. In this context, free speech and independent opinions endanger the organizational performance and, therefore, imperil or jeopardize the survival of the group.

From an anthropological perspective, this misconception perhaps the most sophisticated. The craving for «unity» seems to stem from an incapacity to process differences in a civilized way –through words and pre-established social mechanisms. The incapacity to properly utilize words and an elaborated social scaffolding seems to stem from the fact that many authoritarian individuals stand in the classification of *animals* described in [3.17] and subsequent sections, and many of their brains operate disjoined as described in [3.137] and subsequent sections. Syncing a mind-set with the group, or establishing a shared mind-set, either diminishes or makes unnecessary the usage of abstract outward sound reasoning and choice-making processes in an interplay with others different. Accordingly, most individuals enacting an authoritarian organization do not need to abstractly reason and process different points of view –thereupon, individuals with scarce abilities may find an incentive to join and build such organizations. Ordinarily the upper-rank authoritarian individuals partially direct the shared mind-set.

As already stated, an organization implies a predefined method to make choices; the effective performance of those choices by each member composes the organizational performance. Homogeneity does not secure organizational effectiveness and achieving the latter does not require the former; rather, the desire for homogeneity stems from the incapacity to enact more complex organizational patterns.

Certainly, cooperative systems make possible to achieve what a single or a few individuals could not, but thriving and succeeding in an organized fashion neither implies nor creates a collective homogeneity. Instead, cooperative systems usually involve a specialization of labor. Thus, awkwardly, typically individuals in authoritarian cultures state: «We develop each different specialized capabilities and enact commands received, but we the same –we think equal at unison– as *one*.»

[7.7]

All these authoritarian misconceptions arise from or result strongly supported by cognitive methodological propensities and deficient *executive functions* in brains glaringly lacking a conscience. Moreover, due to the human brain split (described in [3.137] and subsequent sections) and the cognitive dissonance caused by processing the existence of alternative ways of life or alternative options for action, authoritarian individuals readily develop a tendency towards intolerance as a coping mechanism.

Typically, in an attempt to force the real world to adjust into their world-views and thereby reduce the cognitive dissonance, authoritarian individuals engage in efforts to indoctrinate everybody else into their misconceptions. Those zealous efforts for indoctrination do not happen in individuals lacking authoritarian tendencies.

[7.8]

In this context, the parasitic psychopathic subspecies developed a methodological propensity towards authoritarianism which serves merely as instrumentality for the goals of the members of the subspecies –as recorded in section [3.171].

Thereupon, the development of typical authoritarian societal schemes within humanity very often comprise and rely on the following sequence:

α.   Bands and formations of authoritarian individuals develop within the society, composed by members of the parasitic psychopathic subspecies mixed with ordinary authoritarian individuals. These constitute fascist bands and fascist formations by all accounts, usually secret or hidden from the normal members of the infected societies.

β.   The state-organization and the population-wide social contract result modified according to the interests of the fascists, who now control them. Consequently, a fascist regime starts operating in the corresponding country.

Alternatively, the fascists may capture the state-organization by violent means: authoritarian uprisings, civil wars, and coups.

γ. The usual well-known events ensue: persecution and prosecution of individuals who engage in different ways of thinking and acting, massive operations of espionage against the population, all sorts of transgressions against human rights, the fascists steal from the rest of the population, and so on. Abundant documentation exists about the calamities of fascist regimes, recall the list in the last paragraph of section [4.93].

δ. The fascist regime, by either destroying or subduing everybody else, and by developing its own authoritarian chains of command, develops into a totalitarian state encompassing all societal activities.

[7.9]

In different countries and in different historical epochs, the bands and formations of authoritarian individuals reached varied successes in the aforementioned sequence; thus, not all of those reached the intended totalitarian state. This failure to reach a totalitarian regime most frequently happens because of the opposition of the rest of society, whereupon any further sliding into totalitarianism would produce an overt confrontation and defiance by the majority of the population.

Hence, most frequently, authoritarian regimes of any degree engage in permanent propagandistic and ideological (indoctrinating) efforts aiming to increase the scope and self-internalization of the volitional submission of the individual citizens; and upon the relative success of those campaigns the regimes advance towards totalitarianism. However, if directly defied or challenged by a large and relatively unorganized sector of the population, an authoritarian regime can rush the passage into totalitarianism by means of widespread repression.

A totalitarian state constitutes the superior phase of authoritarianism. Slow or fast genocides, ethnic cleansing campaigns, and the systematic elimination of every different or non-fascist person already happened when totalitarian states arise, besides the permanent threat of imperial invasions against neighboring countries.

[7.10]

Within an authoritarian regime –either fascist or fully totalitarian– the members of the parasitic psychopathic subspecies and ordinary authoritarian individuals allied with them will always seek to assemble a fascist formation placed and distributed in privileged positions, from which they can control and exploit the rest of the population, eliminate these latter humans when deemed convenient, and take for themselves the assets and social positions of the eliminated persons as bounty. Often such privileged positions result meager because the fascist formations include many members, many of those members dumb, and an authoritarian social structure comprises few posts in the upper hierarchy; nevertheless still poor fascists will proudly stick to the formation, as they will regard themselves as «privileged among the poor».

In a large quantity of cases the main *privilege* of a fascist individual consists in receiving gathered public and private-stolen information about normal individual humans, as part of the massive espionage and stealing of fascists against the rest of the members of the societal cooperative system.

How the members of the parasitic psychopathic subspecies distinguish between themselves and ordinary authoritarian individuals already addressed in sections [3.177] and [3.178].

Despite the magnitude of their activities within a totalitarian state, as a matter of usual business, the fascist formations will keep themselves as hidden and secret as possible from the rest of the population.

[7.11]

Many fascist individuals do not regard themselves as fascists. This discrepancy between their perceived identity and the (objective) reality, apparently stems from the fact that fascist individuals frequently deem the allegiance to a formation as something natural to a human.

Accordingly, not all authoritarian individuals (humans with an authoritarian culture) espouse a fascist way of living, or actively seek to join a formation. Thus, authoritarian non-fascist individuals will just interact in an authoritarian fashion with others whenever they deem necessary to interact with someone at all.

Societal Cooperative Systems and the State-Organization

[7.12]

Placing aside the subject of the parasitic psychopathic subspecies and authoritarians in general, a succinct description of the main traits and components of human societal cooperative systems serves as foundation for afterwards understanding *why democracy.*

[7.13]

Remember the basic concepts about cooperative systems recorded in [2.30] and subsequent sections.

Human societal cooperative systems consist of those cooperative systems assembled by a (sometimes or occasionally loosely defined) group of individuals living within a habitable zone or zones, where for this group results convenient to establish and perform habitual predictable social relationships. Those predictable social relationships constitute the headstone of a later social contract.

[7.14]

Hence, humans aggregated themselves into societal cooperative systems for the purpose of using and enhancing the advantages of dwelling within societies, while enjoying some hedge against threats coming from outside the zone where they usually live, and against antisocial individuals.

Later, societal cooperative systems evolved and created permanent state-organizations. These state-organizations initially enacted primitive choice-making processes.

[7.15]

The term state-organization denotes the *formal political organization which directly arises from a society and operates as its arm or limb, thereby enhancing the corresponding cooperative system.*

The *state* –short term for state-organization– consists of a human organization, and does not consist of a set of circumstances or conditions, as the ambiguity of the word *state* would suggest. The english language lacks a univocal word for labeling a state-organization.

Thereat, a state-organization does not arise from vassals, but from citizens who create a shared culture and enjoy a set of basic prerogatives within that group. Thus, the state-organization constitutes a concrete expression of and relies on a population-wide social contract, whether the social contract formal or informal, whether kept steady or routinely modified, whether (the social contract) consciously or unconsciously acknowledged.

Those individuals or groups of individuals treated as vassals who do not furnish an input into the direction of the state-organization, do not belong to the society which created such social order. This latter situation often happens in the case of empires, where a core society creates and manages a state-organization which oppresses and exploits peripheral or subjugated societies.

In authoritarian regimes, the willingness of each citizen to obey commands from a hierarchically superior individual constitutes its input into the direction of the state-organization; and its expressed and implied personal opinions by which regards a command chain as the indispensable backbone of any functional social order, constitute its input into the shared culture, and into the social contract. The aforesaid compliance and acquiescence within authoritarian regimes proceeds reinforced by the shared culture enacted by peers; in contrast with the cases when the subjugation proceeds enforced by an external group.

[7.16]

In many cases, in greater magnitude in failed countries, the state-organization does not fully operate on the aspects of societal living and within the full territory prescribed in the social contract as its field of action. Hence, in many instances happen glaring and extensive gaps where the state-organization should operate, but either does not operate at all, or just does it sporadically and partially. The size of those gaps denotes the degree of failure of the societal cooperative system.

Typically, when the shared culture and the corresponding social contract contain large inadequacies, the individuals within that dysfunctional society resort to avoid enacting those inadequacies in order to survive –frequently without a conscious acknowledgment of it.

[7.17]

Humans created neither societies, nor societal cooperative systems, nor state-organizations for the purpose of securing a source of commands, for providing themselves with someone whom they could obey. This because humans can readily and efficiently make their own choices by themselves.

Rather, humans created and joined societal cooperative systems because doing so provided them with much more choices –much more possibilities– than those available if they thrived alone.

Even in the case that an individual chooses to obey a command chain, the individual seeks to augment its personal effectance through concerted collective action. Thus, by joining a formation, an authoritarian individual seeks to achieve what could not alone, seeks to acquire or augment some possibilities in its life thinking mistakenly that for achieving those goals must unavoidably relinquish the capacity to choose on many aspects.

[7.18]

Analogous to a living organism or enduring self-preserving material organization, any societal cooperative system must engage in activities aimed to produce its own survival and temporal continuity.

And like in a living organism, the components of a societal cooperative system neither exist fixed nor belong perennially to it, as humans do not live forever and, likewise, a human can dissolve its membership into a cooperative system. Nothing binds a human to a societal cooperative system but its own personal will.

[7.19]

Ordinary societal cooperative systems attempt to, at least nominally, provide and secure a *survival spot* –a spot suitable for survival– for all its members. With the excuse of providing and securing such survival spots, some societal cooperative systems engage in static social settings, whether these consisting of castes or hereditary social positions, or these consisting of lifetime posts.

Pretending to provide and secure a survival spot for everyone does not justify static social settings, happens no causality there. Furthermore, typically statically layered social settings merely serve as scaffold for the traditional human intra-species depredatory processes (recall section [2.18]), where those humans in privileged castes depredate and exploit those others in the lower ones.

As recorded in section [7.4], an organization implies a predefined method to make choices and, in any case, in an advanced and fair civilization such predefined method to make choices must involve procedures for creating and securing a survival spot for all the members of the society.

Why Democracy

[7.20]

1. *Equal humans, even if those existed, will make different choices in equal situations; as described in section* [3.45].

   In real-world settings do not exist two identical humans with identical trajectories, and the usual input of guesses in choice-making processes makes their behavior even more distinct. Hence, when dealing with equal situations humans produce a myriad of varied choices and preferences.

   [7.21]

2. *Diversity engenders strength and endurance for any species, as far as this diversity results compatible with the basic behavior that ordinarily secures the survival of the species.*

   Diversity among the members of a species constitutes a pool of resources and capabilities to which the species can resort to cope or deal with novel situations and novel environmental requirements. Thus, diversity furnishes qualities that make more remote the possible extinction of the species which fosters them, while at the same time diversity produces a readiness for prospering and expanding in non-standard conditions.

   Therefrom, a large diversity among the members of a species contributes a lot to the adaptive capabilities of the population.

   [7.22]

3. *For a human societal cooperative system, conscious diversity makes possible and nourishes directed evolution and development.*

   As already recorded in sections [6.87] and [7.18], any human societal cooperative system, similar to a living organism, must perform activities that ensure its survival. But a human societal cooperative system constitutes neither a living organism nor a regular biological species; accordingly, happens no need to use any type of random testing of new mutations and thereupon keep only those instances where the mutation survived within the natural environment; happens no need of so much hardship and so many failures and deaths like in the ordinary evolution of living organisms. Because humans can think, can devise novel solutions, can imagine novel paths, and can thereby adjust their behavior.

Therefore, a human societal cooperative system can reap great advantages from the discussion of ideas among its members, from those expressing their diversity, from all sharing and developing alternative courses of action, from fostering everyone to imagine a myriad of possible solutions to the same problem. Because then the cooperative system can use that richness to transform itself, to reach new heights and unforeseen developments that otherwise a rigid societal structure would suppress.

[7.23]

4. *Every human must choose a cooperative system; competent humans want to choose their own destiny because they can make the optimal choices by themselves.*

As recorded in section [7.18], the sole element that binds a human to a cooperative system consists of its own personal will. The human must choose the cooperative system or otherwise soon or later will defect, and attempts to secure membership by force and negative incentives usually produce endless struggles for freedom that squander the vitality of the cooperative system itself. Threat, if a human must choose a societal cooperative system, any reasonable human will choose a cooperative system which guarantees that the societal choice-making processes will swiftly and efficiently take its interests as input.

The interests of a human involve, among many features, both the direction of societal development and the adequate usage of the resources that the human furnishes to the cooperative system. Hence, a society that can perform transparent and inclusive choice-making processes will gain the support of most capable humans.

[7.24]

That four reasons should suffice for people that can understand. Unless one wishes to live in a world ruled by force, democracy constitutes the best option. Those societies ruled by force, since they lack the advantages furnished by a civilized resolution of disagreements, and do not enact a productive usage and coexistence of differences, typically involve much suffering, systemic violence, material and intellectual poverty, and chronic underdevelopment for their members.

A democratic societal cooperative system constitutes the best option for any human that aspires to develop its own kin, furnish new generations with a stable living environment, and reach new and unforeseen goals.

The Essence of Democracy

[7.25]

The essence of democracy consists in inclusiveness in choice-making processes, where the input of each participant contributes to build a whole.

[7.26]

For democracy to function, derived from what stated in section [7.17], a person must estimate useful or advantageous its participation with other individuals in a cooperative system which manages itself by democratic choice-making processes. If a person does not deem useful or advantageous to associate itself with other individuals for any given purpose, then the person can (and usually do) legitimately refrain from such involvement.

Thereat, if a person finds the individuals available for association too dumb or incompetent, then that person may choose to thrive on its own, rather than wasting time and resources with them.

Thus, democracy implies a *factual minimal human quality threshold* of the participants. The minimum mandatory education that every citizen must receive implicitly establishes a factual minimal human quality threshold in nominally democratic societies. Nevertheless, in many societies the actual average available human quality results too low, and competent individuals just choose to leave that societies and join others with more competent individuals.

[7.27]

Hence, the enactment of democracy by a group of individuals consists in, sequentially:

1. Knowing each other, getting acquainted with each other's needs, generic wants and aspirations, and situations in life.

2. Establishing a common goal, towards whose attainment operates the democratic choice-making process.

   In many instances the first generic common goal consists in establishing a specific common goal, when everyone does not agree unanimously to one without further processing.

3. Sharing proposals, listening to divergences, understanding each other.

4. Rationally considering and processing each other's proposals by:

   a) Explicitly stating the fundamental causes of each relevant aspect of the various inputs.

   b) Understanding the fundamental causes of convergences and divergences of the various inputs.

   c) Merging the shared convergences into a single common proposal.

   d) Negotiating modifications of aspects where divergences exist and/or imagining new proposals which eliminate such divergences, to the extent feasible and acceptable for each participant.

   e) Assembling proposals which, whenever possible, comprise or imply a framework for enacting different solutions for the same problem.

   f) Keeping the insurmountable divergences for a voting stage, as a last resort.

5. Voting for each of the finally crafted proposals.

6. Enacting the proposal that receives a majority of votes.

[7.28]

Here again noteworthy that if the construction of socially-viable proposals proceeds defectively and unable to provide a framework for enacting different solutions for a single problem when divergences in specific proposals exist, then the ensuing voting stage results highly fragmented, where large percentages of the participants do not find their input included.

This failure to provide room for diversity typically ends with the abandonment of democratic processes by those excluded from their output; because of this failure people also leave nominally democratic societal cooperative systems.

[7.29]

If happens that someone mistakenly postulates a falsehood, and the timely intervention of other individual (or individuals) shows that person its mistake, such activity of enlightening constitutes neither an essential nor indispensable part of a democratic choice-making process. However, helping someone else to fix its own mistakes serves to produce a better input for the democratic process and, in many cases, that mutual exchange of reflections proceeds as a matter of routine.

[7.30]

Individuals with an authoritarian culture usually do not understand democratic processes. Thus, usually authoritarian individuals regard the stage of considering and processing divergences as a «debate», which for them constitutes a «win-or-lose» instance. Likewise, authoritarian individuals typically regard the voting stage as an instance where «the strong subdues the weak, where the strongest faction consists of that with the largest number of votes». Therefrom, authoritarian individuals regard the essence of democracy as consisting in «building majorities», where the «ruling party» and the «opposition» can achieve a «majority» by «making alliances». As if warfare.

Ditching the Concept of «Government»

[7.31]

Currently, the so-called «democratic countries» at best constitute failed democracies, and fixing such situation will involve some relatively large indispensable shifts. The first and most obvious mistake consists in the notion of a «delegated will» or «invested *power*» into the «representatives of the people».

Democratic societies –democratic cultures– must completely discard the shared notion that the individuals will choose whom they will «obey» or who will constitute the «authority».

In democratic societies, long ago the shared notion should consist in: «We will choose our state-organization employees who will perform our commands.»

[7.32]

The person holding the highest ranking post within the state-organization of a truly democratic country works as an employee of the people.

[7.33]

The whole idea that a person holds a kind of «political authority» in a democratic society constitutes an anachronistic, backwards, and toxic inertia: a taint by an authoritarian culture.

[7.34]

Correspondingly, the people must denominate the branch of the state-organization specialized in the performance of the prescriptions codified in the formal social contract simply as *executive branch* or *executive branch of the state-organization*, as already many humans do.

The individual performing the highest post within the executive branch of the state-organization should receive the denomination of *prime minister*, instead of *president*.

In a truly democratic society does not exist a «government».

Honest Competent Civilized Individuals

[7.35]

Remember the *golden rule* of civilized behavior: Do to others as you would wish them do to you.

If this the first time you know about it, contemplate its content for a while.

[7.36]

In democratic or harmonious societies people tend to behave with honesty because they understand the importance of the *golden rule* for building the society they want.

In contrast, certain subset of members of fascist societies behave with honesty due to a desire to fulfill «orders received» and thereby avoid punishment or slightly improve their hierarchical status. Typically, these persons who behave with honesty merely to please their masters stand at the lower layers of their social pyramid, while the most psychopathic members of the society hold command posts.

[7.37]

Every society must comprise an indispensable minimal percentage of honest competent individuals within the population for achieving success; without this *critical mass* of honest competent individuals the society degrades into lower civilizational arrangements and/or gradually disappears. This requirement of honest competent individuals apply both to democratic and fascist societies, where the origins of honest behavior differ as described in the previous section.

[7.38]

The appreciation of the *golden rule* within a population produces far-reaching consequences. Accordingly, fascist regimes arising from fascist societies can engage in imperialistic wars with the acquiescence of the population. Meanwhile, when traitors drag democratic societies into imperialistic wars, they must create some cloak for their actual intentions. For example:

a) When at the beginning of the XXI century the United States of America –a mostly democratic society living in a nominally democratic regime– invaded Iraq, the traitors to democracy within the United States of America vigorously disseminated a lie claiming that the purpose of the invasion consisted in eliminating some non-existent «weapons of mass destruction», fighting terrorism, and «liberating» the iraqi people. Thereby millions of naive simpletons inside the United States of America could regard the invasion as geared towards a socially constructive goal.

In fact, the invasion of Iraq happened for the purpose of securing the control of the vast oil reserves of that country by capitalistic corporations. Hence, after the invasion, the United States of America established a failed democracy in Iraq, hired a capitalistic corporation for writing a law regarding the hydrocarbons in that country which secured a profit for foreign capitalistic corporations, and afterwards the failed democratic regime in Iraq approved the aforesaid law against the desires of the iraqi people. Moreover, the United States of America conditioned the withdrawal of its troops upon the approval of the corresponding oil law which guaranteed the profitability of the invasion.

b) In the year 2022, Russia –a fascist society which produced and supports a fascist regime– started a war of conquest against Ukraine. As internal preparation for the war, the russian fascist regime openly claimed that the ukrainian territory belonged to «the historical Russia which stood under the control of the ukrainian people due to past mistakes of russian autocrats and due to the collapse of the soviet empire». In this twisted logic, since the ukrainians lived as vassals in both the russian and the soviet empires, the collapse of these empires did not confer any right of ownership of the land to the ukrainians, and the legitimate owners of the land remained the russians, because those latter constituted the society which owned the empires –in their words: «when you leave, take what you brought with you». Thereat, the russian fascist society actively and passively supported the indiscriminate destruction and military invasion of Ukraine with the aim of eliminating the ukrainian statehood, the ukrainian culture, and any non-compliant or non-fascist ukrainian. The russian fascists aimed to convert the ukrainian territory into a peripheral vassalage as a preparatory stage for rebuilding a full-fledged russian empire, with the ukrainian people either subjugated or destroyed.

Once understood the main goal of the invasion among the fascist ranks, the russian regime focused on disseminating all sorts of lies in order to justify the invasion for both the foreign public and for any true believer within the russian society.

Notably, the russian fascists –since most of them belong to the parasitic psychopathic subspecies– ordinarily mirror and mimic the actions and methods of their adversaries and, likewise, as a preemptive protection, the russian fascists accuse others of the same crimes they themselves commit or pretend to commit. Thus, for example, the lies proclaimed by the russian regime included accusing the ukrainians of attempting «genocide», and the accusations against the very few russian citizens who dissent from the russian fascists focus on labeling the dissenters as «extremists». Consequently, for any incautious observer, the discourse of the russian fascists appears bizarre or upside-down.

[7.39]

Competent individuals that behave with honesty due to an appreciation of the *golden rule* hereinafter characterized as *honest competent civilized individuals.*

Honest competent civilized individuals tend to seek their peers because they can build a functional and advanced society with those. Therefrom migrations of honest qualified people ensue.

[7.40]

The percentage of honest competent civilized individuals within a regime of *representative democracy* typically determines the degree of relative success of such democracy.

Societies nominally democratic with relatively low percentages of honest competent civilized individuals endure more frequent direct attacks to democratic foundations by both traitors and fascists, since the human resources available to deter those result less. Unsurprisingly, notwithstanding if the fascists do not fully control the state-organization or do not reach the ultimate totalitarian regime, societies with low percentages of honest competent civilized individuals tend to constitute failed civilizations, reproduce colonial cultures and lifestyles, live with nasty factual oligarchies, and so on.

[7.41]

Thereupon, honest competent civilized individuals cannot turn into «heroes» and «save the idiots». Rather, ordinary individuals within a society must choose which type of life they want and thereafter they must do whatever it takes to transform themselves. Thus, after achieving at very least a first stage of personal transformation, each individual can engage in building a new society.

An individual cannot relinquish the accountability for the beginning of its personal transformation.

[7.42]

The following paragraph conveys a paramount observation concerning the beginning of a cooperative system.

The aggregated group of founders –the people– creates and defines initially the character of a society, of a civilization. This does not happen inversely: the social arrangement does not build initially the characteristics of the group of founding members.

Societies arise when peers find each other, when peers coalesce into a group; constitutes the task of each founding member to previously reinvent, reform, and refurbish itself into the kind of people he/she wants to live with.

[7.43]

Will not happen a «rescue» of failed societies and failed human groups; no «heroes» will make the labor that each person must do. During the XX century, as recorded in section [1.2], many humans already attempted to aid in the self-transformation of others through public institutionalized education, by fostering the usage of scientific information and general knowledge widely disseminated for the purpose, and by enacting other similar methods; and all those attempts utterly failed. A vast majority of those individuals who evolved in their ways of thinking and behaving during the XX century would achieved the same without active aid.

No reasonable human stands interested in repeating the failed efforts of the XX century, the lesson resulted clear: whether because of deficiencies in their *executive functions*, or because of pure mediocrity, or because of a mixture of those, most stuck populations do not advance even with active aid. The sole viable and sustainable possible aid consists in just placing available to everyone the necessary information for progress, and then those who can and want to move forward must do it by themselves.

In such endeavor, the necessary information for human progress beyond the curricula of standard basic education, and basic scientific and historical facts, should not get distributed without cost. As the parasitic psychopathic subspecies showcased during the last five years before this writing, such altruistic efforts just produce in the parasites a desire to take more and more, and they will even zealously demand the fulfillment of their desire.

[7.44]

The type of democratic regime proposed in this document will require a higher indispensable percentage of honest competent civilized individuals within the population, higher than in a regime of *representative democracy*. The *basic resource* for moving forward a civilization consists of honest competent civilized individuals. Of course, the success of this kind of people happens in an interdependent fashion with the evolution and progress of the civilization built: more of them will thrive in an advanced civilization, and they will build that same advanced civilization.

[7.45]

Failed democratic regimes, like those managed and infested by traitors, thereupon attempt by all means to «capture» honest competent civilized individuals. For such purpose these failed regimes enact a series of programs aimed to «*recover* and/or *convince* citizens», and typically also sabotage and undermine any social class of honest competent civilized individuals who either flock away or act (and think) independently –frequently to prevent those from emigrating and succeeding abroad, after which they could aid to oust the traitors either after returning strengthened to their homeland or while remaining in a friendly country.

Likewise, fascist regimes in times of hardship overtly obstruct and prohibit the emigration of their citizens, albeit ordinarily this obstruction happens by surrounding the individuals with fascist social structures which hinder any development outside or different from the approved paths.

This happens because both traitors to democracy and psychopathic fascists understand that they need honest people to *milk* them, to exploit them, to steal and plunder from them, to enslave them.

[7.46]

In consequence, honest competent civilized individuals routinely fight against traitors within democratic societies, and against fascists everywhere. Fewer traitors to democracy and fewer fascists in the world produce by subtraction an increased welfare for honest competent civilized individuals.

This ubiquitous fight already advanced a substantial extent.

The Failure of the Representative Democracy at the Beginning of the XXI Century

[7.47]

At the beginning of the XXI century in democratic societies became patent the failure of the *representative democracy* for producing prosperous and fair social environments. Every reasonable individual can effortlessly acknowledge the outstanding failures of democratic institutions for effectively executing the people's will.

Caused great damage to the satisfaction with democracy:

1. The noticeable decrease of available personal opportunities and quality of life (which impacted young generations first) within societies relying on the capitalistic expansion described in section [4.88], since the Earth stands now severely damaged, overpopulated by humans, and depleted from resources readily available for consumption. However, even at these times of massive ecological disaster, many hominids lack the capacity to process such information.

2. The organizational volatility of the capitalistic fraud which acerbated after the year 2008 causing all sorts of disruptions of human activities. Thenceforward the capitalistic criminals resorted to emit and distribute among themselves more money than ever before during a relatively short period of time; thereby resorted to rampant stealing –mostly under the brand «quantitative easing», as described in section [4.65]. Most honest competent civilized individuals noticed the ridiculously large amounts of money emitted and distributed among the thieves.

3. The massive, intrusive, and unaccountable espionage from the so-called «state security agencies» against the will of the citizens, which blurred the distinction between a democratic and a fascist regime. Some of the largest capitalistic corporations actively aided in this espionage and, moreover, with the acquiescence of the same «state security agencies», those capitalistic corporations massively spied and stole data from the population for their own particular interests, whether those interests commercial or of any other type.

4. The everywhere-concerted manipulation of information flows, in many countries coupled with inequitable, fake, or rigged electoral processes, although these activities very much a continuation of XX century practices.

The Earth's massive ecological disaster should stand at the top of the causes of dissatisfaction. The fact that a very large percentage of the population lacks the indispensable arithmetic capabilities and *executive functions* for comprehending the ecological disaster makes more dire the situation of humankind.

Furthermore, in a desperate attempt to cope with the consequences of the failed civilization produced by the capitalistic fraud, many humans both quietly and outspokenly promoted a diminution of the rate of expansion of the automation of labor; because of those attempts to hold to the past, in some productive fields the increase of automation either significantly decreased or basically stalled.

[7.48]

In this context, before recording a coherent proposal to reform the current democracy, a description of the fundamental origins and causes of the failure of the *representative democracy* at the beginning of the XXI century, and the corresponding behavioral patterns that produced such failure, will enlighten the targets to reform. Thereupon, in the following sections briefly addressed these subjects.

The Path Towards the Present: Representative Democracy in the «Western» Civilization

[7.49]

Modern *representative democracy* originated in the «western» civilization, its main traits became configured and assembled at the time when mercantile practices displaced the old rigid social structures of the Middle Ages. Those game-changing mercantile practices produced the rise of a new group of commanders of industry, and among that group the capitalistic criminals inserted themselves –such transition already described in previous chapters.

In this commercial and competitive context, the new commanders of industry and accompanying capitalistic criminals deemed useful the establishment of a social order adequate to their needs and interests.

[7.50]

Hence, at the core of the «western» civilization, capitalistic criminals and new industrial barons tolerated and somewhat fostered *representative democracy* merely because it served to displace the old kings and feudal cooperative systems, while at the same time unrestricted thought and unrestricted transmission of ideas inherent to democracy served as an essential foundation for an efficient development of science and technology.

The old kings and feudal cooperative systems constituted an obstacle for the accumulation of profits and the control of political institutions by the capitalistic criminals and new industrial barons. Meanwhile, the development of science and technology furnished indispensable advantages and instruments for:

1. The imperialistic expansion of the «western» civilization during the XVIII and XIX centuries –recalling that the capitalistic criminals obtained a massive amount of undue profits from that human-destructive expansion.

2. The creation and development of new products and services, and their ever-augmenting production –from which the capitalistic criminals also obtained a steady flow of undue profits.

In this way, as already explained in section [4.39], the development of science and technology served as joint backbone for both the «western» imperialistic expansion and the accompanying criminal venture called *capitalism.*

Over time the capitalistic criminals either assimilated or displaced the industrial barons and their descendants, depending on the case, using both the criminal scheme of the «monetary credit» and the capitalistic regime of corporate property. Thenceforth the capitalistic criminals acquired the control of all the major industrial conglomerates; this plutocratic control nowadays stands highly concentrated in a handful of shady capitalistic criminal cliques.

The interested person would find very useful to review the historical records from those centuries. Notice that «the masses» and the social «revolutions» actually played marginal and subsidiary roles for the ultimate outcome of the epoch.

[7.51]

Thus, modern *representative democracy* emerged upon the migration of one type of elite into another, dependent on the new elites, tolerated and somewhat fostered just as a tactical measure, and controlled since its very beginning. And for supporting and reinforcing that same social reconfiguration, the new elites fostered and directed the transition from regimes of widespread slavery and bondage into granted *freedom*, as a means to accommodate the newly variable and flexible hired-labor requirements observed by that same elites; especially at those times when successive industrial revolutions made indispensable to dislodge people from permanent posts while nascent industries required new laborers, as described in section [4.88].

Thereby, as already introduced in section [4.40], true or actual democracy does not constitute an essential part of the modern «western» civilization. Rather, an *appearance of democracy* constitutes an essential part of the modern «western» civilization; fake democracy, managed democracy but not true democracy constitutes an essential component of the modern «western» civilization.

[7.52]

Whenever «western» societies enact a social contract based on an asynchronous exchange and a true democracy, if they ever do it, that will constitute a new historical time, very different from the current one.

Main Social Causes of the Failure of the Representative Democracy

[7.53]

Two social behaviors constitute cornerstones of the failure of the *representative democracy* at the beginning of the XXI century:

[7.54]

a) *Fascism within nominally democratic societies.*

Within every human society dwells an undetermined quantity of members of the parasitic psychopathic subspecies. The subspecies, together with ordinary authoritarian individuals, assemble fascist covert formations, as described in section [7.8].

In democratic countries, fascist formations regard democracy simply as the playground they must cheat and manipulate.

Therefore, those fascist covert formations usually stand ready to collaborate with whatever group may furnish them with parasitic societal positions; hence, the fascist formations eagerly embrace aspiring dictators who command a retinue, capitalistic criminals, oligarchs, and any other socially-harmful group of individuals. The deal for the fascists results simple: «We aid you to steal and manipulate, we cover your tracks, in reciprocity you provide a framework where we develop our parasitic activities.»

In the aforesaid interdependence, fascist formations actively aid and participate in electoral frauds and rigged elections, in diverting the attention away from capitalistic criminals (and capitalistic banks), in protecting the interests of oligarchs, in defending dictatorships, and so on.

Furthermore, the preferred target for infiltration by the members of the parasitic psychopathic subspecies consists of the so-called «state security agencies», where the psychopathic parasites can legally spy the population and then illegally and/or unfairly share the data with their peers; this made worse by the glaring absence of a democratic control over such agencies. This described further in section [7.58].

[7.55]

b) *A giant kindergarten.*

The unwillingness of many people to acquire accountability for their own actions and for the welfare of the world where they live in also causes the failure of the *representative democracy.*

Many humans expect that, without their intervention and understanding, other individuals find and pursue the solutions for common problems; that «specialized people», «experts», or «the authority» make the strategic choices that affect everybody's destinies; and that the state-organization, private organizations, or individual «heroes» enact those choices.

This unwillingness to engage in personal accountability finds support in and becomes intensified by—

α. Regular crafted information flows which aim to direct what the public must think, as described in [7.59] and subsequent sections.

β. The concealment of decisive, uncomfortable, or essential data by the so-called «state security agencies», under the guise that it «could disturb the population».

γ. The covert fascist formations which willingly collaborate to manipulate everyone they can.

Many current, nominally democratic societies thus resemble a giant kindergarten, instead of constituting societies directed by their adult population.

In these giant kindergartens the child-citizens receive only filtered information that may serve for them to continue their lives unaltered. The information therein diffused lacks any data that the child-citizens may use to question their reality and the status-quo, or to establish alternative ways of life.

Main Structural or Organizational Causes of the Failure of the Representative Democracy

[7.56]

Likewise, five structural or organizational schemes constitute cornerstones of the failure of the *representative democracy* at the beginning of the XXI century:

[7.57]

a) *The capitalistic fraud.*

As recorded in [4.41] and subsequent sections, within exchange spaces controlled by the capitalistic fraud, honest hard-working individuals and entrepreneurs toil and compete in a permanent structural disadvantage against the capitalistic criminals and their allies. Honest people hardly prevails in an exchange space corrupted by the capitalistic fraud. Meanwhile, the capitalistic criminals just distribute money and payment promises among themselves and allied criminals.

The capitalistic fraud creates a situation where everybody can see that, within nominally democratic countries, dishonest individuals routinely thrive and displace honest people. Accordingly, those same dishonest individuals frequently realize that the essential source of their «success» consists of an unfair and rigged societal system, and therefore they direct their energy and resources to uphold the capitalistic fraud and pervert democratic processes.

Thus, the capitalistic fraud, as venom, poisons and putrefies whole societies.

[7.58]

b) *The state security agencies.*

In basically every nominally democratic society the so-called «state security agencies» operate factually detached from democratic direction, democratic control, and public accountability. Everywhere most citizens regard the «state security agencies», or «state security services», as the most sinister component of the state-organization.

This situation happens driven further by the failure of the *representative democracy* itself as described in what follows.

Everyone can unmistakably observe that frequently unskilled, treacherous, or incompetent individuals (or any combination thereof) reach high command posts by electoral processes. And such individuals, as prescribed by procedures of *representative democracy*, only last a few years in their posts, at most.

The aforesaid incompetence in upper command posts fostered and served as justification for defensive strategies enacted by the employees of many branches within the state-organization, including the «state security agencies», who resorted to establish parallel, sometimes informal, mechanisms for self-regulation –for surviving while coping with top-rank unfitness and derelict. Otherwise, many state-organizations would collapsed because of instability and ineptitude long ago.

In this context the «state security agencies» handle much confidential information and, as noted in section [7.54], constitute the preferred target for infiltration by the parasitic psychopathic subspecies. Besides, due to the possibility of obtaining an unchecked «control» over other humans, ordinary authoritarian individuals frequently seek to join those agencies.

Thereupon, in many countries the «state security agencies» transformed themselves into a branch of fascism, and the «intelligence community» operates as another, undemocratic society factually above the democratic one.

Consequently, in many nominally democratic countries the quantity, pervasiveness, and intrusiveness of electronic state espionage against the population corresponds to a totalitarian regime; while stealing personal or private information and its illegal covert distribution for commercial purposes happens ordinarily.

Hence, for achieving actual democracy, any reform of nominally democratic regimes must make the «state security agencies» accountable to the people.

[7.59]

c) *The transmission of information about current events.*

Several centuries ago the printed press conveyed the first massively-distributed regular unidirectional information flows. Almost since the beginning of such unidirectional information flows, interested individuals and groups controlled and directed those for their own factional profit, as happens nowadays. Thereupon, massively-distributed regular unidirectional information flows, now conveyed also using electronic devices and electromagnetic waves, typically contain deliberated biases and partial data, when not outright lies. Modern societies face a difficult problem for reliably acquiring accurate and unbiased data about relevant, current events.

Thereon, the transmission of information about current events typically involves several arrangements for social manipulation:

[7.60]

a. In the theory of the *representative democracy*, journalism supposedly would serve to «uncover the truth» and tell everybody about relevant facts and novelties happening in the world, including uncomfortable facts for top-rank state functionaries. Because of that social function, in democratic countries journalism proceeds legally protected and, except for public broadcasters, also proceeds detached from the state-organization. But in current «western» societies the implied honesty and impartiality of journalists rarely happens, and instead everyone with a conscience can observe the synchronized, manipulated, and concerted distribution of selected information by blocks of journalists and the organizations they work at.

To make things worse, nowadays in «western» societies journalists frequently present themselves as «specialists» in every field from which they gather data, and seek to «explain the facts» instead of just reporting them. At some point the couriers attempted to become themselves the center of the attention and saw their job as a source of «power» and «influence» over other humans.

This dysfunctional distribution of information about current events severely impacts and impairs the capacity of «western» societies for building true democracies.

[7.61]

β.   In the age of electronic communications by the internet, which very recently started, several individuals and organizations almost immediately built several mechanisms for manipulating information flows available on that network. In general, fascists and capitalistic criminals sponsor and protect those individuals and organizations that promote and enact the manipulation of information flows available on the internet and thereby delude the humans who regard such information as true. Otherwise, competent unconfederated businesspersons would already vanquished those socially-harmful enterprises. Threat:

i.   When someone submits a query to the so-called «web search engines» or *web indexing services* operated by monopolistic or oligopolistic corporations, typically those return biased and manipulated lists of results. Nowadays, such manipulation typically happens by implementing and configuring automated algorithms.

ii. Unsurprisingly, almost as soon as internet talking forums[6] and other mechanisms for sharing written expressions through the internet became popular, many antidemocratic organizations and individuals deployed

---

6   The first internet talking forums, and so far the most useful, happen asynchronously either in text-only mode or using chiefly text. Even chatting forums still proceed mostly by written statements.

scores of fake internet users and hordes of actual fascists who targeted and actively engaged with specific groups of genuine users.

Software built to mimic an interlocutor –optionally characterized as «discussion robots»– at the time of this writing still does not exist sufficiently developed for proficiently replacing humans. Upon such achievement the aforesaid software more or less automatically could exhibit a behavior resembling a human, thereby deceiving and interacting with real humans for the purpose of making those latter waste their time and energy. The technology available at the time of this writing suffices for building such «discussion robots», and these computer programs constitute an obvious target for development.

iii. Some web services called «social networks» specialized in functioning as platforms for exchanging personal thoughts and life experiences. The programmers of these «social networks» soon developed mechanisms to «boost» supposedly popular trends among users; while, in fact, human operators frequently hand-picked and carefully cured the subjects to «boost». The way of «boosting» content typically consists in showing it more frequently in the user interface. Thus, yet again, humans aiming at and striving for (predatory) social control advertised an information-sharing environment that would serve for building a stronger society and promptly turned it into a tool for manipulation.

[7.62]

d) *The indoctrination of the population lacking a conscience.*

Almost since the beginning of traditional civilizations many individuals engaged in deliberately indoctrinating other humans for the benefit of the manipulators. Hence, nowadays the practice of indoctrinating others happens masterfully developed as usual business.

In this context, in a world of humans lacking a conscience, *basic animals* like those described in sections [3.165] and [3.166] just lack the sophistication for processing indoctrinating data, and this incapacity produces a behavioral advantage in a competition against other humans when all together dwell in primitive social settings, or in proto-civilizations. Therefrom, in social settings where nobody enforces compliance with social standards, while others seek to behave correctly according to their cultural conceptions, *basic animals* know no internalized rules and behave without any significant restraint.

In many instances, the implanted doctrine (the implanted mind-set) furnishes a mental configuration adequate for the indoctrinated human to perform tasks within an organization disproportionately for the advantage of the *puppet masters*, as explained in the following sections.

[7.63]

Many humans lack the indispensable *executive functions* for understanding the consequences of the exercise of their own organizational posts. If someone attempts to explain to those humans the overall actual organizational interactions and dealings, and the far-reaching temporal and spatial relevance and consequences of the performance of their own functions, along with the organizational general goals (the real goals, not those publicized by any doctrine); then those humans deficient in *executive functions* will not understand or, more frequently, will regard such events and consequences as irrelevant for their own organisms.

[7.64]

In this way, few humans with above-average *executive functions* can indoctrinate scores of humans with deficient *executive functions* for performing organizational posts while making those latter think that the goals of the organization at which they toil consist of others different from the real primary organizational goals.

Hence, organizational doctrines also serve for individuals to lie to themselves; doctrines save them from acknowledging or searching for the truth, even privately.

[7.65]

Due to what recorded in section [3.82], attempts to directly implant external, explicitly codified doctrinal sequences into the mind-set hardly produce the intended consequences.

Typically, a doctrine becomes implanted through the exposition to, memorization, and repetition of audiovisual animated representations, histories and myths, graphic figures, and simple statements, among several methods.

The fundamental characteristic of all these doctrinal vehicles consists in that the shown pseudo-events indirectly transmit or imply some or several of the doctrinal sequences aimed for implantation. Thereat, the *logical-operations machine* can obtain or deduce the underlying and essential relationships present in those pseudo-events, ascertain the implications of these former, and pass those implications to the *machine to conform and store the mind-set strings*.

An accompanying operant-conditioning style training coherent with the doctrine can reinforce the whole process.

[7.66]

Thus, in modern times the indoctrination of individuals deficient in *executive functions* (and lacking a conscience) happens mainly through four avenues:

α. Massive broadcasting and display of movies, animated series, and melodramas *(soap operas)*.

β. Publicity by means of «informative transmissions», direct advertising campaigns and, with the advent of the internet, manipulated content displayed to a user of electronic devices –as described in section [7.61].

γ. The culture conveyed by judeo-christian and islamic religions, which comprises a magical theoretical foundation for authoritarianism and the deferral of much welfare for «after death».

δ. The distortion of institutionalized education to indoctrinate the population according to the interests of a few, including (of course) the systematic distortion of history.

Notice the large variability in both scope and complexity of these avenues. As example of comparison: a quickly crafted campaign can produce a direct advertisement which depicts straightforward relationships; meanwhile, an ordinary religious practice, which arises from methodological propensities blended with cultural elements, serves to stabilize personalities and produce functional individuals as described in sections [3.144] and [3.145], albeit those humans mostly functional for societies with authoritarian traits.

[7.67]

e) *«Representatives of the people» in positions of disadvantage.*

The facts in the human world render untenable the theory that, in a regime of *representative democracy* coupled with the capitalistic fraud, anyone could just abandon its productive activity and direct a large amount of its time and resources for competing for an electoral post and reach the public office independently, in such way that the commitments acquired actually reflect the interests of the people that voted for the elected candidate. Rare the cases when someone achieves such feat with its own welfare unharmed.

This detached-from-reality theory befits the dream of a «hero» who carries everybody else, popular among the members of the parasitic psychopathic subspecies.

[7.68]

The *representative democracy* coupled with the capitalistic fraud almost always develops into a plutocratic regime where the electoral processes serve solely as an «escape valve» of popular aspirations, where alternating between individuals from one political party and another as «commanders» of the state-organization just serves for modulating the predefined course of action.

[7.69]

For reaching a public office through an electoral process, in the conditions of the current *representative democracy* coupled with the capitalistic fraud, usually any individual can obtain a substantial advantage by collecting money from its supporters and using that money for paying touring and advertising expenses. Those expenses ordinarily the average citizen cannot afford without damaging its own welfare, even for a relatively minor post as municipal executive officer.

Furthermore, due to the rotational nature of the public electoral posts in a *representative democracy*, anyone who engages in such professional activity after finishing its term and returning to «civilian life» typically must cope with uncertain or weakened future prospects in the exchange space (for earning money), compared with those individuals who did not participate in any electoral campaign and did not deviate their attention from their main income-producing business.

Moreover, usually only the capitalistic criminals and the «owners» of productive cooperative systems –in the framework of human exploitation described in [6.46] and subsequent sections– hold large amounts of spare money which can furnish to a political campaign. Due to these conditions, for achieving success regularly every candidate to an electoral post must convince two audiences:

α. The citizens legally entitled to vote.

β. The privileged elite that furnishes the money for the candidate's campaign and, in many cases, also pays for the living expenses of that same «professional representative» out of the public office.

[7.70]

The show of the «political campaigns», as a means to obtain favorable votes by «differentiating» candidates and communicating slogan-size proposals, ordinarily attains its goal because of deficient *executive functions* in the majority of the population.

Thereof, for example, most humans prefer to choose a candidate by watching a broadcasted «debate», rather than by comparing written detailed proposals and actual projects.

[7.71]

Everywhere everyone can observe the aforesaid perverted patterns and interactions routinary in a *representative democracy* coupled with the capitalistic fraud.

[7.72]

To make things worse, in many cases the «representatives» arrive knowing little or nothing about the particular situation of the state-branch which they join once elected, typically due to the lack of institutional transparency of the current state-organizations.

This lack of transparency coupled with the rotational nature of the electoral posts, and with the absence of a democratic control over the «representatives» once in office, originates and sustains an absence of accountability for the medium- and long-term consequences of the choices made by elected officers.

[7.73]

All the dysfunctional environment usually produces herds of candidates and elected officers ready and eager to sell their will to the best bidder. Once sold, or once within a criminal group, the «representatives of the people» usually champion and make choices that produce customized consequences from which their accomplices, sponsors, and themselves can obtain profits, draw inequitable advantages, or secure privileged positions, before the respective «representative» abandons the public office. Optionally, the «representatives of the people» resort to directly stealing public money and assets, but in countries with fairly functional judicial systems this latter entails a large risk.

[7.74]

Hence, typically happen societal and state behavioral interactions succinctly characterized as «moving forward according to the immediate interests of the sponsors of the sold representatives, profiting fast those who can obtain something from it, and making the indispensable adjustments to quell the population and/or give the impression of democracy».

These behavioral interactions proceeded more or less stable during decades sustained by the plundering of the Earth's natural resources through the expansion of the capitalistic fraud. But at the beginning of the XXI century when truly state choices became indispensable, at the time when societies should behaved as actual cooperative systems, the promoters of the status-quo entered into a type of negation of reality.

Main Failure Modes of the Representative Democracy

[7.75]

All the described causes interplay in the failure of the *representative democracy*, here recorded only two well-known failure modes.

Managed Democracy: Full-Scale Showtime

[7.76]

From the circumstances afforded by the aforesaid causes, regularly arise plutocratic and oligarchic regimes of various degrees and styles.

The most popular style of plutocracy or oligarchy, depending on the case, consists in a *full-scale show*. In this style, the gangs of affluent and privileged individuals reserve for themselves the businesses engaged in mainstream journalism, unidirectional broadcasting, and bidirectional communications. Thereat, those affluent and privileged individuals drive out any competitors from the aforementioned businesses by unfair and/or illegal means; for this latter purpose usually the sold «representatives» within the state-organization furnish them with exclusive licenses, favorable legal frameworks and, in some instances, directly transfer public property and state enterprises into the control of plutocrats and oligarchs.

If the aid directed from the state-organization does not suffice for eliminating competitors in those businesses, plutocrats and oligarchs can still use the money furnished by the capitalistic fraud as an insurmountable advantage against all competitors.

[7.77]

Thereupon starts the full-scale show: what a totalitarian regime would do to achieve sophistication, homogeneity, and pervasiveness of propaganda, the plutocrats and oligarchs do much better.

[7.78]

Plutocrats and oligarchs strive to use the full-scale show to keep entertained the members of the parasitic psychopathic subspecies, by all means, directing the attention of those latter into *something*, into anything, whatever. Such entertainment and diversion fundamental for the purpose of weakening the activity and effectiveness of the fascist formations and thereby securing the prevalence of the interests of the plutocrats and oligarchs within the state-organization.

[7.79]

The full-scale show, coupled with the control and manipulation of every information flow and data source readily available to the population, also serves to disseminate biased and partial information and data upon which the general population makes choices at electoral processes. By those means oligarchs and plutocrats secure a perception of volition and independence for the manipulated citizens who «select» the candidates and political options of their preference.

[7.80]

Consequently, in a managed democracy typically blossom several political parties all supported by aspiring or actual plutocrats and oligarchs, where the political parties differ merely in relatively trivial and irrelevant aspects and styles. Deficiencies in *executive functions* within the population constitute the paramount foundation for the effectiveness of those aspects and styles as differentiators.

[7.81]

Therefrom, if the population desires and demands a development and transformation of the societal cooperative system into a particular direction, or mobilizes towards those goals, then plutocrats and oligarchs can manage and manipulate the related information flows to serve their interests and, if necessary, use that same information flows to directly or indirectly promote a change of individuals and political parties at the top of the state-organization by means of directed electoral processes.

Hence, in a managed democracy routinely change—

1. The individuals at the top of the state-organization.
2. The political party to which those individuals belong.
3. The executive style of the state-organization.
4. A few accessory organizational mechanisms within the societal cooperative system.
5. Some secondary choices regarding the social lifestyle.

But, after all that circus, the general direction and nature of the societal cooperative system remains the same.

A Single Pervading Political Party: Faked Electoral Processes

[7.82]

Also known as «dominant-party system». In the best-case scenario, this status-quo stands halfway between a fascist regime and a managed democracy, although fully fascist societies can enact it as a mask to disguise themselves. For example, currently the fully fascist russians use a pseudo-democratic mask of this type, albeit unsuccessfully.

[7.83]

The concerted interaction of fascist formations and the capitalistic criminals constitutes the foundation of the status-quo where a single pervading political party controls the state-organization and manages many puppet civic organizations to support the same party –for example, authoritarian labor unions typically serve or publicly affiliate with the pervading political party.

[7.84]

As support for providing a minimal appearance of «democracy», usually the single pervading political party surrounds itself with some satellite political parties which serve as pseudo-competitors in electoral processes and public offices.

[7.85]

In this type of undemocratic regimes, the fascist formations usually stand within the ranks of the state-organization and the pervading political party, thereby creating an organizational coalescence which blurs the boundaries between the state-organization and the party.

[7.86]

Meanwhile, the capitalistic criminals stand in privileged positions, including monopolistic and oligopolistic industries, and actively cooperate for the maintenance of the ruling party.

[7.87]

In this case the main control of readily-available information flows and data sources arises from the state-organization. The methods used to control information flows comprise, among several—

    a)   Explicitly banning journalistic establishments. Persecuting and prosecuting non-aligned journalists; if those activities do not suffice for silencing them, then the fascists may resort to physical attacks, including direct sabotage, theft, and murder.

b) Spreading the state budget labeled as «advertising expenses» into journalistic enterprises in exchange for favorably biased editorial lines.

c) Granting exclusive licenses for publishing and broadcasting to the capitalistic criminals and/or transferring monopolistic or oligopolistic publishing and broadcasting enterprises to them.

d) Controlling distribution networks in the case of physically printed materials. Blocking the access to internet websites and proscribing software platforms.

[7.88]

The control and destruction of alternative candidates and political parties typically happens by—

a) Pseudo-legal proceedings against those, frequently ending in jail terms or large material loses for the prosecuted. Additionally, the fascists approve laws unfavorable to the activities of the actual democrats.

b) Systematic sabotage of their political activities and personal lives; including outright espionage, persecution, and direct sabotage by the fascist «state security agencies».

c) Non-existent coverage of their activities and proposals, or active defamation against them in fascist-aligned news outlets.

d) Assassination and direct physical harm.

[7.89]

As sometimes happens, the control, sidelining, persecution, or prosecution of alternative candidates and political parties does not suffice for vanishing those when the population demands a change of direction in the societal cooperative system and, not surprisingly, among the non-fascist population nobody regards as true the ridiculous and implausible explanations attempting to present a single pervading political party as the result of «democracy».

When that happens, and despite persecution or prosecution alternative candidates reach electoral processes, the fascists resort to electoral fraud. Normally, the fascists and traitors perform the electoral fraud as a standard-business routine, does not matter whether the alternative candidates actually reached a fairly large popularity or not.

Usually everyone can notice the electoral fraud but, since the «state security agencies» stand filled by fascists, and the armed forces also stand controlled by fascists, typically the democratic sector of the population cannot revert the fraud in the short-term. Again in this case, deficiencies in *executive functions* of many individuals within the general population hinder the capacity of the society for quickly and efficiently organizing itself against fascist factions.

[7.90]

An electoral fraud which subverted the will of the people produces a fracture when the democratic sector of the population resolves to fight the fascists until their obliteration; but, if those upon whom falls the historical task of fighting for the rule of democracy lack courage and a drive for excellence, and thereupon choose the path of submission and collaboration –as happened in Mexico in 1988– then their choice mars the future of generations to come, and those generations may find unsurmountable or pointless to fix and transform that wasted country.

Democracy as a Bait: International Hypocrisy

[7.91]

The human world ended World War II split between nominally democratic and fully totalitarian regimes, and between those poles many countries displayed traits of the two types. In such civilizational environment many humans fought for their freedom against fascists everywhere and, of course, many regarded establishing a democratic regime as the most effective way to displace authoritarianism.

Hence, many humans made high-stakes bets for democracy throughout the second half of the XX century.

[7.92]

The United States of America ended World War II in an advantageous position for fighting against totalitarian regimes. This happened due to its relative physical isolation, the abundance of natural resources within its territory, and its well-developed scientific and industrial base at the time.

[7.93]

Instead of fully focusing itself and its foreign policy on an authentic fight against totalitarianism and the fascists who supported it, the United States of America enacted an imperial foreign policy where the fight for democracy served merely as a bait to subdue people.

That same imperial foreign policy served as foundation for establishing unnecessary military bases all around the planet, which served to project military might but served nothing to advance the proclaimed causes of democracy and human rights.

In this regard, the United States of America squandered a unique historic opportunity.

[7.94]

Those who expected something different from the United States of America, perhaps due to physical distance, popular myths, propaganda, and the unreliable communications of the epoch, or perhaps just because of a desire to think that a better place existed compared with the abominable authoritarian regimes, did not notice the true nature and unequivocal history of that country.

Starting with the sweeping genocide of native-american people, passing through the Monroe Doctrine, and the late rationalization of themselves as an «exceptional nation» which established secret clandestine jails all around the world[7], and whatever now follows, the United States of America always enacted an imperial project. Such imperial project in time varied in scope, complexity, and specific goals; nevertheless, always placed as main goal the «dominion» of that country's state-organization and its main oligarchic enterprises over all other people.

[7.95]

In the United States of America the idea of democracy serves as sales pitch for internal organization, upon which operates a *managed democracy*, and thereat proceeds an outward imperial project.

---

7   The establishment of secret clandestine jails around the world happened as part of the «war on terror» started at the beginning of the XXI century as a «counterattack» because of the terrorist attacks in New York on September 11, 2001. Many «allied countries» –failed democracies– secretly approved and cooperated with the establishment of those secret clandestine jails within their own territories, the jails euphemistically denominated «detention centers». Within those clandestine jails, the kidnapped detainees suffered systematic and organizationally approved torture, the most outstanding practice of torture consisted in *waterboarding*, the practices of torture also euphemistically called «enhanced interrogation techniques».

[7.96]

Therefrom, the United States of America as a country, as an organized group of humans, typically and historically regards the fight for democracy and against fascism as—

- A business.
- Yet another opportunity to establish an advantageous position for themselves.
- A source of pawns and subordinates.

[7.97]

Furthermore, as happens in many countries, within the United States of America dwell significant scores of fascists. Those fascists within deem reasonable to reach agreements and alliances with every foreign fascist and antidemocratic group. Accordingly, agreements happened with medieval arab monarchies and with several other antidemocratic regimes, upon which the United States of America brought assistance, protection, and support to those.

[7.98]

The aforesaid treacherous agreements with antidemocratic groups led that country and others to an imperial attempt to divide the human world into «spheres or zones of influence» where one or another imperial country would prevail over the subjugated nations. As would happened during the XIX century with a british mind-set, as the fascist russians and fascist chinese nowadays attempt.

Consequently, very often also, when the time of action and actual attack against antidemocratic forces arrived, winning against fascism resulted against the actual interests of the United States of America. Thereat, more than once that country supported, armed, or organized dictatorships and diverse types of antidemocratic warring formations.

[7.99]

Some factions within the United States of America can either covertly or quietly promote and strengthen the antidemocratic traits of independent countries and foreign social groups, for making easier the task of presenting their country as an «indispensable ally for freedom»; thus either creating or attempting to create captive vassals for the actual empire centered in the same «liberating» country. However, strengthening the antidemocratic traits of groups in foreign countries apparently also happens as part of an exchange of favors.

For these tasks, nowadays the manipulation of content shown to users of electronic devices plays a paramount role. Hence, for instance, the Google corporation acts as the flagship of this «soft» imperialism, frequently manipulating the content presented to segments of users for a wide array of purposes, including the attainment of political goals in foreign countries and publicizing antidemocratic ideologies.

The manipulation of indoctrinating content also serves to promote a type of parceled, subsidiary «spheres of influence» by promoting the interests of second-tier nostalgic countries with long-bygone empires.

[7.100]

Adding to the swamp, the capitalistic elites within the United States of America –those that handle the *managed democracy* there– upon their total lack of commitment with democracy established long-term commercial relationships in China, while those capitalistic elites stood fully aware that an openly antidemocratic fascist regime manages that latter country.

Thereupon many capitalistic corporations relocated their productive operations into China, with the explicit purpose of profiting from the low wages paid to chinese citizens. And the chinese laborers, unable to exercise any democratic rights, stand in an outstanding disadvantage against their employers. Obviously the chinese laborers cannot vote for a minimum wage and mandatory adequate social security, obviously they cannot vote to change the laws of that country.

Hence, as part of their treason to democracy, the capitalistic elites within the United States of America in concert with those of other failed democracies established a competition between laborers of democratic countries and laborers lacking basic democratic rights and freedoms in a fully authoritarian regime, with the foreseeable and later materialized decrease in the quality of life of laborers in democratic countries.

[7.101]

Much damage caused the treason against democracy; the democratic world survived it, but thenceforward many humans lost confidence in democracy as a way of life, as a real option against authoritarianism. Nobody wants to fight against fascism just to fall prey of yet another empire; here again every cognizant individual remembers the XX century. And no laborer in a democratic country wants to match wages of poverty or abject hunger.

[7.102]

Within the aforesaid country little or nothing changed in all these decades concerning its foreign policy. Consequently, at the beginning of the XXI century, when the decline of the «supremacy» of the United States of America became evident, its political elite attempted to engage in ways to ensure «another century of *american* dominion» –due to their ethnocentrism they call themselves *America*– and attempted to repeat the path of the second half of the XX century.

[7.103]

In a democratic world no country can present itself as an «exceptional nation» and does not exist such thing as «primacy among peers». Furthermore, in a democratic world no country can declare itself the «world police and judge», and thereupon assassinate suspects in foreign countries.

In a democratic world do not exist «world leaders»; rather, happen democratic processes where everybody chooses a shared destiny without relinquishing its own individual uniqueness.

[7.104]

Fighting and controlling fully fascist societies which strive to kill, render expendable, or exploit everybody else must proceed using a true alliance of democratic people, institutions and armed forces of democratic regimes, and legal and fair processes.

Make no mistake, fascist societies present an *active threat*[8] for humanity; and, in the specific case of Russia, the most rational solution consists in dismantling such civilization.

Democratic societies must externally manage fascist societies since fascist individuals only understand relationships based in force, and they live in a world where they must either rule or obey. Therefore, democratic countries must engage in explicitly and openly prevailing over fascist societies and, at the same time, must establish legal immigration procedures available to any human capable and willing to live in a more advanced civilization.

---

8 An *active threat* implies an entity which actively exerts itself, tends, or desires to inflict damage to a target. In contrast, a *passive threat* implies an entity which only under certain circumstances hypothetically would cause harm to a target. Hence, an expansionist empire poses an active threat for its neighbors, while a defensive military alliance poses a passive threat for any potential aggressor.

Direct Democracy

[7.105]

Considering the causes and modes of failure of the *representative democracy* coupled with capitalism, the following reform for democratic regimes results pertinent.

Parliament Dismissed

[7.106]

Lawmaking bodies or legislative assemblies filled with «representatives of the people» must cease to exist. Instead, the people directly by democratic processes must redact and modify the population-wide social contract.

The current electronic communication technologies make such action possible in an efficient and prompt way.

[7.107]

Henceforward, the people itself manages the law. The people itself proposes and approves (or rejects) law projects. No «representatives» distort the people's will, now directly expressed in the social contract. In the same way, healthy citizens cannot relinquish accountability.

[7.108]

If a majority of the citizens cannot understand any given law, then such law should not exist –democracy cannot exist there! The citizens themselves bear the accountability for understanding which societal cooperative system they want and therefore approve.

[7.109]

Someone could argue that dismissing the parliament prevents the «specialization» of the law-making job, and that to engage everyone in the law-making process implies or produces a squandering of human resources.

However, as explained in section [7.3], a human societal cooperative system does not resemble a single unified organism. The specialization of tasks, as would happen in an ordinary organism, constitutes neither an inherent quality nor automatically desirable feature of a societal cooperative system.

As recorded in section [7.13], a societal cooperative system consists of a functional assembly of individuals gathered into it because of mutual interest; those same gathered individuals compose, enact, and materialize the corresponding societal cooperative system. But that gathering does not create a «connection» with peers; predictable social relationships do not create a «connection» whatsoever.

Besides, gathering and cooperation do not require a close kinship, and those activities do not create it.

Hence, all the humans gathered in a societal cooperative system remain independent volitional organisms who seek their own welfare. Therefore, delegating or «outsourcing» the management and design of one's own living environment into another individual does not secure survival. May a human delegate specific functions within a known framework, and supervise the correct performance of those functions.

And, anyway, a gregarious organism must either continuously or periodically monitor and engage with the societal cooperative system where dwells as part of its basic survival functions.

[7.110]

For providing physical power humans can better use ordinary labor animals and mechanisms. Happens thus no justification for attempting to keep large quantities of humans as «brainless and therefore efficient labor machines».

[7.111]

The information and communication technologies available to a society condition –or determine– the mixture of codified sophistication and actual democratic control that the population can exercise upon the formal social contract. This happens because—

α. The more speedy and capable become those information and communication technologies, a collectivity of individuals can craft and exchange increasingly complex ideas and proposals, besides the content of the social contract, in increasingly short periods of time in an organizationally functional fashion which includes and processes the input and opinion of many.

β. Upon the dearth or insufficiency of information and communication technologies, the population must resort to either build a very simple formal social contract which the citizens can easily exchange using their available means, or delegate those functions to some individuals who can then design a sophisticated formal social contract, as happened with the *representative democracy*, and then theoretically each subset of the population should periodically control and direct its own representative.

For example, a society lacking readily available technologies for communicating by written statements –think before the invention of the printing press, when paper, ink, and pen constituted scarce and expensive items– may, at best, establish a democratic social contract verbally in very simple terms.

[7.112]

In the theory of the *representative democracy*, the citizens entitled to vote could indirectly control their «representatives» by voting either favorably or unfavorably for any individual and political party, depending on the results obtained in the immediately preceding period, in a sort of intermittent «carrot and stick» relationship. However, as described in sections [7.72] and [7.73], the «representatives» in many (or most cases) can more efficiently secure their own welfare by different means, instead of satisfying the actual aspirations and interests of the citizens entitled to vote.

In the organizational scheme of the *representative democracy*, not only the sponsors and business associates of the «representatives of the people» wield a preceding influence over the elected officers, but the allegiance of each elected officer towards its political party typically supersedes the commitments of the individual towards the population.

Therefrom, with or without electronic communication technologies available, a democratic society must remove the intermediaries between itself and the social contract. If electronic communication technologies do not exist available, then a population can:

1. Write a very simple social contract by using paper and ink, which only the population can modify by direct democracy.
2. Delegate the design of subsidiary regulations to any collegiate body of representatives, and celebrate periodical elections to either approve or reject those proposed subsidiary regulations.

Here the evident cost consists of the increased time required to enact convenient modifications to subsidiary regulations.

[7.113]

The direct management of the law by the people turns the expression of the people's will into an habitual affair, which neither requires anyone's approval nor entails a large fanfare. This direct management of the law turns the circus of the *representative democracy* into a set of ordinary administrative procedures.

Moreover, the direct management of the law by the people will force the political parties and political associations to actually function as such, because now whoever wants to modify the social contract will need to campaign within the population to advance each proposal and each idea, instead of just making dealings with a reduced number of secluded «representatives».

[7.114]

A minimum of citizens must sponsor a law-project for the whole law-making citizens to formally consider it within a legislative agenda. In this way, if the legislative period consists of 10 months:

1. At least 5% of the whole law-making citizens must sponsor a law-project for it to reach the plenum, for everybody to formally consider the project. Each citizen can sponsor only one queued project during each legislative period.

2. Everyone can either endorse or reject a queued project in advance, and change its choice, before the project's closing date.

3. Therefore, every 10 months the plenum –the whole law-making citizens– will consider, per-schedule, at most 20 law-projects. Hence, approximately one law-project every two weeks.

However, if at least 60% of the citizens endorse a proposal outside the queue, then such proposal will become thereby approved. The same for a proposal within the queue which will account as presented outside.

[7.115]

Using open pools of candidates who present written commitments, those individuals who obtain the highest number of (modifiable) votes by the people must thereby become 10-year management boards of—

- The state electoral organization.
- A decentralized state auditing organization.
- An organization specialized in championing human rights.

The total votes for each candidate must remain visible during all the selection process, so anyone can adjust its vote towards the end.

A Unicameral Senate for the Executive Branch

[7.116]

A unicameral senate must perform specialized executive functions, this council established for ensuring inclusive choices within the executive branch of the state-organization. In this regard, the senate now belongs to the executive branch of the state-organization, and not to the legislative one.

[7.117]

The citizens must select the members of the unicameral senate through a societal-wide democratic process using the D'Hondt electoral method. Thereat:

a)   Every political association or political party must present a list of candidates whom the whole society will consider.

b)   The candidates must compete not by district or province, but *cooperative system-wide* (nation-wide).

c)   Thereupon, the D'Hondt electoral method guarantees that even a geographically scattered small social group will obtain a post.

Consequently, if the senate consists of 20 individuals, then a social group consisting of 5% of the population will obtain a post.

In the Appendix 1 recorded a detailed description of this well-known electoral method.

[7.118]

At least 0.5% (half percent) of the adult citizens must affiliate to a political party for this latter to obtain the right to participate in elections –the people through the social contract may adjust this percentage. A citizen cannot affiliate to more than one political party.

As any other organization, each political party must establish a particular social contract to which its members legally bind.

A political party does not need to hold fixed physical assets, as it just consists of a group of organized citizens; accordingly, keeping offices, buildings, or alike, must not constitute a legal requisite for establishing a political party. Furthermore, the affiliation to a political party must consist of a relatively simple process, which can also happen by using electronic communication devices. Therefore, the material cost of organizing and maintaining a political party must remain very low.

[7.119]

The senate must remain relatively small, composed by between 20 and 30 individuals. For example, in a senate composed by 30 individuals, a social group consisting of 3.33% of the population obtains a post.

This organizational provision ensures that the members of the senate can engage in genuine peer-to-peer dialog and perform fast choice-making processes.

[7.120]

The law-making citizens must establish a simple procedure in the social contract enabling them to directly supersede any choice made by the senate.

[7.121]

Hence, the senate can engage in activities prescribed by the social contract; those activities should comprise:

1. Redacting organizational regulations and institutional action guidelines required by the citizens through the approved laws, according to the policies delineated in such laws.

2. Nominating and approving who will perform the highest state posts, including:

   a) The members of the cabinet of ministers.

      The cabinet approved in a single batch –the prime minister forms part of the cabinet. Senators from several political organizations may form a coalition that reaches a majority, and must nominate a cabinet that includes members from all the organizations involved in a way proportional to the votes obtained by each political party.

      The same majority or coalition of senators may replace any single minster at any time by selecting another from the same political affiliation, and the newly appointed will just finish the term of its predecessor. Otherwise, if the coalition dissolves or does not reach a majority any more, the senate must select and appoint the full cabinet again.

   b) The highest ranking officers of the armed forces.
      Selected by simple majority.

   c) The highest ranking officers of security, intelligence, and law-enforcement agencies.
      Selected by simple majority.

d) Ambassadors and other prominent members of the foreign service.
Selected by simple majority.

e) The highest ranking members of the judicial branch of the state-organization.
The composition of the supreme court of justice must reflect that of the senate –and the population. Therefore, the senate must select the members of the supreme court by the D'Hondt method, where several groups of senators present each a list of candidates. This implies fixed equal terms for performing the posts of the supreme court.

f) The highest ranking members of public universities and research institutions.
Selected by simple majority.

g) The members of a scientific council tasked with:
   α. Defining and approving research lines and research projects in fields of basic science, basic knowledge, and foundational technologies.
   β. Allocating the corresponding available budget into those research lines and research projects.
   γ. Evaluating the outcomes of those research lines and research projects.

The members of the scientific council selected by the D'Hondt method in the same fashion as the supreme court.

Universities and research institutions can directly select and manage projects pertaining to applied science or technological development where they can forecast much more tangible and immediate profits; this done using as guidelines the available budget, developmental policies established jointly by the cabinet of ministers and the scientific council, internal organizational regulations, and the social contract itself. Nevertheless, universities and research institutions must develop specific technological solutions upon the request of either the cabinet of ministers or the scientific council.

In sections [7.137] and [7.138] recorded further how to evaluate research and development projects.

3. Performing an unrestricted scrutiny of the operation of both the executive and judicial branches of the state-organization, and individually producing a written report every six months.

   Unrestricted scrutiny includes on-site inspections. Hence, for the senators must stand available without restriction all the information about the scope and nature of the activities of security, intelligence, and law-enforcement agencies.

   Each senator should delegate this unrestricted scrutiny into an aide prescribed and remunerated by law –besides the scrutiny directly performed by each senator. That appointed aide must engage full-time in overseeing the state-organization.

4. Reviewing and pre-approving treaties and legally-binding international agreements. The law-making citizens afterwards must either approve or reject those.

5. Examining, modifying, and approving the state budget presented by the cabinet of ministers.

[7.122]

As an extraordinary measure, the members of the senate may, by simple majority, instruct any individual minister to perform any specific task. Thereon, a frequent usage of this capacity by the senate may denote poor or defective institutional guidelines given to the cabinet.

[7.123]

Given the magnitude of the work, the legal framework must prescribe for each senator a small team tasked with processing data, also the members of each team remunerated by law.

[7.124]

The people through the social contract or other directly-controlled ordinance must define the minimum prerequisites that any individual must fulfill for becoming eligible by the senators for occupying the highest ranking posts within the institutions of the state-organization, excepting the post of prime minister. An essential prerequisite must consist in either holding a professional specialized degree in the related field of action, or demonstrating long-term experience in the same field.

The law-making citizens must also establish the maximum term or accrued time that any given high ranking member of the state-organization can remain in its post. Accordingly, the senate must assign other individuals to those posts with a minimum, known frequency.

[7.125]

Ordinarily, the senate should not assemble a cabinet of ministers by the D'Hondt method because doing so may lead to the inclusion of different incompatible personalities within a singe team, and thereby may produce a dysfunctional performance of the state-organization. The time-sensitiveness of the tasks and the margin for possible disagreements within the cabinet of ministers differs from that of the supreme court and the scientific council; thereat, the senate must tune the cabinet of ministers for performance.

[7.126]

The people through the social contract must prohibit the members of the senate from selecting themselves to occupy any high-ranking post within the state-organization, including the prohibition of selecting a member of the senate as minister of the executive branch.

[7.127]

As already happens with the *representative democracy*, many political parties will tend to function around a «leader», whether this «leader» formally appointed or just informally acknowledged. Thereat, the prohibition of selecting a member of the senate as minister of the executive branch will force the «leader» of each political party to, either:

α. Place itself at the top of its party's list of candidates to the senate (that list which obtains votes from the citizens through the D'Hondt method), and attempt to «pull the strings» mainly using its functions within the senate, or

β. Place a set of lackeys at its party's list of candidates to the senate and instruct those to select itself (the «leader») as prime minister of the executive branch, or any other suitable position.

If the «leader» of an authoritarian political party selects the first option and attempts to «pull the strings» within the senate, then anyway will need to reach agreements with other political parties for selecting the members of the cabinet of ministers of the executive branch.

And, if the «leader» of an authoritarian political party selects the second option, then:

1. The voters will need to acknowledge that they select a bunch of lackeys as their representatives within the executive branch, not the «leader». Most people who would vote for a «leader» in a list of candidates will doubt or think twice before voting for the

lackeys, since those voters ordinarily espouse an authoritarian culture and carry scarce *executive functions*; thereby the number of votes obtained by the political party will decrease.

2. The lackeys at any time can change of opinion and act independently, since they do not hold any legal binding to the «leader». Moreover, if the lackeys appoint the «leader» as public official, then formally the «leader» becomes a subordinate of the lackeys.

3. The «leader» runs the risk of remaining out of any public office whenever its party obtains a reduced number of votes. Since the social contract prescribes a professional specialization for performing any high-ranking public post, also the available posts for the «leader» become highly reduced.

[7.128]

The senate must select a very capable individual as prime minister, since that individual will perform critical tasks in times of war, when must both exercise an ability to inspire its people to relentlessly fight and make correct strategic choices for the survival of the cooperative system. Thereon, the social contract must include a *martial law* which comprises an alternative set of procedures for managing the state-organization and provisions for mobilizing the population. Likewise, the social contract must include the specific situations when the senate can approve a state of martial law.

[7.129]

The absence of a single individual who acts as «head of state» in times of peace may annoy (and even confuse) some people with an entrenched authoritarian culture.

And, in international relationships, this absence of a «head of state» will render patently void the nowadays frequent, popular, and useless summits of «world leaders».

Everywhere people must become accustomed to the fact that any single individual should never make alone the fundamental choices that affect a whole democratic nation.

Keeping a Nation Safe and Functioning

[7.130]

No human cooperative system will function properly if lacks adequate humans as members, or if those members do not want to make it work. In this same scope, a democratic social arrangement will not function as a true democracy if lacks a majority of capable humans resolved to make it work.

Arguably, the most easy path for accumulating a large percentage of democratic, competent individuals within a single country consists in organized, carefully filtered, and planned migrations from failed or fascist countries into democratic ones. Yet, the most stable solution for concentrating democratic, competent individuals within a cooperative system consists in furnishing the conditions for those to thrive.

Furthermore, a democratic social arrangement must produce and entail conditions highly harsh, unpropitious, and unsupportive for a non-democratic way of life; thereby, traitors and non-democratic people will deal with systemic adversities and hindrances.

[7.131]

For the aforesaid purposes, a fully transparent state-organization constitutes a cornerstone of a healthy democratic societal cooperative system, as it supports accountability and inclusiveness in choice-making processes in a society managed by its adult population.

Full Transparency of the State-Organization

[7.132]

All the data from the state-organization regarding ordinary activities not directly related with defense and security functions should stand readily available to the citizens of a democratic regime, without restriction and without requiring an express request.

This data includes, among others, all the ordinary records about—

- Local services and infrastructure. Hence, the data concerning fixed distribution networks, roads, reserved and used capacities of local administrations, and so forth.
- Territorial management, urban planning, urban construction permits, and concomitant data.

- All the ordinary expenses of the state-organization. Those expenses include the remunerations of all public employees.
- The management and administration of state enterprises; and all the operational capabilities of those. Hence, the accounting data and the administrative records of those enterprises.
- The quantity, quality, and localization of mineral resources, the data about its current extraction, and the forecasts about them.
- Updated collected statistics, including those regarding the performance, health, and abilities of the population.
- Detailed forecasts about the development of both the societal cooperative system and the natural environment.

[7.133]
The social contract must explicitly include a right for each citizen to request all its personal data collected by the state-organization. Upon request, the state-organization must provide such personal profiles and records without delay. And, as part of its ordinary transparency, the state-organization must routinely publish which data collects from its citizens, the purpose of collecting it, a reference to the law or ordinance which prescribed such collection, and the aggregated findings.

[7.134]
If the investigation of a crime involving a citizen as suspect or any other tracking activity related to security happens at the time when that same citizen requests its personal data, then the state-organization must keep in secret such investigation during at most one month for allowing the collection of evidence, and afterwards the state-organization must inform the citizen about the investigation and the specific charges it may produce. Thereupon the citizen must stand entitled to initiate a judicial proceeding for demonstrating its innocence and thereby dismiss the ongoing investigation; if the citizen fails to actually demonstrate its innocence, then the investigation may continue. The social contract must prescribe a maximum temporal length for active investigations.

In the case of an ongoing investigation, the state-organization must refrain from delivering to the citizen more data than the ordinarily collected from everybody else. But upon the dismissal of the investigation, if either the judicial procedure finds the citizen not guilty or such guiltiness remains unproved, then the state-organization must disclose all the data collected.

[7.135]

The people through the social contract must explicitly prohibit the state-organization from collecting data from specific individuals as a preemptive action.

Alternatively, the state-organization can designate an individual as a *person of interest* according to some predefined standards established by the people in an ordinance for the purpose, and secretly collect an increased quantity of publicly-available data about that individual during a limited period of time (with a maximum also approved by the people); but afterwards, if the *person of interest* does not commit any crime and the designation expires, the state-organization must inform the individual about the fact and disclose the corresponding collected data.

[7.136]

Moreover, based on a personal *right to privacy*, the social contract must prescribe jail terms for the individuals that retrieve, collect, or distribute private data from targeted persons, or otherwise track them without their explicit consent; the corresponding jail terms must increase if the criminals perform the activity as part of an organized group. *Private data* consists of all data not publicly available from an individual, or not voluntarily disclosed by its owner.

The social contract must declare every person the legitimate owner of all the publicly-available data about itself, whenever this data does not relate to affairs concerning the cooperative system.

The Evaluation of Research and Development Projects

[7.137]

The practice of rating or evaluating the usefulness of a scientific publication by the number of citations that receives in arbitrated journals must cease and disappear. Likewise, the evaluation of the work performed by a researcher must not depend on the number of times other researchers formally cited the publications of the former.

Such failed evaluation practices belong to that world managed by incompetent and ignorant individuals who attempt to reduce everything to indexes –hence, belong to the failed capitalistic world.

[7.138]

In the reformed democracy, the scientific council must publish the policies which will use to evaluate the work performed by researchers; and must appoint committees for performing the corresponding task in each branch of knowledge. The ensuing evaluations must stand publicly available to the citizens in a searchable database, such evaluations must include a detail of the costs incurred.

Universities and research institutions must perform the same practices for evaluating the output of applied-science or technological-development projects managed by themselves, and must publish the corresponding evaluations in the same searchable database of the scientific council. However, in these cases, each institution must also publish and periodically update the profits generated by each project.

The costs incurred by a research or development project include the expenses related to the usage of either fixed or long term assets and equipments in laboratories and research facilities.

Reorganizing Academic Institutions

[7.139]

Societal cooperative systems must completely disband all existing *schools of economics*. Any person presenting itself as *economist* must find another job.

[7.140]

In current *law schools*, individuals attempt to learn a specialization related with the operation and construction of societal cooperative systems.

Societal cooperative systems must reform those *law schools* within universities into *organizational crafts schools*. The teaching and academic development concerning productive and commercial relationships must proceed within those *organizational crafts schools*, and thereby the discipline of *economics* must cease to exist.

Hence, a single academic branch must encompass the activity of devising methods and ways for the practical organization of human affairs. Consequently, will begin a new academic branch akin to engineering but specialized in human organization, here proposed the name *organizational crafts*.

[7.141]

The aforementioned *organizational crafts schools* must engage in rebuilding and reorganizing from zero all the academic knowledge concerning productive and commercial relationships.

[7.142]

Accordingly, the *organizational crafts schools* will apply –and provide feedback about– the basic knowledge developed in the fields of psychology, sociology, anthropology, and all others related with the study and research of human behavior.

However, any individual who wishes to join these schools must indispensably demonstrate proficiency in mathematics and an ability to understand basic natural phenomena at the standard of science and engineering schools. A few mandatory courses must reinforce and enhance the aforesaid understanding during the first stages of any specialization. The current and foreseeable challenges and opportunities of humanity make this provision indispensable.

If the developmental stage of a country makes it feasible, any person interested in specializing in the *management of the state-organization* must first obtain an academic degree in either basic science or engineering.

[7.143]

Further, any academic degree in *public administration* or *management of the state-organization* must include legal knowledge together with an extensive knowledge about societal relationships and the construction of cooperative systems as instruments to ensure the welfare of those who participate.

Detaching the understanding of the law from the understanding of societal development, organizational behaviors, and societal productive and commercial relationships must never happen again.

[7.144]

The management of the law directly by the citizens through direct democracy, as described in [7.105] and subsequent sections, will prevent the development of any overly-complicated legal framework within the societal cooperative system. Direct democracy should discourage the professionals engaged in *organizational crafts* from attempting to devise –and proposing– legal procedures and methods that nobody or almost nobody understands.

[7.145]

Additionally, notice the untenability of any such thing as *political science* –remember what described in section [3.142]. Anyone attempting to engage in that field usually can find a place in the disciplines of psychology, sociology, anthropology, or any other related.

News Streams and Information Flows

[7.146]

As described in previous sections, unrestricted transmission of ideas and public data, and the associated information flows readily available to a population, constitute an essential foundation for a functioning democracy. Even without high-quality information flows readily available, humans can still search for the truth elsewhere; nevertheless, this creates a burden for the members of the societal cooperative system who will need to divert resources, time, and attention to perform a basic societal function. In most cases such diversion entails a diminution of the productivity of an individual, and therefore a decrease of its personal welfare and, aggregated, diminishes the welfare and success of the whole cooperative system.

Consequently, a societal cooperative system will derive a structural advantage from establishing a democratic management of any medium used to broadcast data. The mediums most widely used to broadcast data consist of the electromagnetic spectrum and the internet.

[7.147]

In the case of the electromagnetic spectrum, physical constraints limit the quantity of channels or unidirectional data flows possible with any technology –may at best an advanced technology increase the quantity of channels. Thereat, considering the available technology, the people through the social contract or any other directly-controlled ordinance must specify how many channels the state-organization can allocate using any chosen transmission protocol.

A minimum percentage of citizens must endorse any given journalistic establishment for it to obtain an electromagnetic broadcasting license, and any citizen may endorse several of those establishments, up to a predefined limit. Thereby, the citizens democratically grant electromagnetic broadcasting licenses.

Illustratively, if the quantity of available channels equals thirty, then each citizen may endorse up to three journalistic establishments, and any establishment that obtains the support of at least ten percent of the citizens obtains a broadcasting license.

[7.148]

The task of providing equal access to the resources available via the internet stands much closer to completion at the time of this writing, compared with the case of the electromagnetic spectrum.

Nevertheless, the social contract or any other ordinance directly controlled by the people must ensure that any citizen can broadcast data on the internet to the whole population that wants to receive such stream, and that everyone can do it in equal conditions –those equal conditions also for large organizations. For achieving that purpose, the social contract or any other ordinance directly controlled by the people must—

α. Assign a lifetime address of the *internet protocol* to each citizen. The mandatory technological infrastructure and protocols must enable every person to assign its own internet address to its own domestic internet connection, or to any other desired end-point. Ordinarily, a single end-point can obtain assigned several internet addresses.

β. Require equal upload and download speeds without any cap on the total amount of data transferred, for any internet service. Thereat, each person can pay more or less depending on the desired speed.

γ. Define mandatory technical arrangements for internet routers and gateways to—
   - Allow by default the passage of broadcasted data-streams.
   - Perform the corresponding replication and distribution of data to all the interested users.

Well-developed technical standards for broadcasting data using the internet protocol already exist at the time of this writing.

Thereupon, any internet user will stream or broadcast data to the whole population without necessarily resorting to any intermediary beyond its own internet service provider.

Electronic Devices

[7.149]

The manufacturers of electronic data devices –including devices capable of telecommunications– must fully publish detailed technical specifications which allow the users to freely reprogram any purchased electronic data device. Thereon:

+ This requirement does not hinder the possibility of installing hardware modules specialized in processing and displaying copyrighted data which the user should not copy; but the user must retain the ability to disable such module whenever not processing data protected by *digital rights*.

+ The manufacturers of telecommunication devices must build-in or hard-code protocols for those devices to remain constrained in legal civilian purposes.

For enforcing the *right to privacy* recorded in section [7.136], the social contract must prescribe jail terms for those manufactures who install spying or covert tracking hardware within electronic devices.

Organizing Exchange Hubs

[7.150]

The state-organization must sporadically intervene in commercial environments in order to ensure the continuation of the competition among participants, usually by breaking monopolies and oligopolies.

Beyond such remedial interventions, the state-organization can greatly aid to the stability and prosperity of the exchange space by facilitating and scaffolding competitive activities. This scaffolding can consist in organizing exchange hubs where numerous and diverse participants can offer their products and/or services in equal conditions, and thereby happens a dynamic commercial competition.

[7.151]

The first and most obvious targets for creating exchange hubs consist in food selling and transport services.

Thus, the state-organization should build facilities where numerous participants can—

1. Sell fresh food –and other consumable domestic products– by retailing and fulfilling all sanitary regulations. Each retailing spot must include basic sanitary fixtures with running water and space for refrigeration equipments. The whole facility can comprise convenient parking lots for customers.

    The state-organization should lease each space for a small amount, but should never sell those. In this way, the same state-organization can ensure that no single participant occupies more than one space, and can redistribute any space which becomes available.

    This practice, in a sense, constitutes an institutionalization of the ancient and traditional downtown street markets where anyone could approach and sell its products.

2. Pick up passengers for public transport. This includes bus stations, seaports, and airports.

    As with food-selling hubs, the slots for picking up and delivering passengers should never become sold to anyone, or it will become –yet again– just another oligopolistic environment, this time created by incompetence. Hence, whoever wants to use such facilities should just pay for the usage of the slot for the time during which picks up and delivers passengers, per ride, and any new competitor must enjoy the same opportunity to use that same slot.

    The state-organization should not charge any fixed periodic fee to each participant; rather, the state-organization should perform the corresponding forecasts to ensure a profitable operation. In this way, the state-organization minimizes the bureaucratic hassle for the participants and allows those latter to enact simple accounting procedures, thereby encouraging small competitors to join the business.

In general, selecting the place and size of the aforementioned exchange hubs constitutes a matter of urban and developmental planning.

Practices similar to the ones here described already exist, but very frequently defectively implemented, distorted, or neglected. The reader can use this document as a reference about how to enact socially constructive practices.

The End of the Kindergarten

[7.152]

Through this document the reader became familiarized with the following facts:

1. Humans carry different sets of mental functions which produce several distinctly differentiated internal and external behaviors.
2. Many humans perform deficiently in key psychological functions denominated *executive functions*.
3. Among humans dwells a parasitic psychopathic subspecies.

In short, the reader became familiarized with the fact that humans not all the same kind, and will not become a single unified species in the foreseeable future.

[7.153]

Humans must strive to build an inclusive world which utilizes the power of diversity for productive purposes; as diversity constitutes the hallmark of a highly-adaptable, fast-evolving species.

Furthermore, a less-than-ideal capacity for performing a task does not constitute a cause for renouncing to such activity. That does not constitute the quintessence of humanity; rather, humans outstand as species because of their capacity to perform even in adverse conditions, even when those adversities arise from their own deficiencies.

[7.154]

Thereupon, if some individuals carry less-than-ideal *executive functions*, then the best that can do the organizational environment consists in pushing them to develop those further.

May those individuals find or develop ways to perform better by themselves, or may develop prosthetic devices, or may develop supporting social schemes.

To say it again in other words: A human will not stop walking just because it lacks a foot.

[7.155]

Hence, through this document recorded an emphasis in personal accountability and the capacity of each individual to build its own destiny. In the same direction stand geared both the proposed reform to democracy and the asynchronous exchange.

A Place for Everyone

Limits on the Size of Human Cooperative Systems

[7.156]

The codifications of organizational procedures and regulations in sophisticated cooperative systems, or complex organizations, typically upon the development of the organization degenerate into a semi-dysfunctional massive linguistic body. Such linguistic agglomerate typically lacks a logical structure among sections; ordinarily, those sections by their linguistic connections resemble a set of geological layers whose size augments disproportionately faster than the furnished increment in the complexity of the issuing organization.

[7.157]

Thereon, presumably mainly due to insufficiencies derived from the primitiveness of traditional languages, internal processes tend to involve incidental and concomitant aspects which delay the performance of typical structures of command and execution in complex organizations.

[7.158]

Modern technological achievements radically transformed many human lifestyles during the last 200 years, and supported a similarly radical increase in the pace of scientific research and production of further technological innovations. As a collateral consequence, now any average individual in a modern society must process and handle codified information several orders of magnitude larger, and much more diverse and complex, than the information available 200 years ago.

[7.159]

Compared with the hindrances and problems experienced by societies two centuries ago, modern languages nowadays constitute one of the main civilizational constraints for building larger and more sophisticated cooperative systems, in a world where modern societies massively produce and use scientific data and technological tools, and enact complex behavioral procedures and regulations.

The current linguistic primitiveness arguably happens because humans did not evolve their languages at a rate sufficient to meet the requirements of novel situations created by themselves.

Humans attempt to develop large and sophisticated (abstract) informational structures using as main raw material languages which comprise centuries-old ensembles, patterns, and operational paths which almost nobody cared to systematically develop and transform.

Like attempting to build a skyscraper using bricks of mud.

[7.160]

Therefore, for achieving a successful large fusion among nations humans must first build or create an adequate civilizational framework for a cooperative system of such magnitude and complexity.

[7.161]

Consequently, in what follows taken into account the civilizational (and thus practical) limitations on the size of cooperative systems.

A Union of Nation-States

[7.162]

A world-wide unified society would produce very unfair outcomes for the most advanced people, and would operate very inefficiently –assuming that does not collapse because of so much inefficiency and ineffectiveness. Many people behaving below a basic quality threshold would constitute a massive hindrance, as already happens in many countries at the time of this writing. Therewith, since any human must deem useful or advantageous to associate itself with the members of a group, as described in section [7.26], a world-wide unified society would produce an unstable cooperative system.

Describing a few ordinary examples may aid to the comprehension of the severity of the usual hindrances:

a) Reasonable people understand that an ordinary urban street must comprise, at least, a road for vehicles, a sidewalk, and basic public services which include clean-water pipes along with sewerage, preferably also wires for electric energy and lines for communications. Reasonable individuals also understand that they would live much better if the street comprises sections with vegetation, a road for bicycles, and parking places for vehicles –all basic improvements. However, many primitive individuals in many places regard all that sophistication as unnecessary, as they could use the land of the sidewalk for some other purpose –like building yet another precarious house– and people could still walk side to side with vehicles, and anyone could install public services «on demand». For example, primitive individuals can «install services» by placing a bunch of wires almost randomly over roofs and poles, and routinely breaking the floor to lay new pipes when needed.

In this context, advanced humans waste a lot of their time and energy attempting to show the convenience of building a modern street.

b) Civilized people can stand in a waiting line for obtaining something. However, many antisocial and primitive individuals routinely attempt to cheat for the purpose of circumventing the basic civilized behavior of waiting in line and thereby orderly and fairly obtaining something. Usually police officers must control and deter these antisocial and primitive individuals –and process them if results the case. More antisocial and primitive individuals imply more police officers for successfully controlling and processing them.

In this context, advanced humans attempting to build an advanced society will allocate a lot of resources to build large police organizations tasked with controlling and deterring a lot of antisocial and primitive individuals, instead of using those resources for productive purposes.

c) In many societies the concept of *littering* in a space does not exist, or most individuals do not care about such notion. Typically, scattered waste lays over homes, streets, and urban areas where these primitive societies live at, and rivers become sewers. Accordingly, frequently exists no direct translation for the word *litter* into the language used by such people.

In this context, advanced humans simply cannot build a clean country and keep an ecologically sustainable environment.

d) Many individuals relatively well nourished, not destitute, and with ample access to information, still do not understand the convenience of washing their hands before eating; if given the option whether to eat in a closed place with sanitary facilities or to eat in a dirty precarious open «kitchen» placed in middle of a dusty street, they will choose the dust. Furthermore, they typically choose food stuffed with fat, since the «cook» in a precarious «kitchen» without a running-water supply can more easily prepare such kind of «dishes».

In this context, advanced humans attempting to build a world-class country permanently endure the problems generated by those who do not wish to do so. The generated problems include, not exhaustively—

α. The disarray caused by a precarious «kitchen» in a public space.

β. Lost taxes since the «kitchen» usually pays none.

γ. Increased public hygiene problems.

δ. Widespread obesity and therefrom a myriad of undesirable far-reaching consequences.

e) Forward-going individuals want extensive curricula in science for their children in schools. However, many primitive individuals still want to include magical-thinking theories as part of the regular school content.

In this context, advanced individuals spend large amounts of time and resources finding or creating proper schools for their children, and in primitive societies frequently do not exist basic, indispensable conditions for achieving the aforesaid task.

f) Civilized people understand the convenience of relationships based on *gender equality* for the development of humanity.

The concept of *gender equality* involves equal rights and organizational opportunities for women and men, but implies neither equal biological traits and capacities nor equal behavioral leanings; accordingly, differentiated sanitary facilities for each sexual gender and gender-based sports contests remain in use. The sexual orientation of a human neither changes its sexual gender nor causes hermaphroditism.

However, many primitive and retarded individuals still want to enact patriarchal world-views where women and girls live—

α. Subjugated to males.

β. Sidelined and segregated.

γ. Severely curtailed in their development.

δ. In general, treated as second-class humans, or almost as non-humans when exchanged as objects.

Furthermore, individuals with these world-views –which form part of an authoritarian culture– typically attempt to suppress any different behavior of other persons.

When directly confronted with this grave problem, as a first step for ensuring a healthy social and familiar environment, advanced humans frequently exclude those primitive and retarded individuals from any close relationship. Moreover, modern societies already spend a lot of resources attempting to make those primitive and retarded individuals understand the inconvenience of their way of life.

g) Individuals with adequate *executive functions* understand the widespread occurrence of oligarchies and plutocracies. In contrast, people with deficient *executive functions* frequently simply cannot grasp such events and recognize the problem but, at the same time, carry an intellect above the minimum legal for declaring them mentally disabled.

In this context, advanced humans cannot build a functional democracy.

In each of these examples the greatest loss for the advanced people consists of the missed opportunity for association. These missed opportunities for association happen because advanced individuals cannot build a world-class partnership, community, or society –for any purpose, including business– with the primitive individuals.

[7.163]

In general terms, besides the lost opportunities for association, incorporating incompetent or primitive people into a society produces a great hindrance for advanced people since, while incompetent or primitive people tend to make low-quality choices, the more advanced humans will need to explain every time which constitutes the optimal choice in any given situation and attempt to convince all the incompetent ones. In a direct democracy –and usually also elsewhere– in the best-case scenario, campaigning for the optimal choice will only provide a small amelioration of the low-quality societal choices at a great cost for the advanced people.

Low-quality societal choices already produced consequences far beyond the factual failure of democracy during the XX century in many countries. Therefrom, nowadays many failed countries drag systemic chronic failures which must solve or correct previously to any merge with another society which made correct or at least less disastrous choices. Those systemic chronic failures include, among others, chaotic urban growth, overpopulation, and ecological destruction.

As recorded in section [7.130], filtering which kind of individuals join any given society, and sustaining conditions propitious for the personal development of the population, constitutes a more convenient, forward-going, and stable solution for averting and reducing low-quality societal choices. For this purpose, societal cooperative systems must expel all illegal immigrants, and the offspring of those; as many people who disregard civilized and fair societal practices attempt to immigrate illegally as preferred avenue to join another society and thereby the patterns which caused the failure of foreign countries will repeat –recall entry *b*) of section [7.162].

[7.164]

Hence, once established a basic quality control concerning which kind of individuals any given society can accept, cooperative systems can combine direct democracy with an asynchronous exchange.

Two options appear feasible for those societal cooperative systems:

α. A single state-organization managed by direct democracy coupled with an asynchronous-exchange space.

β. A union of nation-states with a supranational state-organization –similar to the contemporary European Union. Thereat:

+   The human quality control applies at the border of the union.

+   The union shares a single asynchronous-exchange space; all the individuals can volitionally transit within, and perform productive and commercial activities in all the exchange space without restrictions.

+   The supranational state-organization acts as arbiter in the asynchronous-exchange space, including the borders. This supranational state-organization also managed by direct democracy by the citizens of the involved nation-states.

+   Each nation-state keeps and performs all the other organizational functions not delegated to the supranational state-organization. Each national state-organization also managed by direct democracy.

Consequently, every citizen can exercise political rights in two overlapping instances:

+ In the country from which holds citizenship if currently resides and pays taxes there.

+ In the union –the unified society– from which arises the supranational state-organization.

Accordingly, every citizen can belong at least to two legislative bodies: the national one, and the supranational one. Both the national and the supranational state-organizations may charge different taxes to the citizen within their scope of action.

[7.165]

Within a union of nation-states, in regional and local branches of each national state-organization the citizens should—

- Choose regional and local councils also by the D'Hondt method. The choices made by these councils also subject to override by the citizens.

- Redact and approve by direct democracy local ordinances subject to the general laws approved in the national and supranational instances.

Regional councils should perform administratively according to national and supranational laws and ordinances, without the citizens creating differentiated regional regulations. Meanwhile, local ordinances should attend all those detailed and/or small-scale issues which directly impact the desired lifestyle of a community.

[7.166]

Within each nation-state, the individual citizens must assimilate into a heterogeneous mix, in harmony with what described in section [3.159]. Thereat, ethnic or linguistic divisions and tribal affiliations must not exist within any integrated nation-state.

[7.167]

A union of nation-states managed by direct democracy coupled with an asynchronous-exchange space can provide flexibility where different living styles –different ways of life– can coexist fruitfully.

In my personal opinion, this constitutes the best path for a diverse civilization, far away from monolithic cultures and useless homogeneity, and much more forward-going, fair, and prosperous than any other that preceded.

Appendix 1

D'Hondt Method

[A1.1]

The D'Hondt method consists in allocating posts in an election in a way that the collegiate body thus created approximately resembles the percentage of votes that each option received.

Each political party must present a list of candidates at the electoral process, each citizen votes for a single list and, after counting the votes, the allocation of the posts proceeds according to the output of the D'Hondt method, starting with the candidates at the top of each list.

Thereat, the distribution of the posts submitted to the electoral process happens through several computing rounds, allocating one or more posts per round, until exhausting all the initially-available posts.

[A1.2]

At each computing round, for each political party, the entity which performs the method must calculate a *quotient* as follows:

$$quotient_i = \frac{votes_i}{1 + posts_i}$$

where

- *quotient_i* – the quotient obtained by an *i-th* political party during a specific round of computation.
- *votes_i* – the total number of votes received by that same *i-th* political party during the election.
- *posts_i* – the number of posts allocated so far to that same *i-th* political party.

After computing a quotient for each political party, a comparison proceeds and the political parties which obtained the highest quotient gain each a post. In typical real-world scenarios only one political party obtains the highest quotient of a computation round and accordingly receives a post.

Hence, the number *posts$_i$* of any *i-th* political party which recently obtained a post will increase by one, and the increased number serves as input for the next computing round.

[A1.3]

Example

If 4 political parties participate in an election competing for 10 posts, then a distribution of posts by the D'Hondt method can happen as shown in the next page, using simplified quantities for easiness of understanding.

	Votes received		Round						Total posts obtained	Ratio of votes received
			1	2	3	4	5	6		
Party 1	40 000	Posts obtained so far	0	1	1	2	2	3	4	40%
		Quotient	**40 000**	20 000	**20 000**	13 333	**13 333**	**10 000**		
		Posts obtained in the round	**1**	0	**1**	0	**1**	**1**		
Party 2	30 000	Posts obtained so far	0	0	1	1	2	2	3	30%
		Quotient	30 000	**30 000**	15 000	**15 000**	10 000	**10 000**		
		Posts obtained in the round	0	**1**	0	**1**	0	**1**		
Party 3	20 000	Posts obtained so far	0	0	0	1	1	1	2	20%
		Quotient	20 000	20 000	**20 000**	10 000	10 000	**10 000**		
		Posts obtained in the round	0	0	**1**	0	0	**1**		
Party 4	10 000	Posts obtained so far	0	0	0	0	0	0	1	10%
		Quotient	10 000	10 000	10 000	10 000	10 000	**10 000**		
		Posts obtained in the round	0	0	0	0	0	**1**		
Total posts allocated after the round			1	2	4	5	6	10		

$$quotient = \frac{votes\ received}{1 + posts\ obtained\ so\ far}$$

Appendix 2

Cryptocurrencies
A Lesson Not Learned

Introduction

[A2.1]

At the beginning of the XXI century a group of purportedly anonymous individuals, with the outstanding assistance of the russian fascist regime, started to promote an alternative payment system called «bitcoin» through the internet. The tools of exchange in the «bitcoin» payment system consist of records in an electronic ledger; the electronic ledger stored, updated, and distributed by supposedly independent operators of such payment system.

[A2.2]

The protocol of the «bitcoin» stands available to anyone; thereupon, several other entrepreneurs replicated or tweaked the original protocol and started similar electronic payment systems with different names. The collectivity of electronic payment systems based in the «bitcoin» protocol became denominated *cryptocurrencies*.

Herein, any tool of exchange consisting of a record in an electronic ledger similar to a «bitcoin», called *cryptocurrency*.

[A2.3]

Similarly to the capitalistic fraud, the crooks that promote the cryptocurrencies created a code of lies and misrepresentations to mislead the population, and use almost the same capitalistic sales pitch recorded in section [4.3]. Hence, for example—

- The word «bitcoin» can refer to the payment system itself, or to the respective tool of exchange.
- «Mining» refers to a deliberately inefficient computational operation whose output constitutes a deliberated systemic burden.
- «Proof of work» refers to the output of the aforesaid deliberately inefficient computational operation, as if building a systemic burden amounted to a somehow productive «work».

More detailed explanations of these concepts recorded in [A2.9] and subsequent sections, together with the operative characteristics of the «bitcoin» payment system.

[A2.4]

The main supposed «advantage» of the cryptocurrencies consists in the intended anonymity of payers, payees, and anyone who controls the electronic record which constitutes the cryptocurrency. This anonymity achieved by means of concealing –or attempting to conceal– everybody's identities on the internet. Thereat, the cryptocurrencies present an unmatched opportunity to conceal, store, and distribute the monetary proceeds of criminal activities. Hence, the individuals most interested in using cryptocurrencies very well can consist of terrorists, autocrats, drug-dealers, swindlers, and so forth.

[A2.5]

The second supposed «advantage» of the cryptocurrencies consists in an absence of a centralized arbiter of the exchange space, namely, the supposed advantage consists in the absence of direct state regulation.

This absence of a centralized arbiter happens because supposedly independent and unbound participants act as intermediaries to perform the payments and, at the same time, those same intermediaries update and distribute the electronic ledger where all transactions, and the corresponding amounts of tools of exchange, remain stored. In this way, the «bitcoin» constitutes a private business where the operators obtain a straightforward revenue by charging fees from acting as intermediaries in payments.

The «bitcoin» involves a second straightforward revenue from the operations of «mining» performed by the same intermediaries, as explained in [A2.9] and subsequent sections.

However, when considering the actual real-world consequences of the practice, the reader will understand that the main source of revenue of the promoters, operators, and merchants of «bitcoin» and other cryptocurrencies arises from either starting or participating in very early stages of those payment systems.

[A2.6]

Another aim of the promoters of cryptocurrencies consists in allowing the holders of those tools of exchange to store them during an unlimited time; as already said, with complete anonymity.

Thus, by using a cryptocurrency someone can anonymously receive payments, store anonymously large amounts of tools of exchange during an unlimited time, and then spend those savings likewise anonymously.

[A2.7]

Thereupon, the propaganda made in favor of the cryptocurrencies proclaims that the main aim of such payment systems consists in providing more «freedom», very much as the capitalistic propaganda does. In this context, such augmented «freedom» results achieved by circumventing the regulations of state-organizations; in this mythology the state-organizations share the same traits proclaimed by the failed capitalistic «market theories» described in [4.79] and subsequent sections.

Many of those who promote and use cryptocurrencies did not learn or do not want to learn that, if the state-organization becomes captured by authoritarian or antidemocratic individuals, the solution consists in fixing the same state-organization.

In fact, seems that many of those who actively promote the cryptocurrencies actually do not want to become inserted in any sort of civilized behavior –democratic, or not. Thereat, they seem to strive to live in an environment where cheating and abusing others constitutes the norm, where societal rules remain weak notwithstanding if the people democratically chose those rules; they want to live in a world where crooks and thieves can survive.

At the beginning of the XXI century, once understood that capitalism may not withstand much longer, thieves and crooks look for ways to form a new stronghold where they can survive.

[A2.8]

The endeavor of the cryptocurrencies constitutes yet another attempt to delegate a core societal function into private organizations, and by that means the crooks that promote those payment systems attempt to massively suck resources from societal cooperative systems without performing any actual productive work, presenting themselves as «enablers», very much as the capitalistic criminals do.

Operative Characteristics of Cryptocurrencies

[A2.9]

Here presented an abridged explanation of the essential operation of the «bitcoin» payment system, in a way that a non-specialized reader can grasp how it actually operates. Therefore, the concepts explained without resorting to technical jargon. All other *cryptocurrencies* use either the same or tweaked versions of the original «bitcoin» protocol.

[A2.10]

A «bitcoin» payment system starts when the members of a group of associates distribute among themselves the «bitcoin» protocol codified into a software, and thereupon this group of associates operates any variable group of computers connected to the internet with such software. Thus, the first ones to know about the payment system result the associates who launched it, upon which they start promoting the system as a means to perform commercial transactions through the internet.

Therefrom, for a «bitcoin» payment system to function, in real-world settings, first someone –the group of founding associates– must hold a minimal amount of «bitcoins» which then they sell to those individuals who want to use the payment system. Thereat, when acquiring new participants, the founding associates sell parcels of the initial «bitcoins» in exchange for an already widely accepted currency or real assets which these founding associates can use within already existing commercial environments.

Could not happen otherwise, since the «bitcoin» payment system constitutes a private business; therefore, the founding associates neither command the capacity to assign any initial amount of «bitcoins» to each citizen, nor hold any obligation to do so. If happened that the founding associates of a «bitcoin» payment system assigned an initial amount of «bitcoins» to each citizen, then the founding associates would constitute the state-organization or some other entity with the same capacity, and the promoters of the «bitcoin» payment system precisely present themselves as bound neither to a state-organization nor to any legal framework, but present themselves as private individuals and organizations.

[A2.11]

In real-world settings, the aforesaid initial amount of «bitcoins» distributed among the founding associates constitutes a large part of the available «bitcoins»; therefore, constitutes a large pool of resources that anonymous individuals hold and can resort to at any time.

The propagandists of the «bitcoin» and other cryptocurrencies assert that «anyone can run a computer with the bitcoin software, and thereby obtain its *fair share* of the business»; however, in real-world scenarios, most individuals cannot divert a significant portion of their time to perform an activity that will produce a marginal and very small income for them, if any at all. In this context, the operation of any «bitcoin» payment system remains concentrated with those participants who resolve to make large investments of material resources and time for obtaining something from it, besides some peripheral enthusiasts.

In this way, the professional operators of a «bitcoin» payment system will always stand in a structural advantage for obtaining very large amounts of «bitcoins» from any newly initiated payment system. And likewise, the professional operators will obtain most of the fees charged when acting as intermediaries in each transaction.

[A2.12]

In addition to the fees obtained from acting as intermediaries, the operators of a «bitcoin» payment system obtain a fixed amount of «bitcoins» created when processing a collection of payments which henceforward constitute a batch of transactions; this latter fixed amount corresponds to the income of the so-called «mining».

Thereon, as designed in the «bitcoin» protocol, all the operators of a «bitcoin» payment system simultaneously perform an artificially expensive and repetitive computational operation for processing every collection of payments, and the first operator that performs successfully such operation obtains a fixed amount of «bitcoins».

Since all the «bitcoin» operators perform concurrently the same artificially expensive and repetitive computational operation, the amount of real-world energy wasted directly corresponds to the number of electronic computers used to compete.

The artificially expensive and repetitive operation consists in randomly searching for a number which completes a predefined algorithm. The «bitcoin» operators compete among them to find the aforesaid number, the first one to succeed publishes the answer along with the processed batch of transactions and, at the same time, obtains the fixed amount of «bitcoins» prescribed in the protocol for the so-called «mining». Upon someone publishing a correctly processed batch of transactions, the rest of the «bitcoin» operators attach this batch to their copy of the electronic ledger which contains the records of all transactions since the beginning of that «bitcoin» business –although some operators may use a pruned version of the electronic ledger.

As introduced in section [A2.3], the propagandists call «mining» to the activity of performing an artificially expensive and repetitive computational operation seldom obtaining success, if ever. Those same propagandists refer to the number found randomly as «proof of work».

[A2.13]

Furthermore, the «bitcoin» propagandists refer to a batch of processed transactions as a «block» and, since the «bitcoin» operators (in compliance with the protocol) utilize the preceding batch of transactions as input for the next processing operation, the propagandists claim that the «bitcoin» protocol comprises a super-novel ground-breaking «technology» called «blockchain».

[A2.14]

The deliberated systemic burden called «mining» supposedly would serve for preventing any single participant from overtaking and capturing the whole «bitcoin» payment system, because modifying the electronic ledger would require yet another equally expensive and repetitive computational operation for each batch of transactions already processed.

For such protection of past transactions to withstand, the «bitcoin» protocol presupposes that the «bitcoin» operators will continually and permanently perform the artificially expensive and repetitive computational operation, and thus the operators will keep incessantly adding batches of transactions to the electronic ledger; and the burden thereby created renders practically impossible and unprofitable to modify those already processed batches of transactions.

In this way, the «bitcoin» payment system involves a massive set of electronic computers permanently performing an artificially expensive and repetitive operation just to avert fraud.

[A2.15]

Hence, a transaction in a «bitcoin» payment system proceeds as follows:

1. An individual buys some «bitcoins» using some already existing currency or paying with assets –typically, the individual purchases its «bitcoins» with capitalistic money or payment promises. This initial amount of «bitcoins» usually sold by the founding associates and professional operators (who then, of course, can spend that received currency in making a very real-world living).

2. The individual posts (uploads) a transaction on a website of one of the professional «bitcoin» operators. This transaction includes a fee to «motivate» all those operators performing the artificially expensive and repetitive computational operation, for those operators to include the newly posted transaction in a new collection of payments, and process it –as described in section [A2.12].

3. Both the individual and the counterpart who expects to receive the payment of «bitcoins» must wait for any of the operators to successfully process a batch of transactions which includes the payment, by finding the random number. This waiting time can protract anywhere from minutes to hours.

4. Upon success, the transaction appears publicly visible; but, remember, the public identities of both payer and payee consist of just a set of account numbers, thus they remain anonymous for the public.

[A2.16]

The «bitcoin» protocol specifies a fixed amount of «bitcoins» to emit through «mining». Therefore, whenever the amount of «bitcoins» becomes insufficient, the main operators will start yet another equally inefficient «bitcoin» payment system as already described.

[A2.17]

For formal purposes, here defined the concept of *cryptocurrency*:

[A2.18]

Cryptocurrency

Noun.

A tool of exchange consisting of a record in an electronic ledger, this ledger managed by several supposedly independent participants in the exchange. This tool of exchange conveys unmarked ambiguous data referring to possible unaccomplished transactions, where the data cannot separate from the corresponding electronic ledger and depends on the data of any previous transactions. A cryptocurrency arises from peer-to-peer agreements, where any peer can bring more data into the exchange space by means of extremely inefficient reverse-cryptographic operations.

Real-World Consequences of Cryptocurrencies

[A2.19]

The usage of cryptocurrencies will not eliminate the so-far prevailing plutocracies and oligarchies among human populations but, rather, will create other very grave problems. Thereat, with a widespread usage of cryptocurrencies—

+ The free creation of money and payment promises by capitalistic criminals becomes replaced by starting a cryptocurrency business and participating as operator in very early stages of it, as described in sections [A2.10] and [A2.11].

+ Prosecuting criminals, traitors to democracy, oligarchs, and all other kinds of antisocial individuals becomes extremely complicated, as those can safely hide the proceedings of their activities. No need to resort to «fiscal paradises» when cryptocurrencies already hide the identities of the thieves.

+ Commercial transactions become slow, burdensome, and relatively unpredictable, since the participants now need to wait an undefined period of time for the processing of each individual transaction. Therefore, instant transactions become impossible, such as those which happen in habitual human routines.

+ The availability of myriad of volatile cryptocurrencies promotes instability and duplicity –or multiplicity– of prices.

+ The participants in an exchange space will attempt to «store value» within an electronic record. Magical thinking blossoms.

+ Someone who hoarded very large amounts of cryptocurrencies and then attempts to use those during a very short period of time will promote instability of prices, and can manipulate those latter.

+ Likewise, the founding associates who hoarded extremely large amounts of a given cryptocurrency when started that business instance, will harness a capacity to distort exchange rates and prices.

However, the most serious problem created by cryptocurrencies consists in the massive amount of energy wasted sustaining an artificially-created organizational burden. Attempting to deny the waste of energy, the propagandists of cryptocurrencies frequently claim that the operators of the corresponding payment systems consume energy from «either mostly or 100% renewable sources».

[A2.20]

Therefrom, the usage of cryptocurrencies implies that humankind did not learn the lesson from the civilizational disaster created during the last two centuries. At very least, humankind did not learn that—

1. The fact that one can command many resources –call them «renewable» or not– implies neither that one should waste or profusely expend those, nor that squandering those abundant resources originates or produces negligible consequences.

2. Introducing intermediaries into commercial transactions always entails increased costs and the formation of cartels which operate against both customers and suppliers just to maintain their parasitic positions, typically by creating and enforcing artificial hindrances and inefficiencies –which the gullible regard as «proof of work».

3. Transferring a core societal function from the state-organization into private citizens always produces the emergence and structural encroachment of oligarchies and plutocracies; therefore, produces the failure of democracy and an unfair cooperative system.

Some entity must perform the core societal functions, which do not become accomplished «naturally», does not matter if some humans attempt to minimize or deny these facts, and delegating those functions into the exchange space only degrades the civilization which does it.

Finally, in the current period of the human trajectory, where human civilizations already depleted many of the Earth's resources, destroyed forever many ecosystems, and reduced the planet to a fragile condition, when species massively become extinct, deflecting a massive amount of energy to enact a primitive, deliberately inefficient, patently wasteful organizational procedure will produce a definitive fracture and systemic divergence among humans.

Will not pass unnoticed that, at hour zero, many humans still wanted to keep wasting energy for nothing, instead of focusing that energy on saving the planet.

Index

Anders Baerbock

1984–